AF880417

32/6d. ~~677.21(091): 677.024(091)~~ 28th April, 1970.

TEXTILE INSTITUTE
10 BLACKFRIARS ST.
MANCHESTER 3
LIBRARY

7.52HOP

THE TEXTILE INSTITUTE
10 BLACKFRIARS ST.
MANCHESTER 3
LIBRARY

"A History of the Lancashire cotton industry and the Amalgamated Weavers' Association"

THE TEXTILE INSTITUTE
10 BLACKFRIARS ST.
MANCHESTER 3
LIBRARY

Emblem 1880's

"A History of the Lancashire cotton industry and the Amalgamated Weavers' Association"

by
Edwin Hopwood

The Lancashire Weavers Story

LIBRARY

Published by the Amalgamated Weavers Association, Chronicle Buildings, 74 Corporation Street, Manchester, M4 2BX., and printed by the Co-operative Press Limited, 418 Chester Road, Manchester, M16 9HP.

© *March*, 1969.

Contents

CHAPTER		PAGE
1	INTRODUCTION	1
2	HAND-LOOM WEAVING	4
	Apprenticeship Indenture	5
	Handloom Weavers' earnings	6
3	THE INDUSTRIAL REVOLUTION and MECHANICAL INVENTIONS	8
	John Kay	8
	James Hargreaves	9
	Richard Arkwright	9
	Samuel Crompton	9
	Rev. Edmund Cartwright	9
	Later mechanical improvements	11
	The Automatic Loom	12
4	INTRODUCTION OF POWER	13
	The Factory System	13
5	EARLY ATTEMPTS TO COMBINE	16
	Appalling factory conditions	16
	Early Trade Unions	18
	The Combination Acts	18
	Early Association of Weavers	19
	Cotton Industry Arbitration Act, 1800	21
	Weavers' Petitions	21
	"Blanketeers" and "Peterloo"	24
	The "Philanthropic Society"	25
	General Union of Trades	27
	Repeal of Combination Laws	29
	Fining System	30
6	EARLY WEAVING LISTS	33
7	ESTABLISHMENT OF DISTRICT ASSOCIATIONS	37
	Blackburn	37
	Padiham	38
	Great Harwood	38
	Darwen	38
	Church	39

CHAPTER		PAGE
	Accrington	39
	Haslingden	39
	Preston	40
	Bamber Bridge	40
	Clitheroe	40
	Burnley	40
	Nelson...	41
	Colne ...	42
	Bolton	42
	Oldham	42
	Rossendale	43
	Ashton	44
	Heywood	44
	Todmorden	44
	Rochdale	44
	Longridge	45
	Hyde ...	45
	Whitworth	45
	Bury ...	45
	Wigan	45
	Skipton	46
	Stockport	46
8	THE FIRST AMALGAMATION, 1858	47
9	THE PRESENT AMALGAMATION, 1884	53
	Original objects	54
	Early strikes ...	55
	Emblem	55
	Reelers	56
	Uniform List, 1892 ...	56
	Brooklands Agreement	57
	Breaches of Agreements	58
	United Textile Factory Workers' Association	59
	"Time Cribbing"	60
	"Slate" System	60
10	THE FACTORY ACTS	63
	Historical	63
	The 1937 Act (and "Shuttle Kissing")	66
	Steaming and Artificial Humidification	68
	Temperature	73
11	EARLY 20th CENTURY DEVELOPMENTS	
	Coming-of-Age Celebrations	74
	Passing of three Pioneers	75
	Northern Counties Textile Trades Federation	75
	General Federation of Trade Unions	76
	Joint Rules	76
	Mill Rules	76
	Uniform List for Waste Weaving ...	77

CHAPTER		PAGE
	Parliamentary Representation	77
	Non-Unionists	78
	"Protection" Societies	78
	David J. Shackleton	79
	National Health Insurance "Approved Society"	79
	Trade Union Act, 1913	79
	Weavers' Cough	80
12	FIRST WORLD WAR, 1914–18	81
	Cotton Control Board	81
	Out-of-Work Payments	82
	Textile Workers' Ambulances	82
	Uniform Contributions and Benefits	83
	Post-War Depression	83
	Under-employment	84
	Unemployment Insurance by Industry	84
13	POST-WAR PROBLEMS: 1918 ONWARDS	
	48-hour Working Week	86
	Local Disadvantages	86
	Half-time System	88
	Proposed Federation of Textile Workers' Unions	89
	Passing of Joseph Cross	90
	Late J. C. Parker	90
	Weavers' Charter	90
	General Strike, 1926	91
	Trades Disputes & Trade Union Act, 1927	92
	Fencing of machinery & Prevention of Accidents...	92
	Rigby-Swift Award	92
14	THE "MORE LOOMS" SYSTEM	
	Burnley eight-looms experiment	95
	John Wm. Ogden	98
	James Hindle	99
15	"JOSEPH CROSS" MEMORIAL CONVALESCENT HOME ...	100 (A to G)
	Transfer of the Home to the Trade	105
	Convalescent Home	106
16	THE "MIDLAND" AGREEMENT	
	Serious unemployment	108
	Breaches of agreements	108
	Four weeks' strike	109
	Midland Hotel conferences	110
	More Looms System becomes established...	112
	Amalgamation Jubilee	113

CHAPTER PAGE

17 LEGALISATION OF THE UNIFORM LIST 114
1935 legalised list 114
1937 legalised list 117
Unemployment in the inter-war years 118
Truck Acts & Fining System 119
Legalising of the Waste Weaving List 122

18 OTHER INTER-WAR PERIOD DEVELOPMENTS
Standing Joint Committee of Working Women's Organisations ... 123
Rewound Weft 123
Employment of Women & Young Persons Act, 1936 124
Holidays 124
Holidays with Pay 125
Uniform List for Sheeting Cloths 126

19 THE SECOND WORLD WAR, 1939–45
Emergency Joint Agreements 129
Loan to Government 130
Overtime 130
Cost-of-Living Agreement 130
Minimum Wage 131
1941 Minimum Wage Agreement 132
The "Essential Work Orders", 1941 and 1942 133
Agreement under the Essential Work Order 133
The "Starting-point" Wage Principle 134
Flat-Rate Payment Principle and Minimum Wage for Running Looms Established 135
Guaranteed Wage Agreement, 1946 135
The Present Position of the Guaranteed Wage and Minimum Wage ... 136
Guaranteed Wage 136
Minimum Wage 137
Demarcation of Membership with other Unions 137
Concentration of the Industry during the War 138
Restoration of Pre-War Trade Practices Act, 1942 142

20 POST-WAR PROBLEMS: 1945 ONWARDS
The Cotton Board 143
Working Party Report 145
Winders, Beamers, Doublers, etc. 146
Sweeping and cleaning of looms 148
Combined Fustian and Velvet List... 150
Five-day Working Week 150
Political Rules and Parliamentary representation 151
Staff Superannuation 152
European Volunteer Workers 154
Educational Activities 154
Bangor Summer School 155
Week-end Schools 155
The "C.M.C." Wage System 156
Time and Motion Study 158

CHAPTER PAGE

Developments in Shift Workings:
Double-day Shifts 159
Double-day Shifts on non-automatic looms 160
Three-Shift Working 160
Double-day Shifts 161
Multi-Shift Working... 161
Extension of Multi-Shift Systems 161
Notes 162
Movements in Wage Rates 163
Movements in Wage Levels... 165
Early Wages of Factory Weavers, Winders, etc. 165
Proposed Centralization Schemes 166
Structure of the Amalgamation 167
Cotton Industry Act (1959) 169
Compensation for Redundancy Agreement 171
Appeals Board 176

RECENT PRESIDENTS 177

RECENT GENERAL SECRETARIES 179
Recognition for lengthy service 180

APPENDICES 183

THE TEXTILE INSTITUTE
10 BLACKFRIARS ST.
MANCHESTER 3
LIBRARY

Preface

In the course of the past twenty years or so the Amalgamated Weavers' Association has held a number of Week-End Schools, and has also selected members to attend Schools organised by the General Federation of Trade Unions, the Workers' Educational Association, and other educational bodies. In addition to subjects dealing with contemporary topics interest has been displayed by the students in the history of past struggles and sacrifices of the early pioneers of the textile trades union movement. Very many books have been written, over the years, giving graphic details of early textile history, but until recently there has not been any publication dealing specifically with the work of the Amalgamation.

The present Story deals specifically with the Amalgamated Weavers' Association and attempts to cover in some chronological detail our own particular Union's past history. In my 47 years' work in the Central Office of the Amalgamation I have been intimately connected with many events and developments, and have first-hand knowledge of the considerable amount of work put in by the various chief officers. As working conditions and wages have improved during later years it is as well to recall some of the conditions which existed in the weaving sheds during the nineteenth and early twentieth centuries, and to realise the efforts that have been made by earlier pioneers to secure improvements which have led to present-day working standards.

As I retired from active service with the Amalgamation in 1960 the story from that date to the present time has been continued, under the guidance of the retiring General Secretary, Lord Wright, C.B.E., and with the very valuable help of his successor, Mr. Harry C. Kershaw, who has brought much of the material up-to-date and has had considerable experience, during his period of service with the Amalgamation, of Work Study techniques, Assessment of Work Loads under the C.M.C. System, and, in recent years, work connected with Redundancy Payment cases and similar matters.

In conclusion I would acknowledge the following list of sources of information which I have freely utilised in compiling this historical survey, and recommend students and others to consult these authorities for more detailed surveys of the subjects covered.

EDWIN HOPWOOD,
ex-Assistant General Secretary,
Amalgamated Weavers' Association.

November, 1968.

THE TEXTILE INSTITUTE
[illegible] ST.
[illegible] 3
LIBRARY

Acknowledgments

G. H. WOOD.—*History of Wages in the Cotton Trade During the Past* 100 *Years.* (Sherratt & Hughes).

THOMAS THORNLEY.—*Modern Cotton Economics.* (Scott, Greenwood & Sons).

J. A. TODD.—*The Cotton World* (Pitman).

ANTOINE ZISCHKA.—*La Guerre Secrete Pour le Coton.* (Payot, Paris, 1934).

A. P. WADSWORTH & JULIA DE L. MANN.—*The Cotton Trade & Industrial Lancashire,* 1600–1780. (Manchester University Press, 1931).

C. P. BROOKS.—*Cotton Manufacturing* (E. & F. N. Spon).

SIDNEY & BEATRICE WEBB.—*History of Trade Unionism,* 1666–1920.

Prof. Sir SIDNEY J. CHAPMAN.—*The Lancashire Cotton Industry.*

BRIGGS & JORDAN.—*An Economic History of England.*

FISHWICK.—*A History of Lancashire.*

J. ANDREW & CO.—*Cotton Factory Times,* articles on Lancashire Textile Unions (May, 1933).

W. GWYNN PILKINGTON.—*Lancashire Cotton Industry During the War Years* (Empire Cotton Growing Association).

Prof. A. ASPINALL.—*The Early English Trade Unions* (The Batchworth Press).

H. de B. GIBBINS.—*The Industrial History of England.*

GEO. W. SOUTHGATE.—*English Economic History.*

Prof. H. A. TURNER.—*Trade Union Growth Structure and Policy, A Comparative Study of the Cotton Unions.* (George Allen and Unwin).

TEXTILE INSTITUTE
10 BLACKFRIARS ST.
MANCHESTER 3
LIBRARY

CHAPTER I

Introduction

THE ARTS of spinning textile yarns and weaving textile cloths are amongst the oldest in the world. Engravings and drawings in prehistoric caves prove that man has clothed himself for at least 6,000 years. From excavations in ancient Nineveh it has been proved that about 2000 B.C., there was in existence all over the Orient "a tree which produced white fibres, finer than the most costly wool, of soft silky down." A document of the time of Nebuchadnezzar refers to Cotton as "white gold." Linen cloths were in use in 1700 B.C., and almost five centuries before the Christian era we are told that the ordinary wear of the Indians was cotton cloth. In fact in the pre-Christian era the major communities all had their own exclusive raw materials for spinning and weaving—silk in China, cotton in India, flax and linen in Egypt, wool in Asia Minor, Greece, Italy and Spain, and hemp and wool in Northern Europe, yet none of these communities was aware of the textile fibres used by the others. In 300 B.C., however, Alexander the Great invaded India and broke down the barriers between Asia and Europe, and was impressed by the cotton goods of India.

All historians appear to agree that India was the original home of cotton, and Antoine Zischka, of Paris, writing in 1934, stated that the first cotton cloths known dated from 1100 B.C., and came from India. Zischka thought that although the present modern cotton industry was one of the great industries of the world it had not improved upon nor surpassed the quality of some of the ancient fabrics.

From the East the textile arts gradually spread to Europe, but not until about the 9th or 10th century A.D. The Cotton plant was introduced into Spain by the Spanish Moors about the ninth century, but by the sixteenth century a number of European countries were producing cotton cloths, and in 1560 Venice exported a variety of cottons, whilst Milan manufactured and exported fustians and dimities of many kinds.

Developments had taken place of course, in woollen cloth manufacture in many countries, and up to the beginning of the eighteenth century 86 per cent of all clothing garments were made from linen or wool. Throughout the Middle Ages all over the globe flax and sheep were cultivated. Everyone made their own fabrics in their own homes. Cotton cloths, as with silks, remained articles of luxury. There was a struggle for markets for cotton goods and Chinese silks, but it was a struggle which only affected a certain class of idle rich and merchants of certain importing centres. The common people had no interest in these early struggles, neither as producers nor consumers.

The textile trade gradually spread further West and the first record of cotton being part of English trade is contained in a work written towards the close of the fifteenth century by Hakluyt, who said that the ships of Genoa brought to England, amongst other commodities, cotton. In 1601 it is recorded that cotton was brought to England by the Antwerpians from Sicily, the Levant, and Lisbon.

It had also been found that cotton was developed in the American continent, particularly in Mexico and Peru, and Zischka states that about 1619 the first plantations of cotton were established in Virginia, America, from seeds brought from the Leeward Islands, Brazil, and Mexico.

Until about 1760, of course, the cotton, silk and other textile trades were relatively unimportant in comparison with the woollen cloth trade, although the silk industry received a stimulus at the end of the Stuart period through the immigration of the Huguenots, or French Protestants, after the revocation of the Edict of Nantes, in 1685. Hundreds of thousands of textile workers left France to settle in Britain, Holland, and other Protestant countries, and it is estimated that 70,000 of France's best silk workers settled in England. Everywhere these immigrants created new textile centres, and they learned to use cotton. The Huguenots were industrious and skilled workmen, and were welcomed by the English Government of that time, as—before the days of machinery—skilled labour was the sole means of improving the industrial arts. These new immigrants developed the silk trade at Spitalfields, made sailcloth at Ipswich, and developed calico-printing at Richmond, Yorkshire, besides effecting improvements in paper-making and in the linen industry of Scotland and Ireland.

When cotton yarns came to be spun in England they were only used for the weft threads, the warp being made of linen, as it was not until the end of the eighteenth century that Arkwright invented the machine which could spin a cotton thread strong enough to make the warp.

About 1750, Postlethwaite in his *Dictionary of Trade and Commerce* showed the woollen trade of Lancashire to be still of some importance, nevertheless he estimated that at Manchester, Bolton and the neighbourhood they made over £600,000's worth of cotton goods annually. Fustians, cottons, tapes, etc., were sent on pack-horses to London, Liverpool and Bristol for exportation, and Manchester men travelled to different parts of the kingdom to sell cloths to the tradesmen for home consumption. By 1775 (according to Bryan Edwards) there were in and about Manchester over 30,000 people engaged in the cotton industry, and about this time the cotton industry was also developing in Glasgow and district. The woollen industry was gradually pushed over the borders into Yorkshire and to other parts of England.

One of the main reasons for the early growth of the Lancashire textile industry was the relative freedom of Lancashire from the Elizabethan and Stuart regulation of industry and trade. These regulations were imposed largely on the initiative of the Gilds in the incorporated towns, and were in part directed towards the restriction of industrial development in the country districts. These regulations (e.g., the Weavers' Act of 1558 and the Statute of Apprenticeship of 1563) took the form of limits to the number of looms allowed to be owned by a country weaver; minimum periods of apprenticeship; property qualifications for apprenticeship; and similar limits to expansion. Manchester and Bolton were not incorporated towns and the Acts did not apply to Lancashire or to the West Riding of Yorkshire.

In Dr. Aikin's *Forty Miles Round Manchester*, published in 1795, he says, "the Manchester merchants began to give out warps and raw cotton to the weavers, receiving them back in cloth and paying for the carding, roving, spinning, and weaving." This system was primitive, but the cottage industry gradually spread over the hills, dales and plains of Lancashire. Very many of the farmhouses and cottages had their weaving shops, and the cellars of many labouring people in the towns and villages contained handlooms. It is estimated by Dudley Windel that out of a population of 6,000,000 for all England there were 43,000 cottage and home workers engaged in the spinning and weaving of cloth in Lancashire.

CHAPTER II

Hand-Loom Weaving

IT IS well-known, of course, that handloom weaving was performed in the home for a long number of years, and was allied to farming in many instances. Fishwick quotes an interesting account written by a Samuel Bamford, of Middleton, on the way in which handloom weaving developed in the home:—

> "The farming was generally of that kind which was soonest and most easily performed, and it was done by the husband and other males of the family, whilst the wife and daughters and maid-servants, if there were any, attended to the churning, cheese-making, and household work; and when that was finished, they busied themselves in carding, slubbing, and spinning wool or cotton, as well as forming it into warps for the looms. The husband and sons would next, at times when farm labour did not call them, size the warp, dry it, and beam it in the loom, and either they or the females, whichever happened to be least employed, would weave the warp down. A farmer would generally have three or four looms in his house, and then—what with the farming, easily and leisurely though it was performed, what with the housework and what with the carding spinning and weaving—there was ample employment for the family. If the rent was raised from the farm, so much the better; if not, the deficiency was made up from the manufacturing profits."

William Radcliffe, himself an improver of the powerloom, gives another account of the life of the handloom weaver. In 1770, he says:—

> "the land (in Mellor) was occupied by between 50 and 60 farmers . . . and out of these there were only six or seven who raised their rents directly from the produce of the farms; all the rest got their rents partly in some branch of trade, such as spinning and weaving woollen, linen or cotton . . . The cottagers were employed entirely in this manner, except for a few weeks in harvest . . . Cottage rents at that time, with convenient loom-shop and a small garden attached, were from one-and-a-half to two guineas per annum. The father would earn from 8s. to half a guinea, and his sons, if he had one, two or three alongside of him, 6s. or 8s. a week . . . and when it is considered that it required six or eight hands to prepare and spin yarn, sufficient for the consumption of one weaver, this shows clearly the call there was for labour for every person, from the age of seven to eighty years (who retained their sight and could move their hands) to earn their bread, say from 1s. to 3d. per week, without going to the parish."

Indenture of Apprenticeship

In those very early days it was common for children from the Poor Law to be apprentices to individual weavers (handloom weavers) and in such cases an Apprenticeship Indenture was drawn up and signed. An interesting specimen of an Apprenticeship Indenture of 1767 which also relates to the transfer of an apprentice's services from one weaver to another, was quoted by the *Textile Weekly* in its edition of 31st March, 1944, and is as follows:—

WEAVER'S APPRENTICESHIP INDENTURE

"This Indenture made the twenty-sixth day of August in the year of our Lord One thousand seven hundred and sixty-seven between Bartholomew Hopwood of Marsden (old name for Nelson) in the County of Lancaster, weaver, and Robert Taylor, his apprentice of the same place on the one part, and Daniel Redman, of Briercliffe with Extwistle in the same County, weaver, of the other part. Whereas by indenture of apprenticeship dated on or about Michaelmas in the year of our Lord one thousand seven hundred and sixty-five made between the officers of Goldshaw Booth in the forest of Pendle of the one part and the same Bartholomew Hopwood of the other part the said officers by the consent and allowance of two of His Majesty's Justices of the Peace for the said County put placed and bound the said Robert Taylor a poor child of the said Forest Apprentice to the said Bartholomew Hopwood only till he attains the age of twenty and one and whereas the said Bartholomew Hopwood hath agreed to assign his said Apprentice over to the said Daniel Redman for the residue of the said Term and the said Robert Taylor the apprentice doth hereby consent thereto and being under age doth hereby bind himself to serve the said Daniel Redman for the said Term.

Now this Indenture witnesseth for the considerations above the said Bartholomew Hopwood doth assign transfer and set over unto the said Daniel Redman his executors administrators and assigns the said Robert Taylor and all the right Title and Interest of the said Bartholomew Hopwood of in or to the said Robert Taylor or his service or apprenticeship together with the said Indenture of apprenticeship. To Hold the said Robert Taylor unto the said Daniel Redman his exors administrators and assigns from the date hereof for and during and until the said Robert Taylor attains to age and the said Bartholomew Hopwood doth hereby for himself his Exors Adminors and Assigns covenent promise and agree to and with the said Daniel Redman his exors and adminors by these presents that he the said Robert Taylor shall work and truly serve the said Daniel Redman his exors adminors and assigns as apprentice from the date hereof for and during and until he shall attain to age without any let or hindrance of him the said Bartholomew Hopwood and the said Daniel Redman doth hereby for himself his exors adminors and assigns covenant promise and agree to and with the said Bartholomew Hopwood his exors adminors and assigns shall and will teach and instruct or cause and procure to be taught and instructed the said Robert Taylor in the said Art Trade or Mistery of a weaver and find and provide for the said apprentice all manner of apparell and wholesome and sufficient meat drink washing lodging and entertainment during and until the said apprentice shall attain to the age of twenty and one years.

To witness whereof the said parties to these presents have hereunto inter changeably set their hands and seals the day and year first above written.

Sealed Signed and Delivered in the presence of Jno Walshman. Jonathan Lomax.	Bartholomew Hopwood. Robert X Taylor. his mark Daniel X Redman." his mark

Handloom Weavers' Earnings

In the very early days of handloom weaving wages were very low, and varied between district and district, being fixed between the merchant who gave out the yarns and the weavers weaving them. An attempt was made in 1769 to establish a weaving wage list, and the *Manchester Evening Chronicle*, dated January 10th, 1938, gives a photograph of one such early list. The title page states that the book is "A list of the Prices in those branches of the weaving manufactory called the Strong Plain, Foot Figured, and Flowered Branches; Printed in 1769 at the expense of these manufacturers who were subscribers for carrying on the work. Prices agreed to between a number of masters and journeymen." Five lists were set out in about 30 pages, and the piece rates were complicated and detailed even in those days. Rates covered the black branch, the fancy branch, handkerchiefs, gauzes and nets. The book also contains a commentary on those people objecting to price lists. Signatures to the 1769 list include Flemish and Lancashire names.

In 1769 the average wage in the Manchester district was stated by Arthur Young to be 5s. 6d. to 7s. per week, whilst in 1770 the wages earned at Mellor, near Blackburn, averaged from 8s. to 10s. 6d. per week. From 1788 to about 1803, however, the wages improved considerably. The invention of the spinning jenny, mule and water frame, together with the cylinder carder and the warping mill, greatly lowered the cost of warp and weft, and the demand for cotton goods increased. Professor Chapman says that "every lumber-room, even old barns, cart-houses and outbuildings of any description were repaired, windows made in blank walls, and all were fitted up for loom shops." Radcliffe, writing of this period, said that from 1788 to the end of the century was indeed "the golden age of this trade." Increased yarn supplies enabled higher wages to be earned, and whole families concentrated on handloom weaving. In Mellor it was found that a family could make total wages of 40s. up to 100s. and even 120s. per week.

After 1806, however, a different picture is shown, when, upon the development of the factory system, the handloom weavers' wages began to decline. By 1808, information from Bolton shows handloom weavers earning about 15s. per week, and 13s. 2d. in Glasgow. Ten years later the Bolton wages had fallen to an average of 9s. per week, and in Glasgow 5s. 9d. This decline continued, until by 1834 we have evidence of weekly wages of 5s. 6d. in Bolton, and from 6s. to 9s. in Glasgow. Other sources of information confirm that handloom weavers' wages in the Colne area dropped to 5s. 4d. per week for a good weaver in 1833, and 4s. 6d. per week near Oldham.

In fact the early 1820's became an Age of Distress. In 1829 for instance, when a census was taken in the village of Higham, near Padiham, it was found that there were 103 weavers earning an average weekly wage of 2s. The cost of bread at that time was 1s. 2½d. for a 4-lb. loaf, and the weavers, therefore, had to live on oatmeal. A census in Burnley about the same time revealed that the average weekly wage per head of the population was 1s. 8½d. A man, therefore, had to live on 2d. per day.

The following table shows the variations in handloom weavers' wages, collected by G. H. Wood from a number of authorities, from the commencement of the nineteenth century until the demise of the handloom:—

HANDLOOM WEAVERS' WAGES

(Estimates of averages)

	Bolton	Manchester	Glasgow	near Colne	near Oldham
	s. d.	s. d.	s. d.	s. d.	s. d.
1800	25 0	—	13 1	—	—
1805	25 0	—	15 4	—	—
1810	19 6	16 3	11 6	—	—
1815	14 0	13 2	11 6	17 1	11 9
1820	9 0	11 0	10 0	11 8	9 0
1825	8 6	6 6	9 0	8 6	8 9
1830	5 6	—	7 0 to 8 0	6 0	5 0
1834–5	5 6	—	—	5 4 (1833)	4 6 (1833)

CHAPTER III

The Industrial Revolution and Mechanical Inventions

WITH THE greatly expanding demand for cotton goods a number of handloom weavers and others engaged in the trade began to experiment with improved methods of production, and a number of mechanical inventions followed one another rapidly during the period which has become known as the Industrial Revolution. It would be more proper to refer to this period not as a sudden break or upheaval, but rather as an exceptional acceleration. As Briggs says in *Industrial Revolution* "The theory that the Industrial Revolution was a sudden and violent transformation between 1760 and 1800 by a few men of inventive genius, is now discarded. By 1760 private capitalism large scale production and even competition had obtained a grip on most trades. This does not mean that England had become industrialised by 1760. It was predominantly rural. Textiles and the conversion of bar iron and steel into light usable goods was still carried on in the homes of the workers."

John Kay

The first of the notable series of inventions occurred when in 1733 John Kay (a native of Walmersley, near Bury) invented the fly shuttle, and by 1760 the fly shuttle had come into general use in handloom weaving. About 1769 his son Robert Kay invented the drop box, by which the weaver could use shuttles containing different coloured threads without substituting one shuttle for another directly by hand. As the trade developed it became clear that means would have to be found to multiply the yarn supply, as Kay's invention had upset the balance, and expanding trade was in danger of being lost. The genius of early inventors was therefore largely spent in the development of the domestic spinning wheel. Experiments were made with the use of rollers in spinning, particularly by John Wyatt and Louis Paul. Other inventive minds were at work, and in 1763 the Society of Arts offered a prize of £50 for the "best invention of a machine that would spin six threads of wool, flax, hemp, or cotton at one time and require but one person to work and attend to it." This incentive caused many model spinning-wheels to be submitted for approval, none of which furnished what was required.

James Hargreaves

The solution of the difficulty fell to James Hargreaves, a weaver of Stanhill, near Blackburn, who had for years been making improvements in the carding machines, which displaced the hand-cards then in use for clearing and straightening the cotton fibres preparatory to their being spun. In 1764 he secretly made a machine in his house, which he called the Spinning-Jenny. In the *Textile Weekly* of 12th February, 1943, Mr. W. A. Hunter (of Messrs. Howard & Bullough Ltd.) gives a very interesting account of James Hargreaves and his invention, and relates the story of the attack from the Blackburn mob who broke up the machines which Hargreaves had produced in 1768, with the assistance of a local factory-owner, Mr. Robert Peel.

Richard Arkwright

About this time another inventive genius was at work in Preston, when Richard Arkwright, the barber, patented a system of spinning by rollers, by which a cotton thread strong enough to make a warp was produced. Arkwright also took out patents for improvements in carding, roving and other spinning machinery, and, like Hargreaves, had to flee the county. A man named Highs, or Hayes, invented a machine for spinning, but through lack of means did not follow up his invention.

Samuel Crompton

Samuel Crompton, of Bolton, learned to spin on one of Hargreaves' jennies, when 16 years of age. The systems of spinning then in use produced rather soft weft and were not sufficiently fine to be used in delicate fabrics. The production of fine yarn on a large scale was achieved by the "mule" invented by Crompton between 1774 and 1779. It was a combination of the principles of the jenny and the rollers, hence its name. Like the jenny the first mules were made of wood, but in 1783 an improved design with metal rollers and wheels was made. A clever mechanic named Henry Stones, residing near Bolton, improved the mule, and in 1790 William Kelly invented the automatic mule fitted with several hundred spindles. By 1800 the mule had displaced the jenny in the cotton trade.

It will be obvious that these inventions to increase the output of yarn succeeded so well that loom improvements became an absolute necessity. Long before 1760 a highly intricate machine known as the Swivel loom had been introduced for the weaving of many narrow pieces or tapes at once. In 1724 Stukeley wrote of the people of Manchester, who had looms that worked 24 laces at a time "which was stolen from the Dutch," Professor Chapman quotes from the rules of the Manchester Smallware Weavers, dated 1756, who spoke of the masters having acquired by the use of the Dutch swivel looms "such large and opulent fortunes as hath enabled them to vie with some of the best gentlemen of the county".

Rev. Edmund Cartwright

In 1785 the Rev. Edmund Cartwright, a Kentish Minister, solved the problem of so adding to the rapidity of weaving as to exhaust the increasing output of yarn, by inventing the powerloom. He experimented upon this machine for some time, and in 1786, 1787, 1788 and 1792 he patented improved models. These looms produced more uniform cloth with far greater rapidity, although they were only adopted slowly. In 1787 a small factory was opened in Doncaster, worked by a steam engine brought over from Birmingham, but the enterprise failed, and the inventor was almost ruined. The powerloom first achieved commercial success in Scotland, and in 1793 Robertson set up powerlooms at Glasgow and Dumbarton. In 1790 Messrs. Grimshaw had partially erected a mill at Knott Mill, near Manchester, which was burnt to the ground by a mob of handloom weavers. According to Brooks one of the first really successful weaving sheds was built in Glasgow in 1801 by Monteith, and contained 200 looms.

A "wiper" loom, invented by Miller, was a big improvement upon the Cartwright loom, as it provided a means of protecting the warp threads by stopping the loom if the shuttle failed to reach the shuttle-box. In addition, the use of direct motive power, in place of springs, to actuate the shuttle, was the germ of an improved principle upon which many subsequent inventions were based.

Prof. Chapman points out that new machinery is generally inefficient machinery, and the new powerlooms were no exception to this rule. Cartwright sank a fortune in trying to make them pay, and probably the burning of the first powerloom shed in Lancashire, at Manchester, was no great loss to its owners, since they were but experimenting with the new machinery. For many years certain fabrics could not be woven by the powerloom so well as by the handloom. One defect of the early models was that the loom had to be stopped frequently to dress the warp as it unrolled from the beam. It must be recalled that in the handloom each weaver stiffened or dressed his own warp whilst it was in the loom by applying size with a flat brush. A length of about two yards was sized in this manner and dried by means of hot irons, paper first being laid over the damp twist. In the face of our modern systems, this old-fashioned method hardly appears credible. The paste used was a mixture of flour and water, boiled over the fire, and stored in a stone vessel not unlike a swine trough. Probably from this the term "sow box" arose. The necessity for this sizing was removed by the invention of the dressing machine by William Radcliffe and Thomas Johnson, his assistant, of Stockport, in 1803 and 1804, by which warps were sized before putting them in the loom. This dressing machine was in vogue until 1830, but soon after this the tape frame, producing five times more work than the dressing machine, was invented and continued in use until in an improved form—delivering the yarn direct on to the weaver's beam, and with still further capacity for large output—it took the lead, under the name of the "slasher," among all sizing systems now current. To James Bullough (a native of Westhoughton, though resident in Blackburn) may be credited this last invention, which brought in its train the beam-warping frame, and found increased employment for the winding frame invented early in the century by the Senior Robert Railton.

Between 1803 and 1813, Horrocks, of Stockport, produced an efficient all-metal loom, and thus the modern powerloom assumed its modern form. Horrocks himself derived no profit from the invention, but his ideas were developed by Roberts and Sharp, who placed an improved model on the market in 1822. This machine, which was a tappet loom, was the first capable of competing seriously with the handloom industry, hence its importance.

Joseph Marie Jacquard, of Lyons, France, made a success of his apparatus in 1804, based on previous inventions of Falcon in 1728 and Vaucanson in 1745, and it was introduced into this country early in the nineteenth century. The Jacquard apparatus could be applied to the handloom or used in conjunction with the powerloom, and enabled more intricate patterns to be woven.

Later Mechanical Improvements

A new mechanism was also invented which enabled the cloth to be taken up mechanically, instead of having to be pulled forward by the weaver. These looms became known as "dandy looms". Even then the powerloom was far from perfect. It did not stop running when the warp or the weft broke; so, in 1834 Messrs. Ramsbottom and Holt patented the weft stop motion, which was seven years later perfected and patented in its present form by Messrs. J. Bullough and Kenworthy, of Blackburn. They, too, patented the loose reed loom and roller temple, as well as a taking-up motion, although from records of the time and tales told by the older section of the community in Blackburn (writes Brooks in 1888) apparently it was to John Osbaldeston that the honour is due of breaking the concussion of the shuttle in the shuttle-box (check-strap) and inventing an improved temple. He also originated many of those appliances so essential to adapt the powerloom for weaving fancy goods.

He invented a system of making healds of brass wire, in 1835, and in February, 1842, Osbaldeston improved the mechanism connected with the weft-fork and knock-off mechanism. In that year Railton invented the two or more roller temple and certain mechanisms for the shuttle-box.

An attempt to improve the dobby mechanism was made by Railton and Lang in December, 1858. This was double acting and was referred to as a "double" dobby. Since the two inventors had their works in Blackburn, and the dobby was first introduced into Blackburn mills, it became known as the Blackburn dobby. This dobby was improved upon in 1873 by Bowker, who operated the two lifting knives by means of a strap, and it was often referred to as the "strap" dobby.

In 1827 William Dickinson, of Blackburn, also invented a loom, and made improvements upon it during the subsequent years. A model of the Dickinson loom is at present in the possession of the Textile Department of the Blackburn Technical College, and was shown in an Exhibition in 1862.

If a comparison is made between handloom weaving and powerloom weaving it will be found that a good handloom weaver could weave about 172,000 picks per week, whilst a powerloom weaver, in the early days, could weave 604,800 picks per week on two looms. By 1825 a powerloom weaver could attend to two looms without assistance and could weave 1,000,000 picks per week. By 1835 the loom mechanism and the system of warp preparation had been so improved that a weaver could attend to four looms, with the assistance of a tenter, and weave 1,750,000 picks per week. In 1850 a plain calico weaver on narrow looms could attend to four looms without a "tenter," and could weave 2,000,000 picks per week. Thus we find that in about twenty-five years the productive capacity of the powerloom weaver had been doubled.

It is therefore obvious that the handloom was no longer a serious competitor for the production of average cotton goods, and as the following comparative table shows, the changeover from handloom weaving to powerloom weaving had been completed in about 50 years.

	Handloom weavers	Powerloom weavers
1806	184,000	A FEW
1813	212,000	3,000
1815	200,000	7,000
1817	228,000	10,000
1819–21	240,000	10,000
1829–31	225,000	50,000
1832	225,000	75,000
1844	60,000	150,000
1859–61	5,000	203,000

The Automatic Loom

The earliest public reference to the first fully automatic loom—the Northrop loom as we now know it—is probably to be found in a paper read before the New England Cotton Manufacturing Association, at their meeting in Atlanta, United States of America, in October, 1895. It would appear from an advertisement by the Draper Corporation of America, in a copy of Skinner's Cotton Trade Directory, that the Northrop loom was first placed on the market in America in 1894. Amongst the first of the firms to adopt the Northrop loom in this country was Messrs. Ashton Brothers & Co. Ltd., of Hyde, who started to install them in 1903.

CHAPTER IV

Introduction of Power

FROM THE figures just quoted it will be seen how handloom weaving gradually declined, the weaving rooms in the cottages were closed one by one, and the stalwart self-reliant weavers came into the towns and villages to work in the mills which were being built all over the country. These drastic changes were accelerated by a number of factors operating about the same time. Between 1760 and 1840, over $5\frac{1}{2}$ million acres of common fields and wastes were enclosed by a series of private and general Acts of Parliament (the Enclosures Acts). Under these Acts the common land was divided, in the manor, between the lord of the manor (who got the lion's share), the more prosperous farmers, (who got the bulk of the remainder) and the poor got little or nothing. If land was allotted to the peasant it was burdened by conditions as to fencing or draining which made it impossible for him to utilise it. The effect of enclosure was to take away from the rural worker his independence. Formerly he had his land, his rights of putting live stock on the waste or common lands, rights of cutting fuels, and so on. The poorer peasant therefore gradually became dependent upon the capitalist farmers for his livelihood, and on the landlord for the right to stay in the village in which he was born. Concurrently with this state of affairs in agriculture, spinning mills, and some weaving mills, were being established, which absorbed much of their labour from amongst the country folks, and the farmers who remained in their farms concentrated the whole of their attention to stockbreeding and farming, instead of dividing their activities between cultivating the land and producing cloths.

The Factory System

The two earliest factories in Burnley, of which records have been kept, were Halstead's Mill, near Orchard Bridge, which dates from 1736, and the "Dandy Shop" in Massey Street, erected in 1787. Both these factories contained hand-looms for woollen weaving, the "Dandy Shop" deriving its name from the later "dandy" looms, the cast-iron frames of which formed a marked contrast to the clumsy wooden structure of the earlier looms.

In 1776 half-a-dozen mills were built in Oldham, three being worked by horses and three by water-power. The mills were generally built in the valleys in order to get the advantage of the water-power from the rivers and their tributaries.

Spinning mills, actuated by water-power, began to be built in the Burnley district, such as Extwistle Mill, Jewell Mill, Heasandford Mill, and Mill Dam Mill. The Peels were first to introduce steam power in their factory at the bottom of Sandygate. This mill was built in 1790, and was destroyed by fire eight years later. These early mills, says George C. Miller, in the *Northern Daily Telegraph*, were "lit by candle light, lacked ventilation and proper sanitary facilities, and the operatives laboured from 12 to 18 hours a day, in conditions which must have been veritable breeding-grounds of disease and poverty."

The first real mill was built in Nelson in 1790 by a Briercliffe clothier named Eckroyd, who bought land at Lomeshaye for this purpose. In this small woollen mill, Mr. Eckroyd employed whole families. There are records of children aged three and four earning their own living at this time, according to Mr. W. Bennett, M.A., in the Nelson *Leader*.

Although the inventions which had developed were the products of the concentrated Lancashire industry, with its traditions of enterprise and adaptability, their application was by no means restricted to Lancashire. In the era of water-power (from about 1760 to the 1830's) cotton mills were established in almost every county in the British Isles where water was available. Landowners everywhere offered sites and water supplies on attractive terms. Imports of raw cotton increased from an average of 7,000,000 lbs. a year in 1776–1780, to 31,000,000 lbs. in 1790, the greater part being used for calicoes and muslins, and a smaller proportion for fustians (cotton mixtures). A list of cotton mills (of rather doubtful accuracy) made in 1787 and quoted by Baines, shows 143 mills in Great Britain, of which only 41 were in Lancashire, 22 were in Derbyshire, 17 in Nottinghamshire, and 19 in Scotland. (These mills would be spinning mills). Although steam was used in a cotton mill in 1785, the bulk of these mills were operated by water-power. It will be seen that the use of water-power encouraged the establishment of mills all over the country, in sites often remote but well-placed in relation to water supplies. Mills were erected in the hilly regions of North East Lancashire, Derbyshire, Yorkshire, Westmorland and Scotland. Fishwick estimates that the value of cotton goods manufactured rose from £600,000 in 1766 to £3,304,371 in 1787, showing over a five-fold increase in twenty-one years.

Just as man and horsepower had been superseded by waterpower, this was found to be insufficient and not always available. Steam-power was evolved through many experimentations. The first working steam-engine appears to have been invented by the Marquis of Worcester in 1663 but it was little used. Papin also made an engine, which was theoretical rather than practical. In 1698 Thomas Savery used an engine for pumping water out of mines. This rather clumsy invention, however, was soon superseded in 1705 by Newcomen's steam pump. Newcomen is the greater name before Watt; he separated the boiler and the cylinder.

Watt (1736–1819, born at Greenock) made the next big steps in steam engine progress, though Smeaton had improved on Newcomen. Watt suggested improvements whilst repairing one of Newcomen's engines, and produced his own models between 1763 and 1769. His steam engine was patented in 1769 and was first used in mining operations. It was first applied in a spinning mill in 1785 by Robinson at Pepplewick, in Nottinghamshire, and other well-known spinners followed this example; Robert Peel; Drinkwater; Samuel Oldknow; and Richard Arkwright. Watt's steam engine was also adopted in Bolton, Glasgow, and Oldham. As manufacturers became convinced of the usefulness of the Watt steam-engine a large number of the first powerlooms were driven by steam, hence the name "steam-looms" and the class of operatives as "steam weavers".

In fact, during the first half of the nineteenth century water-power was gradually replaced by steam and the wide dispersion of the industry was simultaneously reduced. According to Baines, by about 1835 the number of mills in Great Britain had increased to 1,125, of which 627 were in Lancashire, whilst the proportions in Scotland, Derbyshire and Nottinghamshire had fallen. The mills outside Lancashire still largely used water-power, and the greatest development in steam-power took place in the Lancashire mills. Hence the concentration of the industry in Lancashire, after its comparatively wide dispersion in the short era of water-power, was closely connected with the greater facility of establishing steam-power mills in Lancashire.

Ogden, in the Journal of the Textile Institute, 1927, suggested that the main factors affecting the actual manufacture of cotton goods appeared to be those of water supply and coal. The main requirement of the industry is a regular supply of soft water, and millowners would naturally prefer the higher ground where the rainfall was greater. The humidity of Lancashire is often put forward as a principal reason for the location of the cotton industry in certain areas of Lancashire, but it cannot be regarded as a primary factor. There is a considerable belt of Lancashire, around Ormskirk, for instance, where the atmosphere is at least as humid as in the Manchester-Bolton area. Humidity might help to explain the presence of the industry in Lancashire, but it does not explain why the industry should cling to the hilly regions of East Lancashire. Proximity of coal is of some importance, but was of much more importance in the past than today. The principal geophysical factor in the concentration of the industry in Lancashire, therefore, appears to be the ample supply of good, soft, water.

Another of the earliest mills in South Lancashire was that founded by Mr. Benjamin Ashton, at Hyde. According to the *Textile Weekly* of 30th November, 1945:

> "One Benjamin Ashton, born in 1718, was weaving hand-made linen warp and cotton weft cloth at Gee Cross, Hyde, in 1745. The first mill on the site now occupied by the Company (Ashton Brothers & Co. Ltd.) was built in 1810. From its inception it was a vertical concern, comprising spinning, weaving, finishing, etc., right up to merchanting."

In the early days in the 1800's the centre of gravity of the industry was far more to the south of Lancashire than it is now. In 1841 about three-quarters of the workers in the industry were in mills to the south of Rochdale and Bury, largely due to the rapid development in power spinning in the Manchester area. The later northward movement of the industry took two forms—Oldham, Bolton, and Rochdale partly replaced Manchester as centres of cotton spinning; secondly, a large number of independent weaving firms were established mainly in the northern part of the county. In 1841, 109,500 persons were employed in combined spinning and weaving firms, whereas only 8,300 were employed in purely weaving concerns, and it must be mentioned that the first powerlooms were installed by power spinners. By 1884, 78 per cent of the spindles were in the southern area, south of Rochdale, and 62 per cent of the looms were in the northern area.

CHAPTER V

Early Attempts to Combine

Appalling Factory Conditions

FROM THE foregoing brief survey of the development of the Lancashire cotton trade it will be seen that Lancashire became one of the chief centres of industrialisation in the country, and this brought with it appalling problems of child labour, long hours, and bad conditions of employment. When factories were first built there was a strong repugnance on the part of parents who had been accustomed to the old family life under the domestic system to send their children into these factories. It was, according to H. de B. Gibbins (*The Industrial History Of England*) considered a disgrace so to do; the epithet of "factory girl" was the most insulting that could be applied to a young woman, and girls who had once been in a factory could never find employment elsewhere. It was not until the wages of the workman had been reduced to a starvation level that they consented to their children and wives being employed in the mills. But the manufacturers wanted labour by some means or other, and they got it, from the workhouses. They sent for parish apprentices from all parts of England, and pretended to apprentice them to the new employments just introduced. The mill-owners systematically communicated with the overseers of the poor, who arranged a day for the inspection of pauper children. Those chosen by the manufacturers were then conveyed by wagons or canal boats to their destination, and from that moment were doomed to slavery.

Gibbins says:

"Sometimes regular traffickers would take the place of the manufacturer, and transfer a number of children to a factory district, and there keep them, generally in some dark cellar, till they could hand them over to a mill-owner in want of hands, who would come and examine their height, strength, and bodily capacities, exactly as did the slave-dealers in the American markets. After that the children were simply at the mercy of their owners, nominally as apprentices, but in reality as mere slaves . . . It was often arranged by the parish authorities, in order to get rid of imbeciles, that one idiot should be taken by the mill-owner with every twenty sane children . . . Their treatment was most inhuman. The hours of their labour were only limited by exhaustion after many modes of torture had been unavailingly applied to force continued work. Children were often worked 16 hours a day, by day and by night. Even Sunday was used as a convenient time to clean the machinery. The author of *The History of the Factory Movement* writes: "In stench, in heated rooms, amid the constant whirling of a thousand wheels, little fingers and little feet were kept in ceaseless action, forced into unnatural activity by blows from the heavy hands and feet of the merciless overlooker, and the infliction of bodily pain by instruments of punishment invented by the sharpened ingenuity of insatiable selfishness.

"They were fed upon the coarsest and cheapest food, often with the same as that served out to the pigs of their master. They slept by turns and in relays, in filthy beds which were never cool; for one set of children were sent to sleep in them as soon as the others had gone off to their daily or nightly toil . . . Some of these miserable beings tried to run away. To prevent their doing so, those suspected of this tendency had irons riveted on their ankles with long links reaching up to the hips, and were compelled to work and sleep in these chains, young women and girls as well as boys suffering this brutal treatment. Many died and were buried secretly at night in some desolate spot, lest people should notice the number of graves; and many committed suicide . . . During this period of unheeded and ghastly suffering in the mills of our native land, the British philanthropist was occupying himself with agitating for the relief of the very largely imaginary woes of negro slaves in other countries . . . The spectacle of England buying the freedom of black slaves by riches drawn from the labour of her white ones, affords an interesting study for the cynical philosopher."

George Southgate, in his *English Economic History* says that factories were "specially built with a view to securing the maximum of profit for their owners, and no thought was given to the health, comfort, convenience, and safety of the employees . . . Dangerous machinery was not fenced off, and serious, and even fatal accidents were common."

In referring to the employment of child labour recruited from the workhouses, Southgate says: "the majority (of the factory owners) saw in the system of child labour nothing but a means of profit . . . It is no exaggeration to assert that the condition of these young workers was indistinguishable from slavery. The truth about the conditions of child labour in the factories was not realised by the general public, and even when knowledge of it spread, people were not shocked at the idea of children of five, six or seven doing factory work. The notion that a child of the working classes should not begin to earn his living until he reaches the age of 14 or 15 . . . is of quite modern growth."

Illiteracy was general, and industrial development outran social and political progress, violently disturbing the whole life of the community.

G. D. H. Cole says: " . . . The new towns, hurriedly built and often without any form of local administration were centres of pestilence and squalor. The old-established craftsmen (the handloom weavers) were being displaced by the new machines, and children and women, under abominable conditions, were being largely employed in the new factories. In face of severe repression, working-class organisation was difficult and dangerous; but Trade Unions were being formed, and strikes were frequent and often accompanied by violence . . . Socialist ideas were beginning to develop and movements, forerunners of Chartism, were beginning to arise. The workers were, however, badly organised, and no match as a rule for the organised power of the employers and the Government."

Special misery had been caused by bad harvests and the prolonged Napoleonic Wars between 1793 and 1815. Newly established associations of cotton operatives poured petition after petition into Parliament, showing that the rates for weaving had steadily declined, and reiterating the old demands for a legally fixed scale of piece work rates and the limitation of apprentices. A Parliamentary Committee of 1808 took voluminous evidence on the subject of minimum rates. Sir Robert Peel (the elder) whose own factories swarmed with boys, opposed a Bill brought in by Sheridan to limit the number of apprentices in the calico-printing trade, in the name of industrial freedom, and carried the House of Commons with him. Meanwhile, the despairing operatives baffled in their attempts to procure fresh legislation turned for aid to the existing law. Unrepealed statutes still enabled the magistrates in some trade to fix the rate of wages.

Early Trade Unions

Comparatively little is known about the history of the English trade unions previous to the repeal of the Combination Laws in 1824. Being illegal, they were necessarily underground organisations. In documents from Home Office papers, published by Professor A. Aspinall in his book *The Early English Trade Unions*, it is found that very few references are made to trade unions before 1790, but that does not, of course, mean that trade unions were then only just emerging. The fact that at the end of the eighteenth century there were more than forty Acts of Parliament to prevent workmen from combining is suggestive both of the widespread existence of trade unions over a long period of years and of the willingness of the legislature of that time to support the labour policy of the employers, i.e., to suppress combination and to keep down wages.

There is evidence that a Weavers' Club existed in Glasgow in 1778, although its history was short. It must be remembered that in those days there was no railways system, nor was there a penny post to facilitate rapid communication. In the Manchester Constable's accounts of 15th February, 1754, mention is made of the apprehension of some persons for entering into "The weavers' combination." In 1759 twenty-one worsted smallware weavers were sent to Lancaster for "combining against the manufactury". A copy of the rules of these worsted smallware weavers, printed in 1756, is in the Manchester Library, and one of the articles is assigned to so early a date as 15th August, 1747, in the preamble of which it is stated that an informal club had existed for many years.

In 1758 the check-weavers were being solicited to enter into a "box" (or club) to oppose the unlawful practice of the masters, and Professor Chapman refers to a resolution of the Oldham Weavers, dated 18th August, 1758.

The Combination Acts

The Combination Acts of 1799 and 1800 were not the first legal enactments against the right of working men to combine for an increase of wages or a reduction of hours. They were the first Acts to prohibit ALL combinations whatsoever, although they represented no change in actual policy on the part of the Government of the time. The clause prohibiting combinations of employers was very difficult to enforce, and the masters hardly made a pretence to obey the law; but the workmen could be, and were, prosecuted at Quarter Sessions or the Assizes for entering into a combination, and punished very severely. They were charged under the Seditious Meetings Act of 1795, or under the Combination Act of 1800, the latter Act being aimed at "the prevention of conspiracies among journeymen tradesmen to raise their wages. All Benefit Clubs and Societies are to be immediately suppressed". The governing classes had taken fright at the French Revolution just across the channel and saw sedition on every corner.

Early Associations of Weavers

Professor Aspinall, in his book on the *Early English Trade Unions*, reprints a lengthy Manifesto which was prepared and printed by the "Association of Weavers" and issued on 13th of May, 1799. The Manifesto commenced with these words: "The present existing laws that should protect weavers, & c., from imposition, being trampled under foot, for want of a union amongst them, they have come to a determination to support each other in their just and legal rights . . . " The Manifesto argued the case for the right to combine, at great length, and dealt with wages being received. It continued: "We will suppose a man to be married in the year 1792; he at that period received 22s. for 44 yds. of cloth. (Handloom weaving). . . . his family keeps increasing, together with the price of every necessary of life, whilst his wages for labour decreases. Let us look at him in the year 1799, and we shall perhaps find him surrounded with five or six small children, and, lo! instead of 44 yds. they have increased the length to 60, and give him only 11s. for it; and, to make ill worse, he must work it with finer weft." The manifesto concluded: "Ye whose hardened hearts are dead to humane feelings which should always adorn the human mind, may say it is impracticable and are we yet to continue suffering on your barely asserting this? No; we are determined that those who are appointed by the Constitution of our country to redress our grievances, shall have our real state laid before them . . . A peaceful demeanour shall always guide all our actions, and we trust a candid public will give the subject a mature consideration and afford us that support we merit. It was resolved unanimously that this Address should be printed and distributed in the different towns, in the name of the General Committee, assembled at Bolton, on Monday, the 13th of May, 1799.

John Seddon, President."

The names of the Committee followed. There were six from Bolton and neighbourhood, three from Manchester and Salford, two each from Stockport, Oldham, Wigan, Blackburn, Chorley, Newton, Warrington, and Bury; one each from Whitefield, Chowbent, and New Chapel, near Leigh. The handbill also concluded: "This Committee earnestly desire that weavers in general will step forward and give their support, and others who are interested in the welfare of the cause are desired to come forward, as they have nothing to fear . . .

James Holcroft, Secretary."

In enclosing a copy of the above Manifesto to the Under-Secretary of State for Home Affairs a Wigan Magistrate, John Singleton, wrote: " . . . In this paper things are much misrepresented, and are calculated greatly to inflame and mislead the labouring class, who, I assure you, are fully employed, and well—very well—paid for their labour, and before these arts were used to disturb their peace and make them discontented, was both happy and contented."

Professor Aspinall's book produces copies of letters which passed between the Under-Secretary of State and another prominent Magistrate, the Rev. Thomas Bancroft, of Bolton-le-Moors, suggesting that "it would be highly proper that you should employ some confidential persons to attend in those parts from whence the delegates are sent to the monthly meetings, in order that it may be known whether any other subjects are discussed there than those connected with the Petition to Parliament . . ." The employment of "confidential persons" to spy on the Weavers' Associations was also made in another letter written in 1799 by the Under-Secretary, to another magistrate, T. B. Bayley, concerning meetings being held in Manchester, Stockport, and Bury, and on 8th August, 1799, the Home Secretary (The Duke of Portland) wrote to the Rev. T. Bancroft, stating that "whatever the expense may amount to which may be incurred in employing persons for the purposes above-mentioned, you will draw for it upon Mr. King (the Under-Secretary of State)."

Largely upon instigation from the Government a meeting of Lancashire magistrates was held in Salford, on 28th November, 1799, when a document was produced, containing this preamble: "We, the undersigned, taking into consideration the various and repeated attempts that have lately been made to excite a spirit of dissatisfaction amongst the weavers and others employed in the manufactures of this County, and by violent handbills and other inflammatory publications, to encourage an illegal opposition to the Act passed in the last Session of Parliament ("To prevent unlawful combinations amongst workmen") do hereby signify our determined resolution to maintain, as much as in us lies, due obedience to the laws . . . "

Beatrice and Sidney Webb, in their book *Trade Union History* quote White and Henson's description of the Act of 1800 as a "tremendous millstone round the neck of the local artisan, which has depressed and debased him to the earth; every act which he had attempted, every measure that he had devised to keep up or raise his wages, he had been told was illegal; the whole force of the civil power and influence of the district has been exerted against him because he was acting illegally; the magistrates, acting in unison with the views of the legislature, to check and keep down wages and combination, regarded in almost every instance every attempt on the part of the artisan to ameliorate his situation or support his station in society as a species of sedition and resistance of the Government; every committee or active man among them was regarded as a turbulent, dangerous instigator, whom it was necessary to watch and crush if possible."

The Webbs cite one instance given in evidence before Hume's Committee, that in 1818 certain Bolton millowners suggested to the operative weavers that they should concert together to leave the employment of those who paid below the current rate. Acting on this hint a meeting of forty delegates took place, at which it was resolved to ask for the advance agreed to by the good employers. A fortnight later the president and the two secretaries were arrested, convicted of conspiracy and imprisoned for one and two years respectively, although their employers gave evidence on the prisoners' behalf to the effect that they had themselves requested the men to attend the meeting, and had approved the resolutions passed. In the following year fifteen cotton spinners of Manchester, who had met to receive contributions to bury their dead, under "Articles" sanctioned by Quarter Sessions in 1795, were seized in the committeeroom by the police and committed to trial for conspiracy. After three or four months' imprisonment they were brought to trial, the whole Bar being briefed against them. It was urged in court that "all societies, whether benefit societies or otherwise, were only cloaks for the people of England to conspire against the State," and most of the defendants were sentenced to varying terms of imprisonment.

Cotton Industry Arbitration Act, 1800

Constant appeals were made to the Government for measures to be taken to improve the weavers' position, and as the result of many petitions an Arbitration Act was conceded in 1800. A special Committee of the House of Commons had taken evidence, and Mr. James Holcroft, of Bolton, had given evidence. This Act was called "Arbitration Act for the Cotton Industry (Statutes 39 and 40, Geo. III.90) 1800" and the preamble was as follows:

> "An Act for settling disputes that may arise between masters and workmen engaged in the cotton manufacture in that part of Great Britain called England."

The Act provided for the appointment of an Arbitrator to settle disputes upon prices, cloth lengths, workmanship, and so on.

Under the new Arbitration Act the weavers set out to make the best of what they thought were the powers given by the Act, and one master had 108 notices of arbitration served upon him in one day, all by the same man, probably the secretary of some formal or informal trade union. The magistrates decided, however, that the Act was never meant to be used as the operatives expected it to be. On the other hand a Mr. Thomas Thorpe, who had acted as arbitrator in some 200 cases, reported that the Act worked well so long as it was carried out. Eleven cases only in which he was concerned had been referred to a magistrate, and of these all but one had been settled in the men's favour. In all, hundreds of applications for arbitration were made, many of them through James Holcroft, but in many cases the magistrates ruled that the Act was never intended to be used as the operatives expected it to be used. The Government appeared to change its mind, when an amended statute was passed in 1804, after which it was understood that no magistrate had power to interfere in the matter of new agreements as to rates of wages. The 1800 Act was repealed in 1824.

Weavers' Petitions

Further efforts were made to bring pressure to bear upon Parliament. On February 26th, 1807, a monster petition was presented to Parliament, signed by no fewer than 130,000 cotton weavers of Lancashire, Cheshire, and Yorkshire. This petition set forth that:—

"whenever the demand for goods becomes slack many master manufacturers adopt the expedient of reducing wages, thereby compelling the petitioners, in order to obtain a livelihood, to manufacture great quantities of goods at a time when they are absolutely not wanted, and that great quantities of goods so manufactured are sacrificed in the market at low prices, to the manifest injury of the fair dealer, and the great oppression of the petitioners," who could often earn only 9s. a week.

In 1808 the weavers again petitioned Parliament asking that a minimum price should be fixed below which goods should not be manufactured. Reference was made to the growing distress occasioned by the masters becoming bankrupt. It was stated that the average earnings at this period were only 6s. per week. A petition also went up from Bolton masters who represented that they had suffered greatly from the fluctuation of wages, which during the preceding three years had been more than 100 per cent and at least 33 per cent on the value of a great portion of the goods in a finished state. The petition stated that this fluctuation of wages gave no increase to the demand from foreign markets, whilst its direct tendency was to ruin the fair manufacturer by reducing the value of his stock on hand. Capital, ingenuity, and industry could not ensure success in the cotton trade, the Petitioners said, till some limits were fixed by the legislature below which the wages of workmen could not be reduced. A Bill was introduced into the House of Commons, but was talked out. Failing to obtain any satisfaction the weavers were driven to desperation. They struck work to enforce better wages, and as might have been expected disorder here and there occurred. A salutary means was found of dealing with "knobsticks", by the simple expedient of entering houses and factories and taking away the shuttles of those who continued to work. Among the numerous places affected in this way were Stockport, Rochdale, and Wigan. It is on record that a gentleman who went with a force of 100 volunteers to stop a party of strikers near Manchester was, on parleying with them, much impressed by their reasonableness. A remarkable incident occurred at Rochdale. Some constables there seized some unguarded bags of shuttles and placed them in the House of Correction. After rescuing five or six of their co-workers who were being conveyed to prison the strikers went and demanded the return of the shuttles. On being refused they broke into the prison and burnt it down. For this exploit one man was sentenced to two years' imprisonment. The offence was not a capital offence as no-one was living in the prison at the time. Various others, guilty of disorder, received sentences of from one to twelve months.

The strikers were encouraged and supported by one Joseph Hanson, a man of some substance and a colonel in the Volunteers, who, popular with the weavers for his advocacy of the Minimum Wage Bill, had stood as candidate for Preston. On the occasion of a great Mass Meeting on May 25th, 1809, he rode on to the field and addressed the people, in opposition to the Captain of the Dragoons. He was arrested and prosecuted for inciting to disorder. Respectable witnesses spoke on his behalf and testified that he used no more provocative expressions than "My lads your cause is good; be firm and you will succeed." "I will support you as far as £3,000 will go, and if that will not do I will go further." He was sentenced to six months' imprisonment and a fine of £100. Grateful for his championship and distressed by the outcome of it the weavers wanted to pay his fine by penny subscriptions, but the offer was declined. Nevertheless, 39,600 subscribers did present him with a silver cup, and Hanson doubtless considered himself well repaid. The strikers had demanded an advance of $33\frac{1}{3}$ per cent, but they compromised for 20 per cent, and in a few weeks they were little better off. The proper sort of combination was lacking to maintain what they had won.

Professor Aspinall, in his book on the Early English Trade Unions, quotes extracts from a handbill which makes strange reading these days. The handbill is dated 16th August, 1810, and is addressed by a committee of weavers to the Manufacturers of Blackburn. It states: "From proper information received, they have reason to apprehend a reduction of their wages (small it is, God knows) will shortly be attempted by a few of those who have ever acted as if their sole wish was to destroy commerce, ruin the fair trader, and bring both themselves and the community at large into a vortex of destruction." The handbill went on to state that the true interest of the master and workman was one, and when the workmen were poor and wretched the manufacturer also suffered. The weavers proposed that by an Association of the manufacturers of Lancashire and the cordial co-operation of the workmen, dreadful evils might be prevented. The plan was therefore suggested that the quantity of goods be reduced when the market is overstocked, and their value will undoubtedly increase with the scarcity." The handbill stated that the weavers of Blackburn had determined not to submit to a reduction of prices, but would agree to a limitation in the quantity of their work, and would bear every privation for a few weeks or months, until a change took place in the markets. They were willing to enter into subscriptions for the relief of small families who might be hurt by the measure.

The *Cotton Factory Times* of 12th May, 1933, published an article giving great details of the sufferings of the cotton operatives in these early times, and they quote copious extracts from a Manifesto which was issued during a strike of Oldham weavers in 1818, which referred to the shamefully low wages of 4s. to 5s. per week. About the same time a delegate meeting was held at Bury, when a handbill was issued, signed by John Hibbert, President, and Robert Ellison, Secretary. It quoted Adam Smith as stating in his *Wealth of Nations* that if the labour of one man would not provide the comforts of life for himself, a wife and three children, such a nation would be on the decline. The address continued:

"Good God! But how must they exist on six shillings per week, which is the sum the greatest part of the weavers must work early and late to procure . . . If such a vast body of ingenious, useful and laborious men must remain in such a state, it must ultimately militate against the State. Gentlemen, we ask you for an advance of seven shillings on the pound. In this you must admit we have confined ourselves within the boundaries of moderation, as several other branches of the trade have called for greater advance than the whole of our income . . . "

We are told that some got the advance and others did not. In Burnley the strikers sent round the bellman to advertise a meeting of strikers, but he was seized by the authorities and thrown into the lock-up as an "agent of the combination." The weavers rescued him and continued to demonstrate until a troop of yeomanry from Manchester came on the scene, arrested seven of the liberators, and lodged them in Blackburn gaol.

Writing of this period Francis Place said: "the sufferings of persons employed in the cotton manufacture were beyond credibility; they were drawn into combinations, betrayed, prosecuted, convicted, sentenced, and monstrously severe punishment inflicted on them; they were reduced to and kept in the most wretched state of existence."

The Webbs state that their employers, instead of being—as in the older handicrafts—little more than master workmen, recognising the customary standard of life of their journeymen, were often capitalist entrepreneurs, devoting their whole energies to the commercial side of the business, and leaving their managers to buy labour in the market at the cheapest possible rate. Cases of gross tyranny and heartless cruelty were not wanting, and the frequent strikes were only passionate struggles to maintain a bare subsistence wage. There were periods of outbursts of machine-breaking and outrages, with intervals of abject submission and reckless competition with each other for employment. Leaders and rank and file were often implicated in charges of political sedition. All these circumstances led to the prevalence among them of fearful oaths, mystic initiation rites, and other manifestations of a sensationalism which was sometimes puerile and sometimes criminal. The most notorious of these so-called "seditions," about which little is really known, was the "luddite" riots of 1811–12, when mobs of manual workers, acting under some sort of organisation, went about destroying textile machinery and sometimes wrecking factories.

Finally, even some of the employers themselves were driven to denounce publicly the ruinous extent to which wage-cutting had been carried. A Declaration dated June 10th, 1819, signed by fourteen Lancashire manufacturers, regretted that they had been compelled by the action of a few competitors to lower wages to the then existing rates, and strongly condemned any further reduction. At Coventry the Ribbon Manufacturers combined with the Weavers' Provident Union to maintain a general adherence to the agreed list of prices, and in 1819 subscribed no less than £16,000 to cover the cost of proceedings, to maintain that object. This combination formed the subject of an indictment at Warwick Assizes, which put an end to the association, the remaining funds being handed over to the local "Streets commissioners" for paving the city.

The "Blanketeers;" Peterloo

In 1817 there was a projected march on London by the working people of Lancashire, with a Petition. The march was designed by the Radicals, but numbers of the weavers who took part in the assembly at Manchester on the day of the start were actuated a great deal more by the failure of their petitions relating to wages than by a desire for manhood suffrage or any of the reforms advocated by the Radicals. The meeting at Manchester was broken up. In March, 1817, a larger meeting was held in St. Peter's Fields, Manchester, at which about 1,000 men appeared, with blankets over their shoulders, and with the avowed intention of marching to London to lay their grievances before the Prince Regent. This meeting was dispersed by the military, and several of the "Blanketeers" as they were called were taken to prison. There was another demonstration of spinners, weavers, and colliers, towards the end of 1818, to press for an advance in wages. Led on by Henry Hunt, the orator, of London, and others, it was decided to hold a mass meeting in St. Peter's Fields on 18th January, 1819. This meeting was held and a resolution was passed calling for the immediate repeal of the Corn Law. In the following August the borough Reeve and constables of Manchester refused to call a public meeting to consider the best means of obtaining reform of the House of Commons, although 700 householders had signed the requisition. The result was that the requisitioners themselves summoned the meeting, which was held near St. Peter's Church, on 16th August, Henry Hunt being called upon to preside.

In recounting the story, Fishwick says that this meeting was attended by members of societies from Oldham, Rochdale, Middleton, Ashton, Stockport, and all the surrounding villages, each contingent being accompanied by its band of music. The magistrates, being determined to disperse the vast assembly, called to their aid 200 special constables, and the Manchester and Cheshire Yeomanry Cavalry; the 15th Hussars, and a detachment of the 88th Regiment of Foot, some pieces of artillery also being ready if required.

The crowd which was estimated at 50,000 was unarmed, but carried a plentiful display of banners with inscriptions more or less revolutionary. Acting under the orders of the magistrates, the Manchester Yeomanry and the Hussars, with drawn swords, dashed through the crowd in the direction of the temporary platform, where they captured Henry Hunt and others. The would-be reformers fled in every direction, and the arrival of the Cheshire Yeomanry assisted to clear the field. After this onslaught—for it could not be called a fight—three or four people were found to have been killed, and about 30 others were carried off to the infirmary. Later it was found that eight persons had been killed, and several hundreds were wounded. Henry Hunt was tried for sedition and sentenced to two years' imprisonment. This tragedy became known as the Battle of Peterloo, from its scene, St. Peter's Fields.

The "Philanthropic Society"

There was considerable uneasiness amongst the cotton operatives during 1818, and Professor Aspinall's book quotes copiously from letters in the possession of the Home Office which passed between the then Home Secretary and the various magistrates in the cotton towns. The following document is quoted in Professor Aspinall's book, dealing with the resolutions of the "Philanthropic Society":—

"Manchester, August 19th, 1818.

"At a meeting of Deputies from the undermentioned Trades from Manchester, Stockport, Ashton-under-Lyne, Oldham, Bury, & c. &c., &c.

"Calico printers, dyers and dressers, hatters, blacksmiths, jenny spinners, cotton weavers, bricklayers, fustian cutters, colliers, sawyers, shoemakers, slubbers, mule spinners, machine makers, &c.

The following Address and Resolutions were unanimously agreed to:

"At a general meeting of trades convened to take into consideration the distressed state and privations to which the working class of society are reduced by their avaricious employers reducing wages to less than sufficient to support nature or purchase the bare necessaries for our existence, with great economy and hard labour; therefore, to render redress in such cases of distress to any body or party reduced as aforesaid.

RESOLUTIONS

"First.—That there be a Union of all Trades called the PHILANTHROPIC SOCIETY, to be held in Manchester on the second Monday in every month, when all Trades shall send a delegate with proper credentials for admission.

"Second.—That every trade be recommended to raise a Fund amongst themselves for the general benefit of all trades joined in this Union, and in particular any trade that may be engaged in resisting oppression, or to alleviate distress, and to enable the labouring part of the community to live in comfort and decency.

"Third.—That any trade feeling the necessity of an advance of wages, that trade shall be bound to give notice to a meeting of delegates convened for that purpose, and their concurrence being obtained, all other trades will support them.

"Fourth.—That if any trade be under the necessity of leaving their employ through the oppression of their employers, they shall first call the general representatives together and inform them, provided that such representatives be not overpowered with too much business at one time, that they may be prepared for supporting the cause and provide for the same; in short, no trade shall leave their employ without first calling the other trades together, and then act by and with their consent in taking the most favourable time for resistance.

"Fifth.—That any body of workmen being oppressed or illegally used, this Society will support them in obtaining legal redress.

"Sixth.—That all printing of notices, &c., with all delegations, or any other necessary expenses, shall be paid out of their separate funds.

"Seventh.—That a Committee of eleven persons be chosen by ballot, out of the different trades who form this Society, and shall be regularly enrolled on the list kept for that purpose. The Committee to go out by regular rotation every month, so that the whole may be changed every three months.

"Eighth.—That in order to preserve decorum in this Society or meeting of representatives, no person shall be allowed to advance any political or religious argument, under a forfeit of 3d. for the first offence, and 6d. for the second, which must be paid the night it is forfeited.

"Ninth.—That there shall be an Auxiliary Society of the different trades in each town; that each trade shall have its own by-laws, and each auxiliary to act in conjunction with the Resolutions of the central Philanthropic Society.

"Tenth.—That the representatives be empowered to alter or amend, add or diminish any Rule or Rules for the benefit of this Society, provided it does not infringe upon or act against any trade or division belonging to the general Philanthrophic Society.

"G. Cave, Printer, Exchange Buildings, Manchester".

This document was at once forwarded by the Home Secretary, Lord Sidmouth, to the Law Officers of the Crown for their advice, and on 19th October, 1818 they replied:—

"We have considered the accompanying paper and we are of opinion it would not be advisable to institute any prosecution for the publication of it. Indeed, we very much doubt whether it could be made the subject of prosecution, and as the spirit of combination amongst the workmen in this part of the country has in some degree apparently subsided, a prosecution now instituted (and particularly if it failed) might rather tend to revive than extinguish it."

Very grave unrest continued to exist in many of the cotton towns, such as Blackburn, Burnley, Padiham, Preston, etc., and at Bury three workers named Pilkington, Ellison, and Kay were committed on 16th September, 1818 for a conspiracy. In a letter dated 17th September, 1818, Dr. T. D. Whitaker, a local magistrate, wrote to Viscount Sidmouth, the Home Secretary, as follows: "The Hundred of Blackburn is in a state of approaching to that of a general insurrection in consequence of a dispute betwixt the weavers and their employers on the subject of wages . . . We have in consequence been compelled hitherto to use conciliation, which has only had the effect of emboldening the mob and encouraging them to acts of greater outrage. The ringleaders which had been apprehended have been liberated by violence . . . The houses of the weavers who are willing to work are visited, their looms and work marked, and themselves inhibited from proceeding, by threats of fire or other mischief."

"General Union of Trades"

In October, 1818, attempts were made to form a "General Union of Trades," delegates travelling from Nottingham, Birmingham, Liverpool, and from weavers in Somerset. The meetings were held in Todmorden for a time, because (as the local magistrate reported to the Home Secretary) "it lays out of view, in a central situation between Manchester, Halifax, Blackburn, and Bolton, and is in a very retired situation."

The following years, from 1819 to about 1824, were eventful in the struggle against the operations of the Combination Acts, and in an issue of a newspaper called *The Courier*, dated 15th September, 1819, there appears an account of a trial at the Lancaster Assizes, held on Saturday, 11th September, 1819, in which two weavers, named James Watson and Laurence Moss, were charged with conspiring to raise the wages of the weavers at Blackburn. The phrase used by the prosecuting counsel was "for a conspiracy to raise the wages of those employed in the art, craft, or mystery of weaving." In answer to a query from the Judge, Baron Wood, as to the whereabouts of Laurence Moss, he was informed that he had not been found. When arrested there was an attack upon the police, and prisoner Moss was released and his whereabouts had not been ascertained. Counsel, in the course of his statement, said that a meeting was held on the 7th September, 1818, upon Blakey Moor, Blackburn, at which 1,000 weavers were present; other meetings were held on the 9th, 10th, 11th, and 12th September, of the same year. Sometimes there were 3,000 or 4,000 persons present, and these had paraded the streets of Blackburn in regular order, marching in files four abreast. Counsel said there was no rioting; there was however, a show of numbers who abstained from work, and endeavoured by the force of intimidation to compel employers to raise wages. The meetings and parades, it was urged, had alarmed the inhabitants of Blackburn. The learned counsel observed that "an assembly, which endangered the peace and security of the neighbours, could not be viewed without anxious interest, particularly as the object of that assembly was an impossible one. A redundant labouring population, and the refinement of machinery (without which, he said, we should have no chance of competition in the foreign market) have reduced the wages of labour, and compelled the master manufacturers to reduce the wages of their men or cease manufacturing." Whatever doubts there might have been about the statement of counsel that the meetings and parades had alarmed the inhabitants of Blackburn, to the accused it would sound alarming when his acts were described as amounting "to an expressed and avowed object to destroy the most fundamental, most important, and essential principle of social security and enjoyment."

We have moved far, in a legal sense, from the days of James Watson and Laurence Moss. The language they were charged with using was "Stand firm; live on air; burn your looms; bear any extremity rather than work." The only exception which could be taken in a legal sense these days would be those relating to burning of looms. James Watson, who was 23 years of age, was sentenced to one year's imprisonment. In delivering judgment, Baron Wood said: "James Watson, you have been convicted upon very convincing evidence of a very dangerous conspiracy, such conspiracies are very mischievous, and if they were allowed there could be no commerce. It is highly necessary, therefore, that they be discouraged. The sentence upon you is, that you be imprisoned in the gaol of this country for one year." There is no evidence that the remaining prisoner, Laurence Moss, was ever captured.

The Government and the employers were, however, slowly becoming conscious of the fact that they were fighting a losing battle. Propaganda through the Press, through public meetings and through the various Radical Reformist Societies, was powerfully contributing to increase the political consciousness of the working class. The great improvement of the postal service, and the multiplication of accelerated stage coaches, enabled the trade unions to organise themselves on something wider than a merely local basis. The Home Secretary sometimes instructed local postmasters to stop all letters addressed to suspected members of these illegal organisations. The workers owed something too to the public houses. However much the Temperance Party might denounce the public-house as an agency of social degradation, or the frightened Tories dislike it as a place where the "lower orders" talked sedition and voiced their discontent, it was immensely useful as a meeting place when trade unions were under the ban of the law. Exasperated employers were for ever calling upon the authorities to punish publicans for extending their hospitality to trade unions, by depriving them of their licences. The trade unions were, of course, greatly aided by the use they made of the "Benefit Clubs," or "Thrift Clubs," of which there were 820 in 1801, and in 1816 the membership was stated to be 700,000.

Repeal of the Combination Laws

By 1824 Members of Parliament on both sides had become convinced that the combination laws had not only failed in their object, but had dangerously antagonised the working class and 1824 saw the repeal of the Combination Laws, largely as a result of the efforts of Place and Hume. This success confirmed in the minds of the operatives the conviction of the justice of their cause, and they felt that combinations to raise wages and shorten the time or diminish the severity of labour were not only innocent but meritorious. For the next six months the newspapers were full of reports of strikes and rumours of strikes. The cotton spinners in the Manchester district were once more striking, and by 1825 the employers throughout the country were thoroughly aroused. Hume and Place had in vain preached moderation and warned the Unions of the danger of a reaction. Various employing interests got the ear of Huskisson, the President of the Board of Trade, and ultimately an Act known as "Peel's Act" of 1825 was passed, which, though it fell short of the measure which Place and Hume had so skilfully piloted through Parliament the year before, effected a real emancipation. The right of collective bargaining, involving the power to withhold labour from the market by concerted action, was for the first time expressly established.

The year 1825 closed with a financial panic and widespread commercial disaster. The four years that followed were years of contraction and distress. Hundreds of thousands of workmen in all trades lost their employment, and wages were reduced all round. In many manufacturing districts the operatives were kept from starvation only by public subscription.

In the midst of all these turbulent conditions efforts were made to establish a permanent organisation in August, 1824, when a Delegate Meeting of cotton weavers was held in Manchester, with the object of preventing reductions in prices and to secure uniform wages. This attempt, in common with previous efforts to establish an organisation, was not too successful, and the weavers of Lancashire had to pass through still greater sufferings and privations before their organisations were effectively established. The spinners formed a Federation of Spinners in 1829, headed by Doherty, whose name will be familiar to students of trade union history. This Federation, however, sank into insignificance before the rising star, The National Association for the Protection of Labour, founded in July 1830. This was a federation of some 150 distinct clubs and included fustian, powerloom and worsted and smallware weavers from Manchester; cotton powerloom weavers from Clitheroe; powerloom weavers from Ashton, Stalybridge, Dukinfield; smallware weavers from Macclesfield; tape weavers from Derby; and nankeen weavers from Blackrod. The National Association flourished for about two years, and then collapsed.

Other "National Guilds" were formed and ceased to exist. These attempts at large-scale organising, stimulated by the failure of the Reform Act of 1832 to enfranchise the working class, culminated in Robert Owen's "Grand National Consolidated Trade Union" of 1834, which soon had half-a-million members, and was as unwieldy as its name.

By this time the employers had begun to combine, and the black-list had been invented for the purpose of victimising obnoxious operatives. The operatives knew how to kick back, however, and some turbulent times followed. The victims of hardship and oppression, it was hardly to be expected that they should be always docile. We read of conflicts with constables and the military and organised machine-wrecking. The year 1842 was notable for "plug-drawing" (i.e., withdrawing plugs from the factory boilers). Some years earlier in Manchester and Glasgow masters and blacklegs were placed in terror by shooting, vitriol-throwing and arson. It was stated in evidence before a Committee of 1824 that blackleg weavers were first treated to the "black-cat" which was a brick tied to a string. The brick was thrown through the window, over the warp, and then pulled away so as to destroy the threads. If this failed to impress the obnoxious weaver, vitriol might be used against him. The burning of Colonel Jackson's house near Blackburn in 1878 must have been about the last of these demonstrations.

Further attempts were made in Oldham in 1834 to form an organisation, and again in 1837, without success. Organisations were attempted in Bolton and Preston in 1836, and at Glasgow in 1837.

Fining System

Another disagreeable feature of factory life at this time was the growing practice of the employers in Fining their workpeople. Fining was no modern invention, as it was older than the factory system itself. At the time when the merchant put out warps to be woven by the handloom weaver he reserved to himself a "power of abatement" for deficiency in workmanship. With the commencement of the factory era the system developed into something of a fine art. In the hands of the greedy designing employer it could be made to yield the equivalent of an all-round reduction in wages. In the "Poor man's Avdvocate, 1832," many instances are given of fines upon spinners, for "rubbed cops" i.e., over-large cops, 1s. to 2s. 6d.; waste found in the necessary, 1s. each spinner; ten minutes late, 1s.; day off without permission, 12s.; gas, six lights, 2s. 6d.; three lights, 1s. 3d.; gas, reelers, 1s.; hot water for tea, 3d., 2d., or 1d.

In another mill operatives paid the engineer a penny a week to send up the steam early to heat the spinning room. There was also a fining system known as the "grassing" system, where an operative was suspended for several days. The spinners and others vigorously resisted this method, with success.

A copy of Mill Rules issued by a Haslingden firm in 1851, will be interesting to modern readers:—

1.—All the Overseers shall be on the premises first and last.

2.—Any person coming too late shall be fined as follows: For five minutes 2d.; ten minutes, 4d.; fifteen minutes, 6d., etc.

3.—For any bobbins found on the floor, 1d. for each bobbin.

4.—For single drawing, slubbing or roving, 2d. for each single end.

5.—For waste on the floor, 2d.

6.—For any oil wasted or spilled on the floor, 2d. each offence, besides paying for the value of the oil.

7.—For any broken bobbins, they shall be paid for according to their value, and if there is any difficulty in ascertaining the guilty party the same shall be paid for by the whole using such bobbins.

8.—Any person neglecting to oil at the proper times shall be fined 2d.

9.—Any person leaving his work and found talking with any of the other workpeople shall be fined 2d. for each offence.

10.—For every oath or insolent language, 3d. for the first offence, and if repeated they will be dismissed.

11.—The machinery shall be swept and cleaned down every meal time.

12.—All persons in our employ shall serve four weeks' notice before leaving their employ; but (the proprietors) shall and will turn any person off without notice being given.

13.—Any person wilfully or negligently breaking the machinery or damaging the brushes, making to waste, etc., they shall pay for the same to the full value.

14.—Any person hanging anything on the gas pendants shall be fined 2d.

15.—The masters would recommend that all their workpeople wash themselves every morning, but they shall wash themselves at least twice every week—Monday morning and Thursday morning—and any found not washed will be fined 3d. for each offence.

16.—The grinders and drawers, and slubbers, and rovers, shall sweep at least 8 times in the day as follows: In the morning at 7½, 9½, 11½ and 12; and in the afternoon at 1½, 2½, 3½, 4½ and 5½; and to notice the board hung up: when the black side is turned, that is the time to sweep, and only a quarter of an hour will be allowed for sweeping. The spinners shall sweep as follows: In the morning at 7½, 10 and 12; and in the afternoon at 3 and 5½ o'clock. Any neglecting to sweep at the time will be fined 2d. for each offence.

17.—Any person found smoking on the premises will be instantly dismissed.

18.—Any person found away from their usual place of work except for necessary purposes, or talking with anyone out of their own alley, will be fined 2d. for each offence.

19.—Any person bringing dirty bobbins will be fined 1d.

20.—Any person wilfully damaging this notice will be dismissed.

The Overlookers are strictly enjoined to attend to these rules, and they will be responsible to the masters for the workpeople observing them.

Later the Truck Act of 1896 was passed to deal with the fining system and the system of paying wages partly in goods, but by Order dated March 3rd, 1897, persons engaged in all branches of the weaving of cotton in Lancashire, Cheshire, Derbyshire and the West Riding of Yorkshire were exempt from the provisions of the Act. The exemption was granted at the request of the cotton operatives, who disapproved even of the systems which the Act legalised. This subject is also dealt with in later pages.

The period between about 1830 and 1850 appeared to have been lean times so far as effective trade union organisation was concerned. The "Short Time Committee" had obtained in 1847 the Ten Hours Act, but the Committee appeared to fall into a state of disorganisation and disunion.

In fact it can be said that the period of active organisation of the working-class by non-working-class politicians was ending. It will be recalled that much of the workers' dissatisfaction with their conditions had been crystallised and utilised by "outside" reformers, politicians, and socialists, such as Robert Owen, Joseph Hume, Francis Place, and the leaders of the Chartist movement. Historians have emphasised that many of these leaders of working-class revolt have had as their objects questions which were wider than the mere bread-and-butter politics of the workers themselves. Robert Owen, for instance, was a prominent Socialist propagandist and his idea was for a general strike which would transform society. Instead of the national stoppage, regional strikes broke out in many places, and the Government of the day retaliated with heavy sentences on their leaders under the 1825 Combination Act and other Acts directed against political uprisings, which tied the unions' hands when it came to action. Outstanding examples of the Government's attitude were the savage repression of the "last labourer's revolt" in the agricultural south of England in 1830, and later the conviction and transportation to Australia in 1834 of the "Tolpuddle Martyrs" for forming a local union of agricultural labourers as part of the Grand National. The Scottish textile workers were others among the many victims of ruthless oppression, while in Durham the miners who struck for fairer conditions were evicted from their homes. The Grand National ultimately broke down, and the era of revolutionary trade unionism was followed by the Chartist Period, during which political activities held the workers' attention while the unions were revising their aims and methods.

From about this time onwards the development of trade unionism, particularly in the textile trades, was slow but it succeeded in throwing up leaders from amongst its own ranks, and for a considerable number of years concentrated its main interests upon the improvements of the wage levels and the standards of working conditions.

In 1853 the present Amalgamated Association of Cotton Spinners was established, although this federal union was weakened in its early stages by abstensions of Oldham and Bolton districts, who did not join up until 1869. The cotton weavers were in a somewhat similar weakened position. As mentioned earlier there had been evidence of a weavers' organisation in 1836 in Preston, and there was another attempt made in 1842, although the present Society dates from 1858. The Radcliffe Weavers' Society was established in 1852, and much later in 1911, became merged with the Bury and District Association.

CHAPTER VI

Early Weaving Lists

THE NUMBER of weaving lists which were formulated in the early 1840's is further evidence of the existence of some form of organisation amongst the operatives in many districts. Lists of weaving prices existed in Ashton-Dukinfield, Stalybridge and Mossley districts in 1843; and a Stockport Standard List of Prices existed in 1844. Leading manufacturers in Oldham had agreed upon a list amongst themselves in 1834, which they revised in 1846. (Both these lists are reprinted in "British Association Report on Weaving Lists, 1887").

As a matter of interest the following is a copy of the "List of Prices Paid for Weaving by the Association of Master Manufacturers, of Ashton-under-Lyne, Dukinfield, Stalybridge, and Mossley, 1843".

"For a 72 reed, 36-inch Plain Shirting, 22 Picks per ¼-inch, 25 yards at Twelve Pence Farthing is taken as Standard.

"For the Reed, give and take for every four Ends in the inch, One Farthing per piece of 25 yards. Three or more Ends in one dent to be paid according to the number of Ends per inch.

"For the Picks, for every Pick below 22 in the ¼-inch, give and take, One Half-penny for 25 yards, for every Pick above 22 in the ¼-inch, Three Farthings for 25 yards.

"Width, for every two inches below and above 36-inches, give and take One Farthing for 25 yards.

"For 60, 64, and 68 reeds, 44-inches and above, Three Farthings for 25 yards in addition to the regular calculation, and for the same widths in a 72 or finer reed, One penny for 25 yards.

"Twills, Four Shaft Twills to be paid One Half-penny for 25 yards less than Plain Cloth.

"Fancies, Seven to Twelve Shafts, inclusive, to be paid One Half-penny more than Plain Cloth for 25 yards. Thirteen Shafts One penny more than Plain Cloth for 25 yards.

"Drills, Jeans and Sateens to be paid as Plain Cloth.

"For Coarse Materials the list gives Twopence more for 25 yards than Medium Counts, but does not state for what Counts of Twist or Weft.

"This List is now paid 10 per cent less than here given. (June 4th, 1883).

"Jacquards are paid the list price at both mills in Hurst, less 5 per cent. whether figures, spots or stripes."

The Burnley Weaving List was first formulated in 1843, and a further List was formulated in 1873, but did not give satisfaction, and in March 1880 a new Weaving List was negotiated in the Bull Hotel, Burnley, this List remaining in operation until the establishment of a Uniform List in 1892.

In view of the historic importance of the 1853 Blackburn List, which was later adopted by many other towns, the following is a copy, showing how certain principles of calculation became established:—

BLACKBURN STANDARD WEAVING LIST, 1853

The Blackburn list is based on a 40-inch loom, weaving from 36 to 41-inch cloth, 60 reed Stockport counts, 16 picks per ¼ inch, 37½ yards, from 30's to 60's weft, and from 28's to 45's twist, for 12.25 pence.

Reeds.—A 60 reed or 30 dents, being the standard, is made the starting point, and ¾ per cent is deducted for every two ends or counts of reeds, from 60 to 48; but no deduction is made below 48 reed, and ¾ per cent is added for every two ends or counts of reed above 60.

Weft.—All weft from 30's to 60's, both included, is considered medium, and reckoned equal, but all weft above 60's to be allowed 1 per cent for every 10 hanks,

and all below	30' to 26's	to be allowed	2	per cent on list
”	26's to 20's	”	5	”
”	20's to 16's	”	8	”
”	16's to 14's	”	10	”

Twist.—All twist from 28's to 45's, both included, is considered medium, and reckoned equal, but all twist above 45's up to 60's, to be allowed 1½ per cent, and all above 60's 1 per cent for each 10 hanks.

and all below	28's to 20's	to be allowed	1	per cent on list
”	20's to 14's	”	2	”

Additions for Picks.—All picks above 8 and up to 18 are considered proportionate, but 8 picks and all below and all above 18, to have 1 per cent. allowed for every pick over and above the proportionate difference in the number of picks.

Width of Looms.—A 40-inch loom being the standard, is taken as the starting point, and all additions or deductions are made therefrom. The reed space is measured from back board to forkgrate.

26 inch loom	has	2½	per cent	deducted	from	30-inch loom
30-inch	”	5	”	”		35-inch ”
35-inch	”	5	”	”		40-inch ”
40-inch loom (45-inch reed space) the standard						
45-inch loom	has	5	per cent	added	to	40-inch loom
50-inch	”	10	”	”		45-inch ”
55-inch	”	10	”	”		50-inch ”
60-inch	”	10	”	”		55-inch ”

Looms of Intermediate Width.—1 per cent per inch to be deducted from 40 down to 30-inch looms; below 30 to 26-inch loom ⅝ per cent per inch to be deducted. Above 40-inch and up to 45-inch loom, 1 per cent per inch to be added, and all above 45-inch 2 per cent per inch.

Narrow Cloth in Broad Looms.—Suppose a 40-inch loom should be weaving cloth 36 to 31¼ inches in width, take off one-half the difference between 40 and

35-inch loom price; and if weaving cloth 31 to 27¼ inches wide, take off one-half the difference between 40 and 30-inch loom price; or if weaving 41¼ to 46-inch cloth in a 50-inch loom, take off one-half the difference between 50 and 45-inch loom, and so on with all other widths.

Range of Cloths:—

26-inch loom allowed to weave cloth up to 27 inches			
35-inch	,,	,,	from 31 to 36 inches
40-inch	,,	,,	,, 36 to 41 inches
45-inch	,,	,,	,, 41 to 46 inches
50-inch	,,	,,	,, 46 to 52 inches

Basis of Calculations:—

The calculations in the Blackburn List are based upon the picks counted by the glass when the cloth is laid upon the counter. Forty yards short stick to be taken as 39 yards long stick."

The Blackburn Standard List was also adopted during subsequent years by Padiham, Great Harwood, Church & Oswaldtwistle, and Darwen.

The Preston Standard List of Weaving Prices (compiled by the local Employers' Committee) was adopted by the Preston Weavers' Association in 1860, and was a codification and improvement upon previous Lists which had existed in that area. The List was a complicated one, containing 33 pages of tables for the payment of Plain Cloth, with adjustments and additions for fancier cloths. The basis for Shirtings, Cambrics and Tanjibs was 11d. per piece for two 46-inch reed space loom, 60 reed Stockport counts, 37½ yards long stick, 60 picks per inch. Provision was made for variations in Reeds, Picks, and Counts. The basic price for Jacconets and Mulls was 6d. per piece for 20 yards short stick. Hair Cords were paid 40 per cent over the Jacconet price. Satin stripes with spots were paid Plain Cloth prices. Brocades were paid from 30 to 50 per cent over Plain Cloth price. Provision was also made for Narrow Cloth in Broad Looms, and for different Loom Widths. The Preston List remained in operation until 1878, when it was superseded by the Blackburn Standard List.

In 1861 a Chorley List was established, and in that year the Bolton Quilt List was adopted. In 1866 a Plain Cloth Price List was adopted in Nelson, and later in 1886 agreement was reached in Nelson upon the terms of the Nelson Satin List, which provided (amongst other things) for 8 per cent extra to be paid upon the Nelson List plain cloth prices. This Satin List gave prices considerably lower than the weaving prices prevailing in the Preston area, and later, largely due to the installation of narrower looms in the Nelson Mills much of the Satin cloth trade left the Preston mills and developed in the Nelson area.

The Hyde Weaving List was adopted in 1867. On April, 12th 1887, Thomas Birtwistle signed a List on behalf of the Northern Counties Weavers' Association called the "North and North-East Lancashire Fancy List," which applied to Grey Goods, and was a combination of the Chorley and Nelson Lists. The new List covered jacquards (plain and satin grounds), leno and velvet cloths, and dobbies, handkerchiefs, satins, drills, & c.

By 1887, according to the Report of the British Association, on Weaving Lists, there were in existence twenty-two of these district weaving lists, the Report stating that "the most important are the Blackburn List of 1853 for plain cloth, and the North and North-East Lancashire List of 1887 for fancy cloths. The Burnley Weaving List (1844) the Chorley Weaving List (1861) and the Preston Weaving List (1860) were mainly based upon the Blackburn Standard List, the two latter relating particularly to fine goods. The Stockport List, the Ashton List, and the Hyde List (1867) were gradually superseded by the Blackburn List as regards plain cloth. The Nelson Satin List and the Chorley Fancy List were combined into the North & North-East Lancashire Fancy List."

In dealing at length on the subject of Piecework Lists for cotton workers, the Webbs say in their *History of Trade Unionism:—*

> "The best and indeed the only exact account of these early cotton lists is that prepared for the Economic Section of the British Association by a Committee consisting of Prof. Sidgwick, Prof. Foxwell, Sir Arthur Acland, Dr. W. Cunningham and Prof. J. E. C. Munro, the report being drawn up by the latter. The principles upon which the lists are framed are so complicated that we confess, after prolonged study, to be still perplexed on certain points, and though Prof. Munro clears up many difficulties, we are disposed to believe that even he, in some particulars, has not in all cases correctly stated the matter."

The year 1890 was an historic one so far as Weaving Lists were concerned, when the "Colne Coloured Goods List" was negotiated at Colne. This List has been retained, with amendments and additions, right down to the present time. In that year also, the Oldham Velvet List was adopted.

CHAPTER VII

Establishment of District Associations

From about 1840 onwards, with the formulation and adoption of District Weaving Lists, there also developed a more or less permanent form of organisation amongst the weavers, winders and other preparatory workers in our Lancashire districts. It is almost impossible to state exactly how or when many of the associations were formed, because of the peculiar and difficult circumstances existing in those early days, when the pioneers of our movement had to work very much in secret. The strength of the early pioneers was in their zeal and devotion to the cause of trade unionism—and not in record-keeping.

Blackburn

One of the earliest of the important district associations was the Blackburn Association, formed in June 1854. The first Secretary was Mr. Edward Whittle—a local character known as Ned Whittle—described by one writer at the time as a "sound, profound, and wonderfully proficient mathematician, who contributed frequently to scientific periodicals and magazines, and in their pages proposed for solution many difficult and interesting problems". Whittle had taken a prominent part, along with another man named Cowel and a Great Harwood man named Mortimer, in a prolonged strike of weavers in the Preston district, which lasted from August 1853 until May 1854. According to the writer mentioned, these three men "became the heroes of continental novels in consequence, and had their likenesses taken to illustrate the Parisian and other European Metropolitan newspapers." Whittle remained as Secretary for four years, also acting as Secretary for the Great Harwood Association, which worked at that time as part of the Blackburn Association. Subsequently, for about twelve years, John Whalley was Secretary of the Blackburn Association. During 1878 there was severe rioting during a dispute and the chairman of the local employers' association (Col. Jackson) had his house at Wilpshire burnt down. A later Secretary was George Barker, who took a leading part in the formation of the Amalgamation. The Blackburn Association took a vigorous part in the agitation for the Abolition of Steaming in weaving sheds, and during the Steaming Enquiry of 1888 valuable evidence was given by a courageous Medical Officer of Health, Dr. Stephenson. For eleven days operatives and other witnesses gave evidence before the Enquiry Committee, who reached the following conclusions:—

"That the weight of evidence given is to the effect that steaming in weaving sheds has been largely and excessively used throughout Blackburn District; that the practice is injurious to health, and that weavers as a class have suffered in health in consequence."

From 1894 to 1906 the Secretaryship of the Blackburn Society was held by Mr. Joseph Cross, who became Secretary of the Amalgamation in 1906. During Mr. Cross' term of office at Blackburn he introduced the mill representative system. The Blackburn Association grew in numbers and influence, and was destined to play a leading part in many problems which the operatives were called upon to deal with. The recorded history of the time indicates that Blackburn must have been the hub of many developments, for one district after another within the immediate neighbourhood successfully formed local associations within a very short period.

Padiham

For instance, the Padiham Weavers' Association was formed in the year 1856, and the first Secretary was Abraham Pinder. It was not long before the newly formed association began to make its presence felt, for in March 1859 a dispute occurred and a demand made for the adoption of the Blackburn List. In order to maintain this strike, collections were made all over Lancashire for a period of 29 weeks. In October, work was resumed and the struggle which had taken place strengthened the determination to establish and maintain an organisation which would more adequately represent the desires and aspirations of the weavers.

Great Harwood

There is evidence that a local Weavers' Association existed in the Great Harwood district long before 1858, and for a time it was a part of the Blackburn Association. In 1858 the association was re-formed as a branch of the East Lancashire Powerloom Weavers' Association. The earliest meetings took place in a delph at Clinkam, as nobody dared to lend a room in their house for a meeting, nor did the officials dare to meet in public. No minutes of business were kept and the utmost secrecy was observed. The earliest minutes were for 1873 and the Secretary was John Calvert. The present office and meeting rooms were built in 1879–80, at a cost of just over £320. During 1884 the Great Harwood Association joined the Amalgamation, and in 1885 they purchased two houses in Accrington (17 and 19 St. James Street) for £930. These houses were let to the Amalgamation as offices and residence for the Secretary, Mr. T. Birtwistle, until they were later purchased by the Amalgamation. When the Great Harwood Association was originally formed it embraced the districts of Great Harwood, Rishton, York, Billington, and Whalley. The members at Rishton withdrew in 1878, and continued as a separate organisation.

Darwen

The Darwen Weavers' Association was formed in 1857 by a few ardent and enthusiastic men who met in the home of one Thomas Singleton. Others were John Kay, William Walkden, Abraham Pinder, and George Holden. The first Secretary was Entwistle Entwistle, who, in addition to his trade union duties kept a stall in the market place. Joseph Cross followed Mr. Entwistle as Secretary, in August 1892, a position he occupied until 1894, when he became Secretary of the Blackburn Society, and David J. Shackleton (later Sir David) was appointed his successor. Mr. Shackleton acted until 1907, when Mr. John Parkington followed as Secretary. Textile operatives in the Darwen locality are mentioned in connection with the "plug riots" and powerloom smashing in 1826 and later, and they were also participators in the Chartist agitations. There was great suffering during the cotton famine in 1862, when every one of the 32 mills came to a standstill.

Church

The Church Weavers' Association was also formed during the year 1858, originating through a dispute at the Stone Bridge Mill. It is believed that committee meetings were held at the homes of those who were trying to create an organisation, but, as in so many other instances connected with our early organisation, no records were kept because of fear. One of the early Secretaries was Mr. Elisha Reddihough, who later became a Trustee of the Amalgamation. He retired in 1899 and after Mr. A. Starkey had served for three years Mr. J. T. Wolstenholme was appointed Secretary in 1902, a position he held for over 26 years.

Accrington

The Accrington Weavers' Association started in a humble way in 1858, in the lower room of a two-roomed house in Briggs Entry, off Abbey Street. Singularly, the upper room was occupied by the Accrington Co-operative Society, which was inaugurated about the same time. The pioneers of the local trade union movement in Accrington were some sturdy men who had come to the town from Settle, Yorkshire, including James Parkinson and the brothers Thomas and Richard Lord, who were also interested in the co-operative enterprise. The early existence of the weavers' union was one of continuous struggle, on a penny per week contribution, and during the later strike of 1878, owing to shortage of funds, a number of officials were sent out begging for the strikers. After a strike lasting for nine weeks the society continued to struggle for existence for several years. About 1884 Henry Heap was appointed a full-time Secretary. David J. Shackleton came to Accrington about that time, and he, along with David Monk and other stalwarts, devoted themselves to building up a stronger and more virile society.

Haslingden

The Haslingden Weavers' Association was formed before 1858, when they had at least 678 members. In the records available there is evidence of a payment being made for the death of a member, and this indicates that the organisation must have been in existence prior to 1858. In 1878 William Henry Wilkinson was the local Secretary, and he later became Secretary of the Amalgamation. About the time of its formation the Haslingden Association had a membership of approximately 1,000, all of whom were paying one penny per week. In 1961 this Association merged with Rossendale District Association under the title of The Rossendale Valley Textile Workers' Association.

Preston

The Preston Power Loom Weavers' Association was officially formed in 1858, though some form of organisation can be traced back to 1842. Mr. J. Swift was the first Secretary, and another stalwart in Amalgamation history, Luke Park, succeeded Mr. Swift in October 1875. Another well-known figure, Thomas Sumner, was first appointed Assistant Secretary at Preston in 1891, and in 1919 was appointed District Secretary. He retired in 1941 after 50 years of continuous service as an official. Another well-known figure in textile trade union history was Jeremiah Woolley, who was appointed President of the Preston Society in 1892.

Bamber Bridge

Although the Bamber Bridge Weavers' Association was permanently established about 1884, an old Rule Book of the Association shows that some form of organisation existed in 1836, when Mr. Peter Sharples was Secretary. The district was a very busy handloom centre and it is possible that the earlier date has reference to a Society which was operating in the district amongst the handloom weavers. The Bamber Bridge district association, whose later Secretary was Mr. Richard Evans, became merged with Preston Weavers' Association in 1940.

Clitheroe

The Clitheroe Weavers' Association has been in existence since before 1860. Evidence of this fact is contained in a diary belonging to Mr. "Chick" Knowles, who at that period was the President of the Association, an extract from which reads: "4th April, 1860. Tonight, being the Annual Meeting of the Weavers' Union, I went up to the meeting, when they put me in the chair. After the secretary had gone through his business, they began to appoint their officials for the ensuing year. I was chosen as president, which I consider a very high honour." The exact date of the formation of the Clitheroe Association is lost in obscurity. It is known, however, that the men who laid its foundations had to meet secretly, and their meetings were held on the outskirts of the town, in fields, or in barns, in order to prevent the employers becoming aware of their intentions and objects. Subsequently a cellar was rented in which to hold their committee meetings. The Weavers' Institute in Whalley Road was opened in 1905 by Sir David J. Shackleton, assisted by David Holmes and W. H. Wilkinson. The first permanent Secretary was Mr. Austen H. Cottam, who acted until his fatal accident in 1921.

Burnley

The foundations of the present Burnley Weavers' Association were laid in 1870, by a few ardent and earnest men. The formation of the Burnley Weaving List in 1843 indicates the probability of the existence of an earlier organisation. The employers did not look with favour on the new Association, and at once began a system of persecution by discharging many who had taken an active part in building up the Society. The employers also exercised a considerable influence with property owners. No sooner were the Committee settled in one place than this was followed by a notice to quit, the owner telling them he was not aware he was letting his property to a Trade Union. This did not damp the spirit of the pioneers of this new movement. Meetings were held in private houses or some out of the way place. Meanwhile small contributions were being made and accumulated and a sufficient amount was raised to enable the Committee to buy the old building in Charlotte Street for £485. Soon after this period the Society, in common with the rest of the manufacturing districts in Lancashire, was landed in the great industrial war of 1878. At that time the Society was ill-prepared to meet the claim of its members, as many of them thought that for one penny per week they could be sustained for any length of time. It is difficult, at this distance of time, to imagine how the Society got through that great crisis without being completely shattered. But all great struggles teach their lessons, and the Committee, profiting by experience, altered the Rules, so as to make the organisation stronger.

It is rather surprising to note that in the Burnley Rules of 1892 it is stated that they had as their "ultimate object the socialisation of the means of production, distribution and exchange, to be controlled by a democratic State in the interests of the entire community." Furthermore, "the political and financial support of the Society shall be used towards the creation of an Independent Socialist Party."

Nelson

Although there was a Nelson Weaving List in existence in 1866 it was not until November 1870 that the present Nelson Weavers' Association was established by a number of operatives employed at the firm of Jack Smith's, Victoria Mill. The leading spirit in the formation of the Society was Mr. Stephen Richmond, and he gathered round him such local stalwarts as James Varley, David Rushton, Robert Barker, John Rushton, Thomas Rushton and Mr. Shaw. The first meeting of weavers was held at the Prince of Wales Hotel, Leeds Road, and was addressed by Mr. William Billington, of Blackburn. A Committee was appointed and the first Secretary was David Rushton, who later became Nelson's Librarian. The original membership was about 400, all of whom paid 1d. per week, which was not a bad start, seeing that there were only 6,000 looms in Nelson and about 1,500 in Barrowford. In a local Souvenir of the Nelson Society, published in 1920, it states of that time that: "the position of a trade unionist was one that required some courage to fill. Men with grit, determination and loyalty to the cause were absolutely essential. The utmost secrecy had to be maintained, and it was carried so far that even weavers employed side by side were unacquainted as to the exact position in the trade union movement their fellow workers occupied, so great was their fear that the employer or management would get to know of their alliance". The souvenir relates the part played by the Nelson organisation in the various lengthy strikes which took place about 1878–80, and the strenuous efforts to maintain and improve the membership. By 1894 the membership had risen to 4,500, and in 1895 the Association was pressing the United Textile Factory Workers' Association to agitate for the Eight-Hour Day. The Society took an early interest in Labour Representation in Parliament, and in August 1902 Mr. D. J. Shackleton was returned to Parliament for the Clitheroe Division. The original Weavers' Institute in Pendle Street was opened in July 1905 by the Rt. Hon. Arthur Henderson, M.P. The Secretary at that time, Mr. Wm. Ward, was presented with a gold watch and chain to commemorate his 21 years' service.

Colne

Colne district was formed in September, 1879, although there is evidence of the existence of some form of organisation previous to that date. A copy of a poster in the possession of the Society shows that there was a strike in Colne as far back as 1861. In 1886 attempts were made to organise the weavers in Trawden and Foulridge, and in 1892 it was decided to form a branch in Earby. The struggles of the early pioneers were extremely arduous, and in 1889, after ten years of active work, the membership had only reached 1,000.

Bolton

The Bolton and District Weavers, Winders and Warpers' Association was formed in September 1865, under the title of "The Excelsior Friendly Society of Toilet and Marseilles Quilt Weavers by Power." Only weavers employed on power-looms weaving Toilet and Marseilles Quilts were entitled to be members. The handloom weavers were only allowed to learn weaving on the powerlooms by permission of the Association, and then only if there was no shortage of work for the other weavers. Members paid an entrance fee of 1s., and a weekly contribution of 3d. In 1878 new Rules were adopted in the name of the Bolton Powerloom Weavers' Friendly Association. Again in 1880 the name was changed, and in 1888 the first permanent Secretary was appointed—William Melling. Finally, in 1902 we got the title with which the Bolton Association is known today.

In the Bolton Weavers' Office there is a Caddow Quilt, into which is woven the following inscription:—

> "This piece was presented as a token of respect, to Mr. Hugh Gillibrand from the Counterpane Weavers' Association, 1846."

The quilt is a beautiful specimen of the art of the old handloom weaver. It appears that Mr. Hugh Gillibrand was the landlord of the "One Horse Shoe Inn," and the Counterpane Weavers Association used to hold their meetings in a room at the inn. None of the records of that early Association arc in existence, and it is assumed that the present Bolton Society is a successor to that Association.

Oldham

The first record of the formation of the Oldham Weavers, Winders, &c., Association, is a copy of an old Rule Book dated 1859. It formerly covered a much wider area than at present, as the minutes contain references to Fustian Cutters at Hebden Bridge, and to strikes of members at Castleton. In its early days it was one of the most prosperous of the District Associations and rendered valuable financial assistance to other sections of the textile workers. The first full-time Secretary was Abram Buckley, and in 1905 James Bell took up his duties as District Secretary, later becoming President of the Amalgamation.

We are indebted to Mr. F. G. Hague, Secretary of the Ashton-under-Lyne Weavers' Association, for the loan of a printed handbill containing an appeal "to the Power Loom Weavers of every Town, and a generous public," for financial support in a local strike of weavers in the Oldham District—the weavers had been on strike for twelve weeks. The handbill is dated 8th June, 1844, and was issued by the "Power-Loom Weavers late in the employ of Mr. John Clegg, High Crompton." The leaflet states:—

> "Take notice! There are nine weavers at Spring Mill Iron Works, Royton, employed by Seville & Co., who have left their work in consequence of not being fairly remunerated for their labour. We have been receiving 7d. per cut, 29 yards, 28-inches wide, 14 picks per quarter-inch. The standard price in Royton is 9½d. and 10d. per cut for the same sort of work. This is the third week of our strike and we sincerely hope that the calico weavers in this borough will come forward with their cordial support . . . We can assure you we are reduced to the utmost distress, having only worked a fortnight since the establishment commenced, and some of us were unemployed for many weeks before. 'Withhold not good from them to whom it is due, when it is in the power of thine hand to do it.'—Proverbs iii.27 . . . The Committee would be glad to see a very strong meeting of weavers on Wednesday evening, in the Chartist Room, Oldham."

A very detailed list of subscriptions then follows, varying from individual subscriptions of 6d. to a total of £1 0s. 4½d. from the weavers at Wallshaw Mill. The total subscriptions were £20 15s. 9½d., and amongst the expenses were, Rent of Room, 6d.; Secretary's Wage, 6d.; Benefits to 76 weavers at 5s. 1d. each; Benefits to Seville & Co.'s weavers at 2s. 6½d. each.

The handbill also contains the following remarks: "Wallshaw Mill—there is Elizabeth Nield, Sarah Nield and a few others, that will be exposed if they do not pay. Greenbank Mill—Old Bill Beverley has two shares in the Hen-Pecked Club and his wife will not let him pay."

Rossendale

The Rossendale Weavers' Association was formed in 1873, and in 1933 celebrated its diamond jubilee by taking all its members to Blackpool. Many of the early pioneers have now passed away. One of the early pioneers was Councillor John Hamer, Treasurer, who was Mayor of the Borough in 1934. The first Secretary was a cousin, Mr. John Hamer, and Mr. John Farron was appointed in 1894 as first full-time Secretary. In 1961 this Society merged with Haslingden District Association, and the two Districts adopted the title of The Rossendale Valley Textile Workers' Association.

Ashton-under-Lyne

The Ashton-under-Lyne Power Loom Weavers' Association was established on a permanent basis in December, 1877, following a dispute at the firm of Gartside & Co. Ltd., Wellington Mills, in September of that year.

Mr. William Booth was the first Secretary and he served until 1907. He was one of the original members of the Amalg. Central Committee. Mr. Sam T. Goggins followed Mr. Booth as Secretary in 1907. The Association had a great struggle to establish itself, and victimisation was rampant; anyone who was known to be a member was instantly discharged from their employment. Swinton and Pendlebury Districts became part of the Association, following a dispute in 1890. The present Secretary, Mr. F. G. Hague, is also President of the amalgamation.

Heywood

The Heywood & District Weavers' Association was formed in 1877 by a number of devout men and women. Recruitment of new members began by canvass and meetings and very soon the membership reached 750. In 1884 the Association was prevailed upon to join the newly-formed Amalgamated Weavers' Association. Mr. J. W. Odgen was appointed the first permanent Secretary of the Heywood Association in 1891.

Todmorden

In 1878 notices were posted at all the mills in Todmorden to reduce wages by at least 10 per cent. Meetings were held of the operatives when it was decided to form a Todmorden Weavers' Association. Not until two years later was it possible to establish an organisation. At a meeting held on 14th February, 1880 the following resolution was passed: "That we, the Weavers of Todmorden and District, form ourselves into an Association to keep up our present rate of wages and prevent one employer paying less than another for the same amount and quality of work." A house to house canvass was at once begun, and a membership of 438 was recorded at the end of the first year. Victimisation was not infrequent, and it required strength of mind as well as of heart to pursue the task that had been embarked upon.

Rochdale

The Rochdale Weavers' Association was formed in the years 1878–80 and in its earlier period the Society was principally concerned with weavers engaged in the Woollen industry. About 1880 the Association became more definitely an organisation of cotton workers. Not only weavers, but Warehousemen, Twisters and Drawers, and other cotton workers are found amongst its early officials. The Association had a very precarious existence for about ten years, and its membership, including woollen, cotton, silk and carpet weavers, was not more than 600.

Longridge

The Longridge Weavers' Association was formed some time in the year 1878. For some years the Association experienced great difficulties and made very little headway. The hostility of the local employers was most marked. In a rural area the difficulties of organisation were great, but by dint of perseverance the Association ultimately became firmly established. The Longridge District Association later wound up in 1964.

Hyde

The Hyde Weavers' Association, which covers a very large area, was formed in March 1880. A number of male weavers employed at the firm of J. & J. Ashton & Co. Ltd., Newton Moor Mills, were responsible for the initial steps. They were very active in the work, for within three months the membership was 1,469. A branch of the Association was established at Hadfield in May of the same year, 660 joining within six weeks. There had previously been a Friendly Society operating, the secretary of which was Mr. Patrick Maloney, who was largely responsible for the Hyde List and the Hyde Sheeting List. In 1922 the Hyde and District Association absorbed the Glossop Weavers' Association, which had been in existence for a considerable length of time.

Whitworth

The actual formation of the Whitworth Vale Weavers' Association dates back to 1882. Great difficulties were experienced in organising the operatives. Family ties were strong and the winning of one family generally meant the winning of a whole host of near and far relatives. The Association was linked up with the Rochdale Weavers' Association until 1884, when, as a result of a dispute on financial matters, separation took place for a number of years. Later, in 1935, the Whitworth Association again merged with the Rochdale Weavers' Association.

Bury

The Bury Weavers' Association was formed in 1884 by a few pioneers who met on the banks of the Elton Reservoir. A small Association had been functioning in the Radcliffe district since 1852, and was merged with the Bury Association on 4th March, 1911.

Wigan

The Wigan Weavers' Association was established in December 1890. Many local strikes had occurred on account of the intolerable conditions that prevailed in the mills. From 1893 to 1897 the Association remained in membership with the Amalgamation, when, in consequence of financial difficulties, membership ceased. The Local Association continued its struggles and during this period was affiliated to the Women's Trade Union League, who gave assistance in organisational work. During 1909 the Association rejoined the Amalgamation and has remained in membership since. In the early part of this second period the Amalgamation was responsible for the temporary services of three organisers, who devoted full-time work to the building up of a sound organisation. Membership increased, and weaving prices, which were at one time about 20 to 30 per cent below list prices, were quickly brought up to standard.

Skipton

The Skipton Weavers' Association is in one of the outposts of the Lancashire cotton industry, in an old town with historic connections. The Association was formed in 1902, its first Secretary being Mr. James Stratton. Mr. Walter Wykes was appointed President, and occupied that position for nearly twenty years. The branch progressed and in 1907 Mr. Luke Bates was appointed as permanent Secretary, and an office was opened in Newmarket Street, Skipton. In 1910, Mr. Bates went to Blackburn as Secretary of the Blackburn Weavers' Association, and was succeeded in Skipton by Mr. Samuel Snell, who had been a member of the Colne Committee. At that time each firm had its own price list, and in 1912 a strike was necessary to secure uniformity of payments in all mills. This was accomplished after a dispute lasting three weeks, and each firm agreed to pay by the Uniform List, less 5 per cent for "local disadvantages". In 1923 Mr. Alvery J. Barker was appointed Secretary. At one period, the membership of the Skipton Association rose to over 1,300, but due to the contraction of the trade, involving the extinction of a number of firms, the membership has declined somewhat.

Stockport

An organisation had existed in the Stockport District for a long number of years, but there are no records available earlier than 1906, when Mr. William Pope of Hyde, was acting as organiser. In January 1907 the first permanent Secretary was appointed, and the Society has continued. Weaving in Stockport has for some time been declining. Three mills, containing at least 2,000 looms have been dismantled, and where there were formerly over 3,000 looms in the district there are today not more than 500 looms running. The bulk of the membership of the Stockport Association is composed of winders, reelers, warpers, and other preparatory workers.

CHAPTER VIII

The First Amalgamation, 1858

NOT ALL the District Associations of Weavers which came into existence in the second half of the nineteenth century were centred in the large and more important weaving towns; Weavers' Unions were also to be found in the smaller towns, but the efforts made by the Weavers' Unions in these smaller towns to secure adequate wages for their members provoked endless disputes with the employers, and in the end the weavers were still compelled to return to work on the old terms.

Most of the employers in these less important districts were members of either the Preston, Burnley, or Blackburn Employers' Associations, and in disputes with the operatives the combined weight of these Associations would be utilised in one great effort to break the back of the strikes.

Thomas Birtwistle, who, as an official of the Accrington Weavers' Association, had experienced several of these bitter disputes at the opening of the second half of the nineteenth century, and decided to try to remedy the weaknesses of the independent District Weavers' Associations, and to work for the ultimate unification of the separate unions into one single Weavers' Amalgamation. By this means an effective countervailing pressure group, composed of the majority of workpeople in the weaving section, and equal to the combined power of the employers, would come to the assistance of any single District Association involved in a dispute with the local employers.

The form which that Amalgamation would eventually take was perhaps even unknown to Birtwistle himself, for it would depend very much upon the willingness of the established District Associations to sacrifice their vested interests for the greater concentration of power amongst the weavers in a single all-powerful Amalgamation. Several of the more important Districts—including Preston and Blackburn—as well as those Weavers' Associations in South East Lancashire, were not attracted by Birtwistle's idea of Amalgamation. For the time being, the more important Districts were able to manage their relationships with the local employers without undue strain and without sacrificing the whole of their independence in other Union affairs for outside assistance.

Thus, in 1858, the East Lancashire Amalgamated Power Loom Weavers' Friendly Association was formed.

The Objects of the newly formed Amalgamation contained little else besides wage matters, the first Object reading:

"To keep up our present rate of wages to the standard list and to be able to resist any attempts to reduce the same, and also to prevent one employer paying less than another for the same amount and quality of work, and more particularly to bring up the prices of those who are paying the lowest rate of wages."

This East Lancashire Amalgamation was, therefore, a federation of local Weavers' Societies situated within a small radius of Blackburn, although, as already explained, Blackburn was not a member. There are no records available concerning the first few years, as the earliest copy of an Annual Report is the Fifth Annual Report for the year ending September 1863.

This Report shows that there were seven societies affiliated:—

Over Darwen	1,102	members
Church	550	"
Accrington	550	"
Harwood	700	"
Padiham	700	"
Chorley	493	"
Haslingden (about)	500	"
	4,645	

The Total Worth of the whole of those Societies was shown as £932 3s. 11½d.

The Ninth Annual Report for 1867 shows there were ten societies affiliated (Clitheroe, Enfield, and Ramsbottom having joined), and the total membership was 8,470. In his Report Mr. Thomas Birtwistle, the General Secretary, referred to "the opposition of the employers when the Amalgamation was established a little over nine years ago, when they tried as a body to crush the Union in its infancy. Public feeling and opinion was also against us, but by dint of perseverance honest and upright dealing, we have very near, if not quite, removed this prejudice from the public mind." The Report also states: "In many districts the members have begun to talk about an advance of wages; it may be quite right to begin to talk; but we think that the staple trade of this Shire is not in a sufficiently prosperous state as to warrant us putting any such claim into a practical shape, although that day may dawn upon us quickly; it is therefore our duty to be prepared for the opportunity whenever it presents itself." (In passing it should be mentioned that this was written at a time when the Cotton Famine, which started in 1862, was nearing its end).

Cotton Famine

It will be interesting to make a passing reference to the experiences of the Lancashire cotton workers during the Cotton Famine. During the whole of 1862 and the greater part of 1863 the price of cotton continued to rise. Between June 1861 and October 1863, Middling Orleans cotton had risen from 8d. to 2s. 5d. per lb.—nearly four-fold. To complicate this situation was the fact that cotton cloths were produced under the constant apprehension that a sudden close of the war in America might throw open the American cotton ports, let into this country large supplies of American cotton suddenly, and inflict heavy losses on those who had manufactured cotton goods from high priced cotton. This fear compelled manufacturers to run short-time or close altogether. In May 1862 there were 11,000 operatives out of work in Preston alone, and 8,429 in Blackburn. The distress increased during that year, and during the winter of 1862–63 there were 36,000 of the Blackburn population on charitable relief. In Oldham, 9,411 workpeople were on relief, and in Rochdale the Guardians were relieving 9,813. In Ashton-under-Lyne nearly 20,000 persons were unemployed, and in October 1862 there was only one mill working in Ashton. Out of a population of 54,000 in Stockport, 23,000 were receiving relief. Sir James Kay-Shuttleworth estimated that by Christmas of 1862 a quarter of a million factory operatives were out of work. Relief was afforded from parochial and county rates, by generous contributions of the whole British people, aided by liberal contributions from the United States and the continent. A great scheme of public works was developed in the county, and a Government credit of £2,000,000 was made available. A special "Union Relief Act" was passed in 1862, and under this and succeeding Acts of 1863 the Government advanced £200,000 for relief. But these and other moneys were quite insufficient, and voluntary relief was organised in Lancashire and London, by which over £1,000,000 was raised. Several Charitable Organisations were established, and in July 1862 Queen Victoria gave £2,000 to the Cotton Districts Relief Fund. Over £46,000 was sent from Australia. Edward Baines, in *Lancashire, Cheshire*, Vol. II, gives copious details of Public Supply works which were undertaken in many Lancashire towns to relieve the distress of these years. Baines concludes: "The unemployed workmen by whom these most useful works were executed, had been overlookers, weavers, spinners, cardroom hands, warpers, piecers, sizers, dyers and bleachers, fustian cutters, roller cutters and hatters . . . The weekly wages . . . varied from 12s. to 20s. per man . . . This great and successful experiment effected the main object for which it was undertaken, viz; that of affording useful and honourable occupation to men most willing to work, but who were deprived of employment by national causes over which they had no control."

In the 11th Annual Report for 1869 the East Lancashire Amalgamation still covered ten societies, Enfield Society having changed its name to Clayton-le-Moors. There were then 8,185 members. The General Secretary referred to the improvement in trade, which was not sufficient to justify an application for a wage increase. He referred to the amount of work falling upon him in connection with detention of wages, law cases, illegal discharges, and so on.

The membership of the early Amalgamation grew slowly, and in 1871 Burnley and Nelson societies had affiliated, making twelve societies in all, with a total membership of 13,495. In the thirteenth Annual Report for that year the General Secretary stated that whilst spinning was lucrative, weaving was very unprofitable. They found themselves launched upon an agitation for Shorter Hours, with every prospect of success, as a great impetus was given to the movement by the Nottingham Trades Union Congress, at which a Parliamentary Committee was appointed to watch measures in Parliament of the most vital importance to workingmen. The Truck Act was also referred to, and a case was reported where "the cutlooker had alleged that the weaver had spoiled some pieces, for which they compelled her to pay and take them home, which she consented to do, after which she left their employment, and although she had agreed to take them, we then sued them for the money they had stopped for the pieces, and recovered it all back. After this, the master applied to the Judge for an order to compel us to give up the pieces, but the Judge ruled he had no power to grant one, as they had made an illegal bargain and must abide by the consequences. Therefore we got both the pieces and the weaver's wages."

Struggles against wage reductions and bad working conditions continued, and Mr. T. Birtwistle, in his Annual Report for 1878, issued from Imperial Chambers (17 St. James Street), Accrington, stated:

"The greatest struggle in the history not only of the Cotton Trade but of all other trades in the world," was taking place. In November 1877, the cotton employers had proposed a reduction of 5 per cent but their action had been temporarily frustrated by the operatives' organisations. Not for long, however, as on the 16th March, 1878, the weavers' organisations were requested to attend a meeting with the employers on the 19th March, to consider a proposal to reduce prices by 10 per cent. The employers could not be moved from their intentions, and as a consequence on 17th April, 1878, between 80,000 and 100,000 factory workers of the north and north-east Lancashire area came out on strike, or were locked out. The *Times* stated that the dispute spread "all the way through a centre of 70 miles." The strikers offered to accept the 10 per cent reduction on condition that the mills would only work four days a week, because of over-production. A heated controversy ensued, but the millowners persisted in their demand for the unconditional surrender of the men, and refused all proposals for arbitration. The cause of the operatives was unfortunately prejudiced by serious riots at Blackburn, during which the house of Col. Raynsford Jackson, the leader of the associated employers, was looted and burnt down.

After a struggle lasting nine weeks the strike ended on 20th June, 1878, the workers returning on the employers' terms. The sum of £4,729 was paid in strike pay, to about 16,000 members of our District Associations, which meant that the strikers received as strike pay a total of about 5s. 11d. for the nine weeks.

The membership of the North-East Lancashire Amalgamation at the end of 1878 was 15,620, and the Association comprised the following districts:—

Church	Clayton-le-Moors
Accrington	Ramsbottom
Great Harwood	Burnley
Padiham	Nelson
Chorley	Bamber Bridge
Haslingden	Rossendale
Clitheroe	Rishton

In 1878 the Rules of the North-East Lancashire Amalgamation were revised, the four main objects being:

1. To maintain as far as possible a uniform rate of wages upon as high a standard as possible, consistent with the true interests of trade as affecting factory operatives.
2. To protect its members from illegal or unjust stoppages, or unjust treatment

of whatever nature that unscrupulous employers may endeavour to subject them to.

3. To render assistance to its members in case of fines, failures and breakdowns.
4. To ensure the respectable interment of its members by the payment at death of an allowance to their relatives or friends.

The Amalgamation now appeared to be strengthening its control over a wider field of Union activities, and although the maintenance of wages still remained of utmost importance, the Amalgamation was also actively concerned in deciding the amounts of Friendly Benefits to be paid to Amalgamation members. This extension of centralised control was inherent in the character of the Amalgamation itself. The real compelling force behind the willingness of Weavers' Associations to join the Amalgamation originally was that a new centralised body would assist in the pooling and equal division of resources according to need. For instance, in the Amalgamation Rules, it was stated that "any branch which became impoverished as to be unable to meet their liabilities were to receive the assistance of the Amalgamation." By this means it was hoped to avoid the situation where, in cases of disputes against the employers, waged over wide areas of the county, some districts had been able to continue the struggle because they held strong Reserve Funds, whilst others, out of necessity, would be compelled to surrender, and there was no real method of transferring the reserves held by one Union to another in order to continue the struggle.

During the period, 1880 and 1883 the North-East Lancashire Amalgamation made serious efforts to draw attention to the evils of Heavy Sizing and Steaming, and as a result a Government Commission of Enquiry was appointed in March 1883, composed of Dr. J. H. Bridges, of the Local Government Board, and Mr. E. H. Osborne, Inspector of Factories. Their instructions were strictly confined to the effect of the system upon the health of the operatives, and did not take into consideration any question of injury to trade or commerce.

In the next report, issued in 1885, the General Secretary referred to the serious slump in trade, and said that "at the present time there is no margin whatever and very few if any cotton spinners or manufacturers are holding their own." It was feared that half the looms would be idle unless there was a sudden change for the better. The General Secretary quoted figures of imports and exports and concluded:

> "From the preceding figures it will be seen that both our Import and Export trade is falling off, while our working population is annually increasing 2 per cent and the rate of production 5 per cent, and if our future Government, whoever they may be, does not turn their attention more to trade and less to party political strife, we shall without doubt go from bad to worse, until all the capital in this country will be in the hands of a few and almost everybody out of work. Nor will this system of Government ever be set aside until working men sink party politics and go in for men who will look to the interests of trade, irrespective of Liberals, Radicals, Conservatives or Tories."

Before passing on to deal with the formation of the present Amalgamation in

1884, it is interesting to quote extracts from Mr. Birtwistle's Annual Report of the North-East Lancashire Amalgamation, of May 1886:—

"We scarcely need explain the heavy expenditure to which the Society has been put as the change of offices from the old dingy quarters at the Imperial Chambers to the splendid, airy and well fitted suite of rooms in Ewbank Terrace, inferior to none, will be sufficient for all. The two houses, one used as offices, the other as Secretary's residence, is the property of the Gt. Harwood District leased to our Executive Council for fourteen years, the conditions being that the Harwood district receive a clear 4 per cent upon the £930 they have advanced upon them, which . . . . will cost the society about £52 per annum including rates, taxes, etc. From this may be deducted Rent from the Northern Counties, £17, and £21 from the Secretary."

Mr. Thomas Birtwistle continued as Secretary of the North-East Lancashire Amalgamated Weavers' Association until taking up his appointment as Factory Inspector in 1892. Mr. E. J. Holmes (son of Mr. David Holmes, a former President of the Amalgamated Weavers' Association) was appointed Secretary. At this time there were only seven districts in the North-East Lancashire Association: Church, Harwood, Haslingden, Clitheroe, Clayton, Bamber Bridge, Rishton, with a total membership of 11,366. Mr. E. J. Holmes remained Secretary, until his appointment as Assistant Factory Inspector in 1896. Mr. A. H. Cottam, of Clitheroe was then appointed to fill the vacancy, and continued until 1903, when the North-East Lancashire Association was disbanded.

In January 1884 the North-East Lancashire Association published a printed report of a census of weaving firms and numbers of looms in the various affiliated Districts, and the following summary is interesting:—

	No. of Looms January, 1884
Church and Oswaldtwistle	10,006
Accrington	12,721
Great Harwood and Billington	7,547
Padiham	10,447
Chorley	8,079
Haslingden	8,482
Clitheroe	4,198
Clayton-le-Moors	3,405
Ramsbottom	7,342
Burnley	46,638
Nelson	8,408
Bamber Bridge	3,137
Rishton	3,243
Colne	7,500
Total	141,171 looms

CHAPTER IX

The Present Amalgamation, 1884

THE PERIOD of usefulness of the North-East Lancashire Amalgamation was passing, and its restricted form of organisation was a source of weakness. There was very little co-ordination and identity of interest. This weakness in organisation was apparent to the hard-headed Lancashire men who were, by that time, leading the operatives, and as soon as a dispute in Blackburn in 1884 was settled, steps were taken to create a much more comprehensive county organisation.

The present Amalgamated Weavers' Association was formed at meetings of representatives of 29 separate District Associations of Weavers, held on 27th April, 3rd and 4th May, and 17th May, 1884. The meetings held on 3rd and 4th May 1884 were held at Bury, and endorsed the first set of Rules and Constitution. The following Districts were represented, by a total of 57 delegates:—

Accrington	Heywood
Ashton	Hyde
Bamber Bridge	Longridge
Blackburn	Macclesfield
Bolton	Nelson
Burnley	Oldham
Chorley	Padiham
Church	Preston
Clayton	Ramsbottom
Clitheroe	Rishton
Colne	Rochdale
Darwen	Sabden
Harwood	Stockport
Haslingden	Todmorden

The original name of the Association was the "Northern Counties Amalgamated Association of Weavers".

The delegates discussed a "Plan of Re-organisation" which had been considered previously by the District Committees. It was decided to establish an "Emergency Fund" of £5,000, to be raised by a fortnightly levy of £1 per 100. At the Sunday meeting on the 4th May, 1884 the salaries of the Central Committee were fixed at 5s. per half-day, or 7s 6d. per day, with 2nd-class travelling expenses. The following persons were appointed as members of the Central Committee:—

David Holmes,
Joshua Barrows,

Luke Park,
G. Barker,
A. Buckley,
W. Booth.

David Holmes was appointed President, at a salary of £5 per annum. Mr. Thomas Birtwistle (who was also Secretary of the older North-East Lancashire Weavers' Amalgamation) was appointed Secretary of the new Amalgamation, but he did not remain Secretary for long. Mr. W. H. Wilkinson, of Haslingden, was appointed Secretary in October 1885. Mr. Birtwistle retained his position as Secretary of the older Amalgamation until 1892, when he was appointed the first Textile Particulars Inspector under the new Factory Act of 1891. Mr. Birtwistle's salary as Secretary of the new Amalgamation was £80 per annum, with second-class travelling expenses. The minutes of the two meetings were signed by John Strickland, of Burnley, who was acting as Secretary *pro tem.*

Original Objects and Rules

The Objects of the new Amalgamation, as stated in the original copy of the Rules, were:—

"The Objects of this Amalgamation are to establish and maintain an uniform and fair rate of Wages, in proportion to the quantity and quality of the work performed, for the Weaving of Cotton Cloths, in the Northern Counties; prevent unnecessary reductions and inflictions, and, when trade and circumstances will admit, obtain an advance in the rate of wages."

The entrance fee was one penny per member, and each Association admitted on the 3rd May, 1884 had to pay a premium equal to 50 per cent of the reserve fund, later admissions had to pay 25 per cent. The Rules governed the election of a General Council, and provided for the payment of levies to an Emergency Fund, which had to be maintained at a minimum of £5,000. The Rules provided for the election of the Central Committee (six members), and for the appointment of a Trustee, who was to be a person not connected with the Amalgamation.

The next meeting of the General Council was held on 17th May, 1884, at Blackburn, when 25 Districts were represented by 44 delegates, covering a membership of 37,539. (Accrington, Heywood, Hyde, Macclesfield and Rochdale were not represented, and Glossop was a new addition). This meeting received a lengthy report by Mr. Josh. Barrows of joint meetings with the employers, when efforts were made, without success, to secure the reinstatement of a previous 5 per cent reduction in list rates. Mr. Barrows was deputed to assist any district who needed help in organisation meetings. Mrs. E. Entwistle was appointed Treasurer, and the following original Trustees were appointed:—

James Craven, Blackburn.
Thomas Heys, Haslingden.
Andrew Harris, Preston.
Joseph Taylor, Blackburn.
Wm. Hesmondhalgh, Harwood.
Elisha Reddihough, Church.
Eli Pemberton, Ashton.

As already indicated Mr. W. H. Wilkinson was appointed Secretary in place of Mr. T. Birtwistle, in October 1885, and he continued to serve with conspicuous success until his death in 1906. In 1885, Mr. T. Birtwistle's son, Mr. J. T. Birtwistle, was appointed an Inspector of Factories, and a resolution was passed by the General Council of the Amalgamation stating that "no Act has given such general satisfaction to the factory workers of this county." Other appointments of trade union officers as Factory Inspectors were made about that time, notably Mr. E. J. Holmes (son of David Holmes, the Amalgamation President).

Early Strikes

The new Amalgamation was immediately confronted with difficulties, for disputes existed in Macclesfield, whilst in Burnley strike action was taken to secure the adoption of the Blackburn Standard List. At the General Council Meeting held on 13th July, 1884 it was reported that there were 37,226 looms stopped through the strike, whilst the strike pay was 1s. per loom. The strike ended in July, and negotiations took place with the employers' secretary, Mr. Rawlinson, for a settlement. The new organisation was fortified by the courageous action of an Ashton-under-Lyne printer, Mr. J. Andrew, who published a weekly paper, *The Cotton Factory Times*, and through the long life of that journal the Amalgamation, along with other textile trade unions, has received the most valuable assistance and encouragement.

During the following twelve months the General Council reports contain references to many strikes which had taken place against attempted wage reductions, particularly in Nelson, Burnley, Ramsbottom, Preston, Accrington and other districts. Many of these strikes about this time had also, of course, for their object the question of the recognition of the Union by employers. On 29th March, 1885 the General Council recorded the following resolution:

> "That the Central Committee merit our best thanks for the able and effective manner with which they have conducted the business of the Council, and which has resulted in unexampled success."

In 1887 there was a 22-week's strike in Barnoldswick, against under-payment of List prices, and a lengthy strike also occurred in Ashton against the prices paid for fancy weaving. Most of the strikes occurring at this time were financed by means of appeals to other Districts, and the amounts paid by members generally ranged around 1d. to 1½d. per loom per week. In January 1887 strike-pay amounted to 2s. per loom.

In 1888 there was a serious strike in Macclesfield against the deduction of 5 per cent from wages for "local disadvantages." It is recorded that in September, 1888, 31 adult weavers and children had emigrated to America, at the expense of the Amalgamation. In an effort to frustrate this move the mill manager telegraphed to the United States, to stop the weavers who had emigrated, but he failed in his object. In the Amalgamation accounts for that year it is noted that the cost of the emigration was £361, whilst the strike itself cost £2,818.

Emblem

In order to stimulate the spirit of brotherhood amongst the members an emblem (*see frontispiece*) was produced and distributed throughout the District Associations, at the price of 1s. 2d. each. It was a common practice in mid-Victorian days—and even earlier—for Trade Associations to represent their craft by some descriptive painting or Certificate of Membership, and our Association was not one whit behind others in seeking to create that pride of craft which was essential to build up a virile Trade Association which would protect their industrial interests.

Reelers

Meanwhile, on 23rd January, 1887, it had been decided to enlarge the scope of the organisation, by taking in Reelers as members. Hitherto the organisation had primarily been engaged in catering for purely weaving operatives. Now it was becoming recognised that operatives employed in the preparatory processes should be organised. Events have proved that a mistake was made when the Amalgamation refused to accept into membership, on 6th March, 1887, the Stockport Yarn Doublers' Association, a small organisation which has since been accepted into membership by the National Union of Municipal and General Workers.

Uniform List of Weaving Prices, 1892

During these years many efforts were made to secure some kind of uniformity in the payment of weaving prices, and a considerable amount of preliminary work and calculation was undertaken by Mr. T. Birtwistle and others, which ultimately led to the formulation of the Uniform List. On 3rd February, 1889 the General Council made a grant of £100 to Mr. Birtwistle for the work he had put into the drafting of a new List. In their book *The History of Trade Unionism*, Sidney and Beatrice Webb said:—

"It is difficult to convey to the general reader any adequate idea of the important effect which these elaborate "Lists" have had upon the Trade Union Movement in Lancashire. The universal satisfaction with, and even preference for, the piecework system among the Lancashire cotton operatives is entirely due to the existence of these definitely fixed and published statements. An even more important result has been the creation of a peculiar type of Trade Union official. For although the lists are elaborately worked out in detail . . . the intricacy of the calculations is such as to be beyond the comprehension not only of the ordinary operative or manufacturer, but even of the investigating mathematician without a very minute knowledge of the technical detail. Yet the week's earnings of every one of the tens of thousands of operatives are computed by an exact and often a separate calculation under these lists. And when an alteration of the list is in question, the standard wage of a whole district may depend upon the quickness and accuracy with which the operatives' negotiator apprehends the precise effect of each projected change in any of the numerous factors in the calculation. It will be obvious that for work of this nature the successful organiser or "born orator" was quite unfit. There grew up, therefore, both among the weavers and the spinners a system of selection of new secretaries by competitive examination . . . the first secretary to undergo this ordeal was Thomas Birtwistle, who, in 1861, began his 30 years' honourable and successful service of the Lancashire weavers. Within a few years he was reinforced by other officials selected for the same characteristics. From 1871 onwards the councils of the trade union movement were strengthened by the introduction of "the cotton men," a body of keen, astute, and alert-minded officials—a combination, in the Trade Union world, of the accountant and the lawyer."

Having all this knowledge of the existence of a variety of Lists in mind, the General Council of the Amalgamation decided on 28th June, 1891, "That the time was opportune to go into Uniform List questions." Considerable discussions took place, and after lengthy negotiations with the employers' representatives the new "Uniform List of Weaving Prices" was adopted by the General Council, on 30th April, 1892, by 54 votes to 9; the new List was established on 24th June, 1892, and came into operation for the first time on 1st August, 1892, for fresh calculations, and in the first week of November for all cloths. The new Uniform List, which was a compromise between the Blackburn, Burnley, and Preston Lists, has continued in force from that time until 1935, when it was superseded by the Legalised Uniform List.

The "Brooklands" Agreement

During a dispute in the South-East Lancashire spinning mills, spinning American cotton, a stoppage took place which lasted from 7th November, 1892 to 27th March, 1893, because of the operatives' refusal to submit to a reduction of 5 per cent in their wages. With a desire to get the operatives' and employers' representatives together, Mr. Robert Ascroft, an Oldham solicitor, on his own initiative, invited a number of these representatives to take dinner with him at Sedgeley Hall, Sedgeley Park, Prestwich, near Manchester, to enable them to have an unofficial talk together. This resulted later in Mr. Ascroft drawing up a few proposals with a view to settling the dispute. These proposals were laid before the operatives' representatives, were accepted, and sent to the employers as the operatives proposals. After considering the proposals the employers replied with counter-proposals, to which the operatives again sent amended proposals. This led to a joint conference being held in the Brooklands Hotel, Brooklands, near Manchester, on 23rd March, 1893. This conference continued its sitting from 2-30 p.m., on the 23rd until 5 a.m. the following morning, when the agreement, since known as the Brooklands Agreement, was signed.

The agreement was amended on 24th December, 1897, and again on 8th August, 1910, and was signed by representatives of the Federation of Master Cotton Spinners' Associations, and representatives of the Operative Spinners' Amalgamation, the Card and Blowing Room Operatives' Amalgamation, and the "Amalgamated Northern Counties Association of Warpers, Reelers, and Winders," (our own Amalgamation).

The Brooklands Agreement has historical importance in industrial relations, as it marked the beginning of an era of joint relationships which spread to other industries in the country. The first clause of the agreement stated that the representatives of the employers and the employed, admitted that "disputes and differences between them are inimical to the interests of both parties, and that it is expedient and desirable that some means should be adopted for the future whereby such disputes and differences may be expeditiously and amicably settled, and strikes and lock-outs avoided."

Subsequent clauses dealt with the manner of handling applications for advances or reductions in wages, and the holding of Local Joint Meetings and Central Joint Meetings before industrial action could be taken. Thus was the foundation laid for the joint industrial negotiating machinery in our industry, which was later codified in the "Joint Rules" in 1908 in the manufacturing section, and reviewed in 1912 in the spinning section.

In order that the Central Committee could have greater power in being responsible for disputes, a new Rule was adopted on 10th March, 1894, giving the Committee authority to act in cases of disputes where not more than 5,000 looms were concerned. In that year efforts were made to create a Federation on the manufacturing side of the industry, but the reply of our Association to the Overlookers' Amalgamation (with whom the Amalgamation had been in consultation) was that until they could obtain a weekly wage for their members by doing away with the system of being paid by poundage no useful purpose could be served by federation. This system of poundage is referred to later in dealing with the Slate System.

Breaches of Agreements

During 1895 considerable dissatisfaction prevailed in the Barnoldswick district against under-payment, and eventually a strike took place at Long Ing Shed against breaches of agreement, this strike ultimately involving the whole of the mills in Barnoldswick. Over 1,200 weavers were reported to be on strike on 7th March, 1896, and the cost was £850 per week. The employers were importing strangers into the locality to take the place of our members, and the attitude of the police in the dispute was of such a character that the attention of the Home Secretary was called to it. In order to maintain the dispute in Barnoldswick levies (which had varied from 5s. to 10s. per 100 members) were increased to 20s. per 100 members. After continuing for many months the strike was lost, due to the successful efforts of the employers in engaging strangers. This dispute amply demonstrated, as did others, that individual employers could break away from agreements with or without the consent of their employees, and it is interesting to note that on the 16th April, 1898, a resolution was adopted by the General Council in the following terms:—"That the Central Committee be instructed to press forward for an Act of Parliament being passed whereby it shall be illegal for any employer or employers to pay less than the standard rate of wages as agreed upon by the Employers' and Operatives' Associations."

Arising from another dispute at a Heywood mill caused by under-payment of coloured goods, the General Council passed a resolution on 18th June, 1898 "That no local district be allowed to make out prices for sorts for which there is no list, but send them to the C.C. so that prices may be fixed for all districts alike."

The question of breaches of agreement continuously troubled the Amalgamation, and it was felt by many that legislative action should be taken to supplement industrial bargains. How to influence Parliament without representation in the

House of Commons was difficult to contemplate, but it was evident that the Amalgamation was not yet ripe for the promotion of representatives of its own in the House of Commons to look after the interests of its members. The mind of the General Council was well revealed in a resolution passed on 22nd September, 1900:—"That the question of Labour Representation in Parliament so far as this Amalgamation is concerned, be not entertained."

In these days such a decision seems strange, especially when it must be remembered that the Amalgamated Weavers' Association was part and parcel of the United Textile Factory Workers' Association.

The United Textile Factory Workers' Association

The United Textile Factory Workers' Association was formed in 1890, but its activities had previously been carried on under the title "Northern Counties Factory Act Reform Association," from 1886. In 1891 (when Mr. T. Birtwistle was Secretary) the Annual Report of that Association expresses disappointment with the operation of the Cotton Cloth Factories Act, which had been in operation for twelve months. The report complained that only one inspector was appointed to cover the whole district, whereas there should be at least six. Legal interpretations were put upon certain clauses which allowed artificial heat to be raised to any extent, whilst the operatives' representatives had been led to believe when the Act was passed that the production of artificial heat was not to go beyond 70 degrees. In that Report there is an interesting reference in a letter (reproduced in full) to Mr. Birtwistle from Sir Henry James, who was then a member of the House of Commons:—

> "I do not wish to refer more than I can avoid to the poor services I have endeavoured to render to the operatives. Still, I must state that whilst I have done my best I frequently felt the drawback under which I labour in consequence of having no technical knowledge of the incidents attaching to labour in a Textile Factory. I need not dwell on the great advantage derived by those who are engaged in certain industrial occupations by being directly represented in the House of Commons . . . it seems strange that the Textile Factory Operatives (numbering, I believe, some 125,000 persons) whose interest you and Mr. Mawdsley, in conjunction with others, have so ably represented in conference, have no direct representation, and I feel strongly that they would do well for their own interests if they endeavoured to secure the presence of one of their own body in the House of Commons.
>
> I do not wish to praise any particular person, or to take part in suggesting any candidate, but I can very confidently bear my testimony to the opportunity the operatives have of choosing men to represent them who could bring to the discharge of their Parliamentary duties not only complete practical knowledge of the work carried on in Textile Factories, but also great ability and rare moderation in the expression of their views . . . "

In the Annual Report of the United Textile Factory Workers' Association for 1893 the then Secretary, Mr. James Mawdsley, gave the text of a Bill to reduce working hours to 48 per week, but expressed disappointment that the Bill was never permitted to be introduced into the House. He said "It is plainly a waste of time for the operatives to instruct the Legislative Council to bring forward certain Bills, and then go home and vote for men who will oppose those measures . . . There is only one way of getting Bills through Parliament, and that is by votes. These votes can only be secured by the operatives bargaining for them at the polling booths. Capitalists will vote for milk and water business in order to keep us quiet, but they will not take on such things as an Eight Hours Day, or stopping steaming in weaving sheds unless they are made."

"Time Cribbing"

In the immediately following years the United Textile Factory Workers' Association spent much effort in securing representation in Parliament, in dealing with the "Time Cribbing" which many employers indulged in, and in helping to place upon the statute book the Trades Union and Trade Disputes Act, 1906. The term "Time Cribbing" was used to describe a practice used by a number of employers to increase production by starting the mill engine a number of minutes before the official starting time and running beyond the usual finishing time).

The Association, which is composed of all the main Amalgamations in the Lancashire Textile Industry, has done extremely valuable work since its inception, and volumes could be written surveying the enormous number of subjects of interest to textile workers and especially the weavers, winders, beamers, &c. In more recent years it has been instrumental in securing the election of several Members of Parliament, who have rendered most valuable service to the textile workers in particular and the trade union movement in general. We recall with gratitude the names of Members of Parliament like the late D. J. Shackleton, the late Thomas Shaw (who was a Vice-President of the Amalgamation, and was Minister for War during the 1914-18 war), the late Captain Albert Smith, the late Wm. C. Robinson; men like James Bell (who became President of the Amalgamation subsequent to J. W. Ogden), Wm. J. Tout, George Tomlinson and Ernest Thornton (Parliamentary Secretary, Ministry of Labour, 1965.)

During 1899–1900 there was a disastrous famine in India, and the Lancashire textile workers generously contributed to the relief of the Indian people. There was much controversy amongst the workers at that time upon the question of Juvenile Labour, and in commenting upon the passing of the "Half Time Bill" in 1900, Mr. A. H. Cottam (who was then Secretary of the older North-East Lancashire Amalgamation) said in his report "although much opposition was shown by the operatives generally to the raising of the age from 11 to 12, there seems to be very little said now when the Bill is in operation." During that year there was considerable agitation to secure a full half-day holiday on Saturday afternoons, by ceasing work at 12 noon, and this benefit was not secured until January, 1902, by the Factory Act of 1901, which also fixed the working hours at 55½ hours per week. These hours operated from 1902 to 1919.

Slate System

During these early years at the commencement of the 20th century feeling ran high amongst the weavers against what was known as the "Slate System," which was a very insiduous method of driving the weavers, by publishing their wages upon a slate exhibited in the shed. There are records in the General Council minutes of numerous suicides during 1901 to 1903, particular reference being made at the Council meeting held on 15th June, 1901, to a Darwen case and in 1903 to an Accrington case which brought prominence to this question. Power was given to Darwen District to take steps to abolish this system and the system of paying commission to overlookers, and a resolution was passed recommending Districts to hold public meetings on the matter. Joint Meetings were held with the employers, but it was not found possible to reach any mutual understanding.

These methods of "driving" were difficult to define materially, but the overlookers tried their best to raise the output of each individual weaver to the level attained by the "best weaver" in the shed. Often a certain degree of victimisation was involved in cases of weavers of limited ability. The weekly output of cloth of individual weavers were often compared and contrasted publicly in the shed. Very often the weavers were recruited by the overlookers, and the weavers were often regarded as the overlooker's team.

Complaints against overlookers of "driving" were difficult to deal with by the Weavers' officials. The overlookers themselves were members of a powerful trade union, and there was the difficulty of defining the term "driving." A description of a weaving shed in 1873 refers to the activities of the overlookers as "drivers" of the operatives in their attempts to raise production:—

"The overlooker is stimulating and driving the weavers all day long, and on making-up day; he goes round to each weaver with a slate and asks the amount of the week's earnings. But before going round, he will generally ascertain, either from the books or some other source, the highest earnings of any weaver in the shop, and everyone who is not up to this mark will receive a severe chastisement at his hands. Very often the earnings were published in a prominent place in the mill, and operatives were often absent on such days, to avoid chastisement and exposure." The overlookers were not paid on any definite Time Rate basis, but upon the poundage of cloth produced by the weavers at work in their shed. It can be seen, therefore, that in periods of bad trade, or immediately after wage reductions, complaints against overlookers for "driving" were at their peak, for overlookers were intent upon making up their losses in earnings which they had suffered by the general reduction in wages, by securing a proportionate increase in output from the weavers.

The various officials of the Weavers' Amalgamation drew public attention to this practice of Driving, and in Haslingden in 1885 Mr. Joshua Barrows (the full-time Agent of the Amalgamation) said:—

> " . . . the 'whip' which had been used so extensively throughout Lancashire during the past dozen years, had conduced very materially to the creation of the state of things which now existed. It was from Thursday morning until Wednesday night one break-neck race with the weavers of Lancashire. It was, over and over again, like starting for the Derby every Thursday morning; sometimes they won by a neck; and sometimes they lost by a head. It just depended on what sort of a mood the tackler was in."

He had no quarrel with the overlookers as a body; they were, as a rule, as intelligent and honest as any other class of men; but there were exceptions to all rules, and there were exceptions amongst overlookers.

The President of the Amalgamation, Mr. David Holmes, also expressed strong feelings against overlookers who were attempting to drive the weavers, at a meeting of weavers held in Clayton-le-Moors in 1885. In 1893, a year of especially bad trade, the *Cotton Factory Times* were still able to describe how, in some Lancashire weaving sheds, boards were placed in the workrooms giving the name of each operative and their individual work performance; against each name was written "This wont do" or "This must be improved upon".

Complaints against driving were so numerous during 1893 that the General Council of the Weavers' Amalgamation decided to consider further action. The following letter was addressed to all District Associations:—

"Driving and humbugging in weaving sheds"

"Fellow Operatives,

"In consequence of the obnoxious system of driving and humbugging operatives in weaving sheds, practised by some overlookers, it has become absolutely necessary that some protection be made against your mental depression, which we believe in some instances had ended in the destruction of life. This being so, we propose trying the following method as a means of improving your present position:—

"Should any tackler (overlooker) speak to a weaver about his earnings at any time or place, or speak unjustly when fetched to tackle a loom, we request such weaver at once to report the same to a member of the Weavers' Committee, and if such tackler be found guilty of doing so, action will be taken against him immediately, as we are of opinion that such conduct is very objectionable and altogether unnecessary. We should advise you not to use any uncivil language to your employers, as such conduct only tends to weaken your case, especially in a court of law. Our only object in taking this action is that we desire your position to be more comfortable than it has been of late, and to do this we require your best assistance, as without this it will be useless attempting to make any improvement. Do not be afraid of reporting your cases, if any, and be perfectly certain they are correctly given, and we assure you that no harm will befall you in consequence . . .

Yours faithfully,
The Executive Council,
The Northern Counties Weavers' Amalgamation.

CHAPTER X

The Factory Acts

Historical

As related earlier in this history the conditions and the working hours of children were abominable, and in the course of time the public conscience began to be stirred. Politicians and economists thought however, that it was essential to the prosperity of industry that the problem should be left alone and that it would be improper for the State to interfere in the "free" contract between employer and employee.

Attention was directed to the evils of the factory system as it was developing in Lancashire, so far back as 1784 by the magistrates of Manchester. They decided to refuse their sanction to indentures of parish apprentices if it appeared that they were expected to work at night, or for more than 10 hours daily.

Early factory legislation, therefore, up to about 1850, was promoted primarily to safeguard children and young persons in the textile industry. These efforts at establishing a code of factory laws were opposed strenuously by many politicians and industrialists, but as one gloomy prognostication after another was proved to be false, other arguments were brought forward. For example, it was asserted in the earlier years that restriction of the labour of young persons and children would be ruinous to industry, and that foreign countries in which enterprising employers were not hindered by factory laws would secure trade which would be lost to Great Britain.

It is interesting to recall that an economist of great repute of those times, Nassau Senior, put forward the view that the profit of the employer was made from the work done by his employees during the last hour of the factory day. If the day were reduced by one hour no profit would be made! Experience has since proved how fallacious such an argument was.

The first Factory Act, which was introduced by Sir Robert Peel, himself a factory owner, was passed in 1802. It was called the "Health and Morals of Apprentices Act," and it dealt only with apprentices in cotton and woollen factories. Their hours of work were to be limited to 12 per day, and after June, 1804 they were not to be kept at work after 9 o'clock at night. Rules were made on such matters as their clothing, their instruction, their religious observances, their dormitory accommodation, the condition of the factory premises, and the provision of medical attention in the event of outbreak of infectious disease. In each district two visitors were to be appointed by the magistrates to inspect the factories, and to report breaches of the Act. The system of visitation was ineffective as occasional visits by amateur inspectors, who were possibly friendly with the factory owner, were useless for the purpose of discovering evasions of the Act.

Employers, however, found a means of evading the Act by ceasing to take pauper apprentices, and employing wage-earning children instead. To these the Act of 1802 did not apply.

In 1819 a further Act (known as the Cotton Mills Act) was passed which applied to all children employed in cotton spinning factories, whether as apprentices or wage-earners, though not to other types of workpeople. Children under 9 years of age were not to be employed, and those who were under 16 years were not to work for more than 12 hours per day. One-and-a-half hours was allowed for meals, so that the attendance of children on factory premises could not exceed 13½ hours per day. This Act was inadequately enforced and easily evaded. Further Acts were passed in 1820, 1825, and 1830, which only amended the law in details, and they were all repealed by the Act of 1831.

The Factory Act of 1831 limited the labour of young persons under 18 years in cotton factories to 12 hours per day, and to 9 hours on Saturdays. It prohibited night work by young persons under 21 years. This Act was openly violated, and although occasional prosecutions occurred, the fines which were inflicted on the factory owners were sometimes paid out of deductions from the wages of the workers.

But such champions of factory reform as Robert Owen, Richard Oastler, and Michael Sadler were at last succeeding in arousing public opinion, and politicians began to realise that the open disregard of the law by factory owners, which had been going on for the past thirty years could not be permitted to continue. Lord Ashley championed the cause of factory reform, and in 1833 a measure which may be described as the first effective Factory Act.

The 1833 Factory Act was applicable to all textile mills (except silk mills), and it continued to prohibit the employment of children under 9 years. Children between 9 and 13 years of age were to be permitted to work in the factory for not more than nine hours per day, or 48 hours per week, and they were to attend school for not less than 2 hours per day, schoolmasters being paid by a penny in the shilling deducted from the children's wages. The labour of young persons between 13 and 18 years was limited to 12 per day or 69 hours per week, and they were not to work at night. Four factory inspectors were appointed, and they were empowered to inflict fines upon manufacturers who violated the law. A surgeon was required to examine the children as being reasonably fit.

Whilst this Act of 1833 was an attempt to secure some improvement in the shocking working conditions of the children, yet from reports of the period it is doubtful whether the new regulations were strictly adhered to. As proof of this we learn that in 1837 a Stalybridge millowner was fined for employing children under 13 years of age for more than the statutory 9 hours per day, whilst a year later 75 children out of 112 children, who had been certified by local surgeons as being over 13 years of age, were proved to be much younger. The working hours and conditions of adult workers were disgraceful, as well. Life for them was "bed and work, and work and bed," and even after the Factory Act of 1833 it was common for a cotton spinner to work from 6 a.m. to 8 p.m., stopping at 4 p.m. on Saturdays, for an average wage of 22s. to 24s. 9d. per week, while the big piecer earned 7s. 6d. and the little piecer 4s. 6d. per week.

In 1844 Peel's Factory Act was passed, which extended and modified the provisions of previous Acts. It applied to all textile factories (other than silk mills). The age at which a child might begin work in the factory was reduced to eight, and while this was a step in the wrong direction it must be remembered that with the establishment in 1836 of the registration of births the proof of age could be more effective. Under earlier Acts it is probable that children of seven or eight were received on the pretext that they were nine.

This Act is notable in that it instituted the "Half-Time System" effectively, as children between 8 and 13 were not to work more than 6½ hours per day, with three hours at school. The limitation of working hours of young persons to 12 per day, was continued, and a similar restriction was placed on the working hours of women, so that by this time the law offered protection to all classes of factory workers except men. Under the 1844 Act a central office was set up in London called "The Office of the Factory Inspector". Dangerous machinery was to be fenced, and the employment of young persons in cleaning and oiling of machinery whilst in motion was prohibited.

The agitation for a ten-hour day continued, and in 1847 Fielden's Factory Act became law. But the Act was so framed that the reintroduction of the "relay" system became possible, and the factory day stretched over a period of 15 hours —from 5-30 a.m. to 8-30 in the evening, and it was difficult to ascertain whether the law was being observed. Lord Ashley drew attention of Parliament to the matter, and Sir George Grey proposed a further Act in 1850, specifying the hours of work for women and young persons. These were to be from six to six and one-and-a-half hours for meals. The daily period of work was thus extended to 10½ hours but there was a limit of 60 hours per week, Saturday work finishing at 2 p.m. The labour of children was, however, still regulated by the Act of 1844 and they might still be employed as early as 5-30 a.m., or as late as 8-30 p.m., and this was remedied only by the passing of an amending Act in 1853.

This "Ten Hours Act" was the culmination of years of agitation, by Oastler, Sadler, Fielden, Hindley, and an Ashton-under-Lyne minister, Rev. Joseph Rayner Stephens. Michael Sadler had, of course, introduced a Bill in Parliament in 1832 to shorten the hours of labour, but public interest was too absorbed in a Reform Bill to pay much attention. Mr. Sadler lost his seat in a later General Election, and Mr. Hindley was elected for Ashton in 1835, and continued to champion the cause in Parliament of Shorter Hours. The Rev. Joseph Stephens continued the struggle outside Parliament, and caused a split in local politico-religious circles, forming a group known as "Stephenites". He was arrested in Hyde in 1838 and sentenced to 18 months' imprisonment for his part in a public meeting in Hyde.

An interval of time elapsed before further legislation was attempted, although employers made unsuccessful attempts to secure the repeal of existing factory laws. The hours of labour remained at 60 per week until 1875. Various Acts were passed in 1860, 1864, 1867 and 1871, extending the provisions of factory legislation to other non-textile industries.

In 1871 textile operatives made an effort to get the working hours reduced from 60 to 58 per week, to enable work to stop at 12 noon on Saturdays instead of 2 p.m. This failed, but the threat to stop the machinery at 12 noon resulted in a lockout of one week in certain districts. On May 9th, 1871 a joint agreement was reached between the employers' and operatives' associations in the Manchester, Oldham and Ashton districts, whereby the hours were reduced from 60 to 59 per week, to enable cessation of work on Saturdays at 1 p.m.

By the Factory Act of 1874 some changes were made in the law as it applied to the textile industries. The maximum number of hours of work for women and young persons, which since 1850 had been 10½ per day, were reduced to ten, and the total for the week was reduced to 56½ hours; in practice this meant a shortening of the working hours for men also. Children under 9—and after a lapse of a year under 10 years of age—were not to be employed in factories, and the half-time age was raised to 14 years, except in the case of children who had reached a certain standard of education. Overtime was forbidden and silk mills were brought into line with other textile establishments.

In 1878 the Factory and Workshops Act was passed, which codified previous legislation, and the provisions governing textile factories remained unaltered.

In 1889 the Cotton Cloth Factory Act was passed, which governed the conditions under which the atmosphere in cotton factories was made humid artificially, and the use of hygrometers was officially regulated.

Under the Factory Act of 1891 children were not to begin work in factories until they attained 11 years and by the Act of 1895 the work of children in all cases was limited to 30 hours per week, and night work was forbidden to children under 14 years.

The weekly hours remained at 56½ until the Factory and Workshops Act of 1901, when they were reduced by one hour, to 55½ hours per week, which meant that Saturday work finished at 12 noon. Under this Act the age at which children were permitted to enter factories was raised to 12, and the long controversy over the "Half-Time System" was ended by the abolition of the System in 1921, due to the Education Act of 1918.

The Factories Act, 1937 (and "Shuttle-Kissing")

The main Factories Act which operates to govern the working conditions, safety, and welfare of our members, dates from 1937, when the Act of Parliament of that year marked a big step forward in industrial legislation. Whilst the 1937 Act consolidated the previous law it also endeavoured to raise the standards of industrial conditions. All workplaces were now termed "factories" and the old distinctions between factories and workshops and between textile and non-textile factories were abolished. Increased powers were bestowed upon the Home Secretary to make regulations, and in fact a good number of such regulations have been made since. Section 50 of the 1937 Act dealt with "Shuttle Kissing" and empowered the Home Secretary to make such special regulations as appeared to him to be reasonable for extending the use of shuttles which were not capable of being threaded by suction of the mouth. The term "shuttle kissing" was commonly used to describe the action of sucking the thread of a new cop through the eye of the shuttle. This was bad for the weavers. The suction affected their teeth and dirty yarn entered the mouth.

In pursuance of that authority the Home Secretary convened conferences of representatives from the industry, in December 1937, to consider the practicability of adopting hand-threaded shuttles, and a Joint Sub-Committee was appointed. This sub-committee has continued its work since, and inspected many types of hand-threaded shuttles. Tests have also been undertaken by the staff of the British Cotton Research Association at Shirley Institute, Manchester, and by 1939 the joint sub-committee had reached such a point in its deliberations that an agreed recommendation was possible.

On 26th April, 1939, the following resolution was passed:—

"This meeting is of the opinion that there are available certain types of hand-threaded shuttles which can be satisfactorily substituted for ordinary shuttles in a great majority of cloths."

Further meetings were held, and on 4th May, 1939, with the Chief Inspector of Factories (Sir D. R. Wilson) present it was agreed that draft regulations should be prepared by the Home Secretary, making provision that after 2½ years from the date of the regulations no more suction-threaded shuttles would be issued to weavers, and that after a further four years (6½ years from the date of the regulation) no suction-threaded shuttles should be used at all on a wide variety of cloths. The periods named were designed to enable individual firms to use their stocks of shuttles and to make the necessary preparations for the change-over. The 1939–45 World War, however, upset all these plans, and it was not possible to proceed with the issuing of the draft Regulations.

The Joint Standing Committee continued to meet, but progress was slow, although in the rayon section of the industry the use of suction-threaded shuttles had more or less become obsolete. The Weavers' Amalgamation continued to press for legislative action, through an Order, to ban the use of suction-shuttles, and in 1950 a lengthy letter was addressed to the President of the Board of Trade pressing for governmental action to implement the desires of the Joint Standing Committee.

Eventually agreement was reached between all concerned, and a new Order was issued. The new Order gave time to the industry to adapt itself to the change, and a period of 2½ years was allowed for the use of suction-threaded shuttles. A further period of 3½ years was allowed for the abolition of the old shuttles, after which it became compulsory for hand-threaded shuttles only to be used.

Thus ended the abhorrent practice of "shuttle-kissing".

The Factories Act of 1937 also provided for the control of humid atmospheres artificially produced by steaming or other means in connection with any textile process. These regulations are contained in Order No. 300, made under the Cotton Cloth Factories Act, and the subject is referred to in greater detail in the later reference to Steaming and Artificial Humidity.

The Act of 1937 also limited Hours of Work in general to nine per day, or 48 hours per week (44-hours per week for juveniles from 14 to 16 years of age).

Certain overtime was permissible, under defined conditions. Specific provision was made for annual holidays, and the previous Section 116 of the 1901 Act (dealing with the requirement of publishing Particulars of Wages) was re-enacted in Section 112 of the 1937 Act.

Steaming and Artificial Humidification

The sizing of warp yarns as part of the weaving process had always been practised, both in Lancashire mills and elsewhere during the first three-quarters of the 19th century. The size originally consisted of flour and tallow, and comprised roughly 20 per cent of the total warp weight. During the cotton famine in the early 1860's, however, the manufacturers were compelled to economise in the use of yarn, and because of the difficulty of weaving the shorter fibred cotton the needful tenacity of the twist was given by a larger amount of size than would be required for better quality yarns. The manufacturers therefore began to add more than 20 per cent of size, and the sizing substance itself was adulterated, the flour or tallow giving way to the use of china clay.

In Todmorden, for instance, one-third china clay and two-thirds of fatty substances were used in sizing, and from 50 to 90 per cent of size came to be used. In the early 1870's therefore thousands of yards of cotton cloth manufactured in Lancashire had been weighted with quantities of size not required for any manufacturing process, but used as an adulteration. This increase in the use of size was accompanied by a deterioration in factory working conditions. There was a great need to keep the weaving sheds damp, and windows and ventilators were kept closed.

In some districts, particularly in Blackburn and Padiham, the required dampness was secured by the injection of steam into the shed from perforations in heating pipes, and by keeping the floor damp with water. It was often difficult to see across a weaving shed for the dust-laden atmosphere. These conditions caused many lung, throat and chest complaints amongst the weavers, and many protests were made by the weavers and by the Weavers' Unions. Over 1,600 weavers in the Todmorden district (without a Union to support them) presented a Memorial to Parliament in 1871, protesting against the practice of cloth sizing and the terrible working conditions which the practice produced. The local Medical Officer of Health, Dr. Buchanan was appointed to investigate the working conditions and to report on the effects of these conditions upon the health of the operatives. His final medical report ended: "All the medical men in Todmorden agree that lung diseases are greatly prevalent and that the circumstances of employment in cotton manufacture conduce to such diseases." But no remedial measures were proposed by the Government after the publication of the report, and working conditions in the sheds continued much as before. Although the Weavers' Unions were weak at that time nevertheless they drew the attention of the Trades Union Congress to the problem, and the Parliamentary Committee of the T.U.C., presented a Memorial to the Government on 17th June, 1882, "drawing the attention of the Government to the practice which in late years has become very common in weaving, especially in the manufacture of goods known as 'T-cloths and shirting'; we allude to over-sizing (50 to 200 per cent of sizing used), and the infusion of steam into the weaving sheds during periods of dry weather;" As a consequence the Government decided to make an Enquiry into the Effect of Heavy Sizing in cotton weaving, upon the health of the operatives.

The Final Report of the Enquiry commented:—

"The means of ventilation were poor in the weaving sheds and in all the factories visited by the Commission no use was made of any of the ventilating means available. It was the practice to exclude fresh air from the shed for at least half the year."

The Commission further reported that, considering the size of the majority of the sheds they visited, the air should have been changed 12 to 13 times a working day, whereas they doubted if it was ever done. The Report was presented to Parliament in 1884; but, again, no ameliorative measures were proposed by the then Government.

But neither the weavers themselves nor the District Associations were content to permit the ill-effects of Steaming to be forgotten at Westminster, and the formation of the Amalgamated Weavers' Association in 1884, provided the means for continuing the agitation on a larger scale than before. In fact, the agitation against Steaming was a means of helping to cement the District Associations together within the Amalgamation in the first years after its formation. The agitation continued during the 1880's, and the Preston Weavers' Association issued a statement, conveying the testimony of 34 Preston doctors "who all testified to the ill-effects of the steaming practice upon the operatives' health." The Preston Weavers' Association collected more than 25,000 signatures for several petitions to Parliament at that time.

In Blackburn, Dr. Stephenson, the Medical Officer of Health, published in 1887 an alarming report on the health of the cotton workers in that district, and in consequence, the Borough Health Committee, in 1888, instituted a Special Enquiry into the question. Several witnesses described to the Commission how they were compelled to work in conditions where the water reached to their ankles, and with water streaming down the walls of the shed, falling directly upon their clothes, which were hung there.

The Commission concluded its final Report: "The ventilation of the mills was unsatisfactory, especially in winter; that heavy steaming as had been practised in Blackburn and the conditions under which work was carried on had influenced the high death rate of the Borough; and that heavy and excessive steaming was injurious to the health of those that work in the sheds, but that light steaming, accompanied by proper ventilation, was not injurious."

The publication of this Report during 1889 brought the agitation against Steaming to a climax. In March of that year a Petition was presented to Parliament signed by "some 220,000 inhabitants resident in textile districts of Lancashire, amongst whom was a considerable sprinkling of medical gentlemen." The Petition took the form of outlining the trend towards the over-sizing of cloth by Lancashire manufacturers, in much the same way as had been made clear by the two earlier Reports. It included a quotation from the Report of the Blackburn Medical Officer, for 1887, to the effect that:—

"It is not the occasional overflow of an ash-pit or excreta tub, nor disagreeable odours, that the death rate of the Blackburn Borough is high. It is by the wholesale slaughter of the inhabitants by infusing steam into the weaving shed."

There was a division of opinion between the weavers themselves and the Union officials as to the best way of dealing with the problem, and David Holmes wrote in the *Cotton Factory Times*:—

"Probably the entire abolition of steaming would be the best solution, but if that is decided upon it would mean an opposition which might take years to overcome, if it were done at all. The evil is at present a crying one, and it is essential that its worst features should at once be remedied. . . . It might be said that in going in for total abolition we should fail to secure our aims, but we should be more liable to get a modification."

Compared with the more reasoned approach of David Holmes a weavers' club official declared at a meeting of Rishton Weavers in July, 1889, that "if the law fails to protect the operatives, then the employers cannot complain of the operatives taking the law into their own hands, as the time seems to have come to employ other means. It may be costly to hamper trade, but the lives of our people must be saved."

Agitation continued during 1889, and during the first week in March, 1889, for instance, the House of Commons heard many Petitions from the Weavers' Unions at Clitheroe, Padiham, Great Harwood, Colne, Heywood, Darwen, Haslingden, and Rishton; from "11,000 adult operatives at Bury, 26,190 inhabitants of Preston; 5,000 inhabitants of Oldham; and 7,000 inhabitants of Nelson."

Sir William Holdsworth called a private meeting of Lancashire M.P.s in the House of Commons on 8th March, 1889, to discuss the possibilities of dealing with the question of Steaming by legislation. No decision was arrived at, but it was agreed to hear the views of a delegation from the United Textile Factory Workers' Association. A delegation, composed of 40 textile Union officials duly met 30 of the Lancashire Members of Parliament, with Lord Cranborne in the chair. He at once suggested that before any action was taken a Select Committee of the Commons should investigate the effects of Steaming upon the health of the operatives; but the Operatives' representatives opposed the proposal, on the grounds that sufficient information had been secured from the various Commissions and Enquiries already instituted. The outcome of the conference was that a joint committee of seven operatives' representatives and seven Parliamentary Members should prepare a Bill—to curb or prevent Steaming—to be submitted to Parliament as early as possible. The members of this Joint Committee were: Sir Henry James; Mr. Mundella; Sir William Holdsworth; Sir H. Roscoe; Mr. H. Hoyle; Lord Cranborne and Mr. T. H. Sidebottom, from the Commons; Messrs. T. Birtwistle (Accrington), D. Holmes (Burnley) G. Barker (Blackburn), James Mawdsley (Manchester) and George Silk (Oldham), representing the Textile Unions.

The reaction of the employers and their Association was to convene a meeting at the Mitre Hotel, Manchester, on 3rd April, with the object of appointing a committee to wait upon the Home Secretary, to urge the necessity for an enquiry before proceeding with legislation on the steaming question.

The Home Secretary, apparently attempting to keep both the Government and himself independent from the question at issue, preferred to secure the employers' views in writing. The manufacturers regarded the attitude of the Home Secretary as something of an insult to the authority of "the most powerful Employers' Association in the United Kingdom." They wrote again at the beginning of April, expressing the view that the time was not ripe for legislation on the subject of Steaming, and they again stated that "the Lancashire employers of the most important trade in the country required the Home Secretary to find time for an interview."

After the passing of six weeks the Home Secretary had not replied, and the North and North-East Lancashire Employers' Association were obviously annoyed, and wrote a third time, demanding that "a full and complete enquiry shall be instituted into the whole question of Steaming . . . " The Home Secretary eventually met the employers' delegation, but it made little difference to the Government's attitude, for, throughout the later passage of the Bill to curb the practice of Steaming the Government remained aloof from taking sides.

Meanwhile the joint committee of textile representatives and M.P.s held many meetings, in order to reach agreement on the nature of the clauses of the Bill. The Unions had already agreed to compromise by allowing some steaming to take place, but the question was, how much? The Unions wished the degree of humidity in the shed never to be raised above that in the atmosphere outside; but they lost their fight, and the final Cotton Cloth Factories Act included a Table of Maximum limits of humidity permissible in the shed. The Unions did not relinquish any of their remaining demands; any employer requiring to practice steaming at any time during the year had first to give notice in writing to the Home Secretary, prescribing details of his premises and the methods of steaming to be used; and whilst such processes were in operation not less than 600 cubic feet of fresh air for each person employed should be allowed into the shed.

Many stormy meetings of weavers were held, when the terms of the new Act came to be explained by the officials, and there were differences of opinion even amongst the officials; but the Bill became law towards the end of 1889.

The Weavers' Amalgamation continued to press for the total abolition of Steaming, and there was a Royal Commission in 1892. Several disputes took place later, and in Padiham, in May, 1895, about 220 weavers employed at two local mills, struck work against the practice of steaming in their mills. The dispute continued until the end of September, when the Joint Committee of Employers' and Weavers' representatives agreed "that steaming should cease when the temperature of the weaving shed rose to 70 degrees."

Agitation still took place on this subject, and progress was made in the right direction, through the Factories Act of 1901, which provided that artificial humidity should cease when the wet bulb exceeded 75 degrees, and there should be no humidification at any time after the first half-hour in any way when the dry bulb reading was below 50 degrees. The regulations provided that two hygrometers should be provided in each humid shed, and additional hygrometers for sheds with over 700 looms.

These provisions were not satisfactory, however, and our representatives continued to press for the abolition of Steaming altogether, through joint meetings and deputations to the Home Secretary. In August, 1913, the Weavers' Amalgamation organised a petition, containing almost 126,000 signatures, and the Petition was presented before Parliament by Mr. Albert Smith, M.P. (Nelson and Colne) and Mr. A. H. Gill, M.P. (Bolton). Textile workers' representatives also met the Lancashire M.P.s during November of that year, to press for the abolition of Fining, and all forms of Artificial Humidification.

The Weavers' Amalgamation also sponsored a Bill before Parliament, dealing with both subjects, but no practical progress was made. A deputation from all the Lancashire Textile Workers' Amalgamations met the then Home Secretary, in February, 1914, and received a somewhat favourable reply on the subject of Fining, but made little progress towards a solution of the Steaming Problem, the Home Secretary contending that to abolish Steaming would seriously damage the industry. He promised to consider ways and means of dealing with the grosser evils of the system. As a consequence of the deputation the Home Secretary (Mr. Reginald McKenna, M.P.) visited a number of mills in Preston and Blackburn, in May, 1914, to see working conditions for himself.

No practical steps were taken, however, until the Labour Home Secretary (Mr. Arthur Henderson, M.P.) appointed a Departmental Committee in 1924, to enquire into the whole subject of artificial humidification. The Committee continued its work for about four years, and in April, 1928 issued its report. Employers, operatives, and scientific representatives sat on the Committee, and they came to the conclusion that (a) there was no evidence that employment in humid sheds gave rise to more sickness than in non-humid sheds (contrary to past contentions) (b) total abolition of steaming would add to the difficulties of a portion of the trade, by increasing manufacturing costs; (c) a certain amount of humidity is essential in weaving, but it should be controlled; (d) although past regulations had been of use there was need for amended regulations. The Committee found on the evidence submitted that there were certain ranges of temperature and humidities which gave most favourable conditions for the weaver's efficiency and for cloth production, and the Committee proposed a number of amendments to the Regulations.

These recommendations were ultimately embodied in the Cotton Cloth Factories Act of 1929. Under that Act regulations which had been made in 1901 and 1911 were codified and strengthened, and were set out in Statutory Regulations and Orders, 1929, No. 300, dated 27th April, 1929. These regulations are still in force and have not been affected by later editions of Factories Acts. The regulation provides that there should be no artificial humidification in a weaving shed at any time when the wet-bulb of the hygrometer is higher than that specified in a table of temperatures in relation to the dry bulb reading given in the table, and artificial humidification should cease altogether if the wet-bulb readings exceeded 72½ degrees. If the wet-bulb readings exceeded 80 degrees, all work should cease in the shed until the readings had dropped to 80 degrees or less, and the workers must leave the shed. On 7th May, 1929 the Home Secretary issued regulations governing the construction and maintenance of hygrometers.

Temperature

Under the 1901 Factory Act regulation 5 provided that in every shed, whether wet or dry, the temperature should not at any time during working hours be below 50 degrees, although half-an-hour was allowed for this temperature to be attained.

This regulation never gave satisfaction to the weaving operatives, and constant attempts were made to secure some improvement. In 1918 a meeting was held of Tenement Factory Owners, Employers, and Operatives, and on 27th August, 1918 a resolution was passed that the temperature should not be less than 50 degrees at starting time (6 a.m.) and should be at least 55 degrees by 6-30 a.m., the temperature not to fall below 55 degrees at any time afterwards during the day.

This voluntary agreement was embodied in the 1929 S.R. & O. No. 300 (mentioned above), and thus became an obligatory regulation. Although the situation had been improved the operatives have never been satisfied, and each winter there are frequent complaints of cold sheds, especially on Monday mornings.

CHAPTER XI

Early 20th Century Developments

"Coming-of-Age" Celebration

A DISTINCT landmark in the history of the Weavers' Amalgamation was the demonstration held at Blackpool on 10th May, 1905, to mark its "coming-of-age". At that time 34 District Associations were affiliated, embracing a total membership of 80,385. Some 480 delegates took tea together in the Grand Hotel Assembly Room, at which presentations were made to Mr. David Holmes (President), Alderman W. H. Wilkinson (General Secretary), Mr. Joshua Barrows (Agent) and Mr. Luke Park (Preston), all of whom had been connected with the Amalgamation from its formation. Mr. D. J. Shackleton, then M.P. for Clitheroe Division, and Vice-President of the Amalgamation and Secretary of the Darwen Weavers' Association, presided, and he was supported by the principal officials. To Mr.W. Melling, of Bolton, fell the duty of making the presentations to the four gentlemen. To Mr. Holmes he handed a tea service, to Mr. Barrows, a tea service, to Mr. Wilkinson, a rose bowl, and to Mr. Park, a clock and bronzes. Mr. J. W. Ogden (Heywood) and Mr. J. Cross (Blackburn) having offered felicitations, the recipients duly returned thanks.

Mr. Holmes stated that the organisation was built upon the disasters and ruins of 1878 and 1883–4. Prior to 1884 their forces were scattered in different parts of the county, the units being called together occasionally for consultation and defensive purposes. The weavers who paid at all, he said, paid a very small contribution indeed, usually a penny per week, and when a society was landed into trouble they expected to be supported through their trials. However, they had managed to see established a regularly organised system of government, but there were still almost 100,000 workpeople connected with the weaving section who were outside the unions. He asked them to put themselves into line. Thirty or forty years earlier it was a delicate thing for a weaver to be known to belong to a society, whereas at that time men were not afraid to join the ranks.

Mr. Wilkinson mentioned that in all his experience as Secretary the Amalgamation had never been six hours without having a dispute in hand. On one occasion at 12 o'clock noon they had a clean sheet, but sure enough the 2-30 post brought a dispute. They had never yet lost a strike through want of money. When they had lost, it had been due to men deserting and supporting the employers.

Mr. Barrows observed that the road in their younger days was not "knocked up with motor cars," it was not then laid. It was all pebbles and thorns, and they who traversed it had sore feet. They had since brushed a lot of the thorns and pebbles out of the way for their children, and they expected their children to look after their progeny in the same way.

Mr. Park said that before the amalgamation days they simply sat under the chairmanship of their friend, Mr. Birtwistle, and all the money they possessed as a body was that which would pay the expenses of what was then the Wages Committee. Prices of all sorts were paid, and scarcely anybody knew what rates others were paying. Most employers paid what they liked.

"Auld Lang Syne" was lustily sung, after which Mr. W. Pope (Hyde) moved, and Mr. William Ward (Nelson) seconded a vote of thanks to the chairman.

For the above account of the celebration we are indebted to the *Cotton Factory Times* of 2nd June, 1933.

The Passing of Three Pioneers

The Amalgamation received a staggering blow when, in 1905 and 1906 death removed three of its chief officials within a year. The Secretary, Alderman Wm. Hy. Wilkinson, J.P., resigned his position through ill health, 6th April, and died on the 25th April, 1906. Mr. Joshua Barrows, who had been serving as Agent from 17th May, 1884, died on 18th July, 1905. and Mr. David Holmes, President of the Amalgamation from 4th May, 1884, died on 14th January, 1906.

In spite of this very heavy blow others were found who were inspired with the same zeal and courage, to build upon the foundations that had already been laid, and Mr. David J. Shackleton was elected President on the 19th May, 1906. Mr. Joseph Cross, of Blackburn, was appointed Secretary on 10th March, 1906, and it was decided that the office of Agent be discontinued. In order to pay tribute to the three officers who had died, the Amalgamation instituted three Memorial Scholarships, tenable at Ruskin College for a period of two years. It was thought that this would be a fine way by which their memories could be held in esteem, and for many years the scholarships were awarded until later, by the wish of the General Council, the scheme was discontinued.

Northern Counties Textile Trades Federation

In September 1896 a delegate meeting was held to discuss the formation of a Federation of all the Unions within the manufacturing section. The scheme fell through, however, as the Tapesizers and the Warp Dressers had already abstained, and the Overlookers' Amalgamation swung against it.

A renewed attempt was made in 1906. Draft Rules were formulated and submitted to the General Council and on 10th February 1906 the Council decided to adopt the proposed Federation Rules. Thus the Textile Trades' Federation came into existence, as a closer unit amongst the Unions in the manufacturing section.

The present day members of the Northern Counties Textile Trades Federation are: General Union of Associations of Loom Overlookers, Amalgamated Textile Warehousmen, Amalgamated Association of Beamers, Twisters and Drawers, Lancashire and Yorkshire Warp Dressers' Associations, Amalgamated Tape

Sizers' Friendly Protection Society, Lancashire Tape Sizers' Amalgamation, Amalgamated Weavers' Association.

General Federation of Trade Unions

On the 19th May, 1906 the General Council also decided to strengthen its affiliations with the general movement, when it was resolved that the Amalgamation join the General Federation of Trade Unions, on the lower scale of contributions.

During 1906–7 a protracted strike took place at the mills in the Hebden Bridge district, on the question of low wages for Fustian cloth weaving, and the financial responsibility for the strike was shouldered by the Amalgamation in the final stages, the total cost to the Amalgamation exceeding £20,000.

During 1907 there had been innumerable disputes concerning "bad work" due to the widespread use of poor quality yarns, and the Amalgamation spent thousands of pounds in strike benefits on this account alone. On 9th March, 1907 the General Council were driven to pass the following resolution:—

> "That in the opinion of this Council it is advisable in cases of bad weaving to endeavour to obtain the payment of a daily wage based on the average wages earned when the work was satisfactory."

Joint Rules

Important years in the Amalgamation's history were 1907 and 1908, when very lengthy negotiations took place with the representatives of The Cotton Spinners and Manufacturers' Association, which led up to the establishment of a code of joint industrial rules, known as the "Joint Rules for the settlement of Trade Disputes." After several attempts to draft suitable Rules the final agreement was reached on 25th September, 1908, and the Joint Rules operated from 1st January, 1909. These Joint Rules have formed the very basis of our joint industrial relationships since, and are still in operation. A copy of the Joint Rules will be found in the Appendix.

The joint industrial machinery existing between the Amalgamation and the Federation of Master Cotton Spinners' Associations was reviewed and strengthened in 1912, and on 28th March, 1912, a joint agreement was signed, continuing to give effect to certain portions of the old Brooklands Agreement made in 1893 (as amended in 1897).

Mill Rules

In 1907 a number of firms in Blackburn, Darwen, and Great Harwood closed their mills on account of bad trade, without giving any notice to their operatives. Legal proceedings were taken in 1908, with the object of getting a decision as to the right of an employer to violate his own mill rules. The cases were heard by the County Court Judge at Blackburn. After a two days' hearing the Judge suggested that the two sides should meet, to see whether they could reach an agreement acceptable to each side. This was agreed to, and the case was adjourned for a few weeks.

Joint meetings took place early in 1908, and the following Mill Rules were jointly agreed between the Amalgamated Weavers' Association and The Cotton Spinners and Manufacturers' Association at joint meetings held on 1st May, 1908, and 25th September, 1908, and came into operation on the 1st January, 1909.

1. Every person employed (except persons casually employed or working as substitutes for sick or absent workpeople) shall give seven days' notice in writing previous to leaving, such notice to be given to the employer or employers on a Saturday, and at no other time and except as hereinafter provided, the employer or employers will give every person in his or their employment (except persons casually employed, or working as substitutes for sick or absent workpeople) a similar notice to terminate such employment; the notice to expire in either case on the closing of the mill on the following Saturday.

2. In case any person shall leave his or her employment without giving the notice aforesaid the employers shall be entitled to reasonable compensation for damages sustained, but such damages shall not exceed an amount equal to one week's average wages of the person so leaving.

3. Should the employers discharge a person without giving the notice aforesaid, such person shall (except in cases provided for by Rule 5) be entitled to reasonable compensation for damages sustained, but such damage shall not exceed an amount equal to one week's average wages of the person so discharged.

4. Any person absent on account of sickness must within a reasonable time give notice to the overlooker or some other person in authority, or in default thereof will be considered to have left his or her employment, and will be liable to pay damages as per Rule 2.

5. Any person guilty of persistently using bad or indecent language, or guilty of any gross misconduct, or wilfully wasting, damaging, spoiling or destroying the employers' property, shall be liable to be discharged without notice.

Arising from these early mill rules developed a comprehensive system of joint rules which were to cover the industrial relations between unions and employers' organisations. (See Appendix).

Uniform List for Waste Weaving

The General Council had been pressing ever since 1905 for the establishment of a Uniform List for weaving Hard-waste Cloths, and negotiations took place over a lengthy period of time. Agreement was finally reached in 1909, and the new Hardwaste List came into operation in January, 1910. Previously prices had varied more than 20 per cent between one district and another, and the task had been a difficult one of reaching accommodation. The operatives' representatives had pressed for a loom and pick basis for the list, but the employers had urged that payment should be by weight, and they could not be moved from that attitude. This system of payment by weight still exists today.

Parliamentary Representation

At the General Council Meeting in August, 1910, a lengthy report was given of the hearing in the Liverpool Chancery Court of an application by a Preston member for an injunction to restrain the Amalgamation and the Preston District Association from collecting levies for the purpose of securing and supporting Parliamentary representation. The injunction was granted, and stated that "such parts of the objects of the Amalgamated Weavers as provide for promoting labour representation in Parliament is invalid and illegal, and that the same are not binding on the plaintiff." The injunction further stipulated that the Amalgamation and the Preston Weavers' Association were not entitled to make payments, directly or indirectly out of their respective funds to the expenses of any candidate for election as a Member of Parliament. Later references are made to this subject in this book.

Non-Unionists

The Amalgamation had been much perturbed at the existence of a fairly large body of Non-Unionists who were enjoying the benefits being so strenuously fought for by the members. In May, 1911 the General Council decided that a district with 85 per cent membership at a mill should have financial support in refusing to work with non-members, and in December, 1911 a two-weeks' lock-out took place, involving almost 400,000 looms, on account of a dispute on this problem, which arose in the Accrington and Harwood districts. This dispute cost the Amalgamation over £15,000.

"Protection" Societies

For a number of years there had existed in certain districts a form of rival organisation, and the Annual Report of 1912 drew attention to the need for good organisation amongst the weavers, and expressed regret that there were a number of people "whose aims and objects seem to be intended for the disintegration and destruction of the present existing district associations. In Nelson the movement to form new societies has been pursued with exceptional energy, and we feel bound to say, pursued in not the very best form of controversy. Circulars had been issued by these societies calling upon the weavers 'not to be allied with Socialism'." The Report continues: "The circular seems generally to be in the direction of stirring up religious and political strife, and to prevent the workers from being able to meet on equal terms their employers . . . It is a repetition of old tactics—keep the workpeople divided, and so effectively prevent them taking common cause for their common good."

Now that this particular menace is a matter relegated to the limbo of past memories it is interesting to recall that these rival societies—"Protection Societies" as they were called—existed in Nelson, Clitheroe, Blackburn, and Preston. The Blackburn Weavers' Protection Society was actually formed as far back as 1888, as a breakaway from the Blackburn Weavers' Association. Later, Protection Societies were formed in the other districts mentioned, and they formed a "Federation of Weavers' Protection Societies." These Protection Societies were not affiliated with the Amalgamation to deal with the situation, following an application by Blackburn Protection Society to become affiliated with the

Trades Union Congress. Conferences were held between representatives of the T.U.C. General Council, the Amalgamation, and the Blackburn Protection Society, which ultimately resulted in the dissolution of the Federation of Protection Societies; Preston branch joined our Preston Weavers' Association; Clitheroe and Nelson Protection Societies were dissolved, and Blackburn Protection Society continued its separate existence, but later became affiliated with the Weavers' Amalgamation, in January 1920. This position continued to exist in Blackburn until 7th January, 1949, when the Protection Society merged its membership and assets with the original Blackburn Weavers' Association.

Resignation of D. J. Shackleton

In December, 1910, Mr. (later Sir) David J. Shackleton resigned his position as President of the Weavers' Amalgamation, on taking up a permanent appointment with the Board of Trade, and in May, 1911, Mr. John W. Ogden, J.P., Secretary of the Heywood Weavers' Association, who had been vice-president, was appointed as President. Mr. Fred Thomas, J.P. (Secretary of the Burnley Weavers' Association) was appointed vice-president. Mr. Thomas later became Superintendent of the Amalgamated Weavers' Approved Society under the National Health Insurance Acts.

National Health Insurance "Approved Society"

An important step was taken by the Amalgamation when, at a General Council Meeting held on 17th February, 1912, it was decided that the Amalgamation should become an Approved Society under the National Health Insurance Act, 1911, for all District Associations affiliated to it. The resolution was referred to the District Associations for their consideration, and after consultation with their members, steps were taken to become an Approved Society, in order to administer the Insurance Act of 1911. All the Districts agreed, with the exception of Nelson Weavers' Association, who formed an Approved Society of their own. At the onset there were thirty-six districts affiliated. The original membership of the Approved Society was 89,682, composed of 24,366 men and 65,316 women, of whom 40 per cent were married women.

This department of the Weavers' Amalgamation continued to function until all the Approved Societies were merged into the State scheme under the 1948 National Insurance Act.

Trade Union Act, 1913

In 1913 a very important piece of legislation was passed—the Trade Union Act, 1913—which cleared up the very unsatisfactory position in which unions had been placed by the Osborne Judgment of 1909—The new Act provided that a Trade Union, wishing to collect contributions for political purposes, could take a ballot of members in order to ascertain their opinions. The Amalgamation took a ballot of its members in November, 1913, which resulted in a substantial majority of the members declaring in favour of paying contributions to a Parliamentary Fund. Previous to the ballot being taken, and during its progress, the opponents of working-class representation in Parliament worked hard and unceasingly to influence members to make the ballot abortive. Separate Political Rules were formulated and received the sanction of the Registrar of Friendly Societies. In writing about the new Act in his Annual Report at the time the Secretary, Mr. Joseph Cross, said:—

> "In these days it is absolutely necessary for the workman to take a direct hand in politics and make sure that his wants and needs shall receive full attention and satisfaction at the hands of the legislators, and the best means to attain his ends are by and through a Labour Party in the House of Commons. It is a cause for congratulation that the members of the Amalgamation gave such a solid proof, by the ballot, of their intention to take an interest in the future legislation of the country by providing the means to support a Parliamentary Labour Party."

By the decision of the Annual Conference of the United Textile Factory Workers' Association an annual levy of 6d. per member was decided upon, and six parliamentary candidates were decided upon, the first list of six candidates being: Messrs. A. H. Gill, A. Smith, J. W. Ogden, T. Shaw, J. Bell, and W. C. Robinson.

Weavers' Cough

During 1913 many complaints were made to the Amalgamation from weavers employed in mills in the Colne and Burnley districts, concerning very violent forms of cough, accompanied by great pain in the chest. The illness caused many of the weavers to give up work. There was danger, according to medical opinion, of persons being left in the first stages of consumption. The epidemic spread to such alarming proportions that it was found necessary to close a number of mills for purposes of investigation. An inquiry found that the air was full of mildew spores. On the advice of a Home Office specialist a disinfectant was used, and eventually the mildew was cleared. The Home Office sent down to Lancashire Drs. Collis and Bridge, and joint conferences were held in Blackburn during March 1913, when agreement was reached that research work should be undertaken by a Government investigator, who would work at the Government's expense, in order to ascertain the true cause of the trouble and prevent a recurrence.

CHAPTER XII

First World War, 1914-18

IN THE early days of August, 1914 half of the world was thrown into a life and death struggle, which was to last for four long years. At the onset the nation seemed stunned and trade was paralysed; the Liverpool Cotton Exchange closed down, and unemployment amongst the cotton workers soared to enormous proportions. Societies who paid out-of-work benefits were soon placed in serious difficulties, and the textile trade unions quickly got together to press upon the Government of the day to render financial assistance. Interviews took place with the President of the Board of Trade, and subsequent arrangements were made to make Emergency Grants through section 106 of the Unemployment Insurance Act of 1912. The Annual Reports of the Amalgamation and of the United Textile Factory Workers' Association complained bitterly of the tremendous increases in food prices during the early years of the war, and of enormous profits which had been made. In the United Textile Report for 1917 we find a lengthy statement on the Food Question, which concludes:—

> "In the early part of this year it was stated in Parliament that the Exchequer had benefited to the extent of £140,000,000 by the Excess Profits Tax. That statement meant roughly that certain people during this war had made £300,000,000 from the opportunity given them to increase prices against their countrymen. Is there any cause for surprise or wonder that the workers of the country are now calling for the Conscription of Wealth? The whole game of profiteering has been merciless and selfish, and the working classes are determined not to submit any longer to the exploitation of their food, to make a few men richer."

Cotton Control Board

As the war progressed it became very evident that other difficulties confronted the cotton trade. Owing to demands made upon shipping the amount of cotton shipped to the country was not sufficient to meet the requirements of the trade. The Board of Trade took the matter up and appointed a Board known as the Cotton Control Board, to deal with questions of supply, distribution, and restriction of machinery in use. The stoppage of machinery caused a large number of workpeople to be idle, and the Board then had to face the problem of unemployment. The workpeople were forced to be idle through no fault of their own, or of their employers. The trade was consulted and a scheme of levying spindles and looms was agreed upon for the purpose of creating a fund to provide a weekly payment to operatives dispossessed of their employment. The Cotton Control Board (of which the Amalgamation Secretary, Mr. Joseph Cross, was a member) decided to pay varying weekly allowances, adult male workers receiving £1 5s. per week, adult female workers, 15s. per week, and youths of both sexes lesser amounts according to grade of employment. A Rota System of working was also instituted, so as to give all operatives a chance to earn some wages in turn, but after some experience of this system some employers expressed dissatisfaction, and the system was ultimately discontinued, much to the disgust of the operatives as a body.

Out-of-Work Payments

The out-of-work payments to operatives by the Cotton Control Board commenced on 15th September, 1917, and the practice was for the District Association to make the payment, which was repaid by the Amalgamation, and the Amalgamation was reimbursed by the Control Board. It is interesting to note that up to June, 1919 (that is, in less than two years' time) a total of £1,174,659 5s. 9d. was paid through the Amalgamation in these benefits.

After the conclusion of the War in November, 1918, employment in the cotton industry remained fairly good until towards the end of 1920, when trade conditions grew steadily worse. The General Council of the Amalgamation decided to apply for permission to administer section 106 of the amended Unemployment Insurance Act, which meant that a society could pay the State Unemployment benefit direct to the member provided the society paid an additional amount of unemployment benefit. In November, 1920 the Districts commenced to pay levies into an Amalgamation Unemployment Fund Account, and these levies continued to be paid until February, 1921. In order to gain experience it had been decided to make payments of the Amalgamation's unemployment benefit for a short period before applying the State benefit; but the experience was so painful that the scheme for the administration of the State's Unemployment Act was never adopted by the Amalgamation. In the period November, 1920 to February, 1921, £16,396 19s. 8d. had been paid in levies, but the Amalgamation unemployment benefits had amounted, in six weeks up to 9th February, 1921, to £69,498 1s. 10d., which caused a deficit of £53,101 2s. 2d. This deficit was later apportioned amongst the Districts affected, and was gradually repaid by them to the Amalgamation.

In the meantime, the newly constructed Cotton Trade War Memorial Fund trustees made payments of out-of-work benefits to textile trade unions, and the Amalgamation disbursed in 17 weeks ending 7th May, 1921, a total sum of £587,462 11s. 7d.

Textile Workers' Ambulances

During the early years of the War the Amalgamation assisted in the efforts of the United Textile Factory Workers' Association to organise assistance to the British Red Cross and the St. John's Ambulance Society, and an appeal was issued to textile workers, which was responded to very generously. The number of single contributions exceeded 10,000, and by 10th July, 1915 the total amount subscribed was over £24,000. Ambulance cars and a movable Field Hospital were provided, bearing an inscription that they had been presented by the United Textile Factory Workers' Association. The Field Hospital consisted of ten tents fully equipped, and some of the best French surgeons were placed at the disposal of the Hospital.

Uniform Contributions and Benefits

During 1919 serious efforts were made in the General Council to secure a system of uniform contributions and benefits throughout the affiliated Districts, and the Central Committee placed a series of proposals before the District Committees, which were discussed by the General Council in November, 1919, along with amendments submitted by a number of Districts.

The outcome of the meeting was such that little actual progress was made, the Council accepting an amendment by Oldham District that "an effort should be made in every district to secure a minimum contribution of 1s. per week." This left the matter in the hands of Districts, and thus uniformity was not secured.

Post-War Depression

Whilst it was felt that trade was good in the early months of 1920, when an advance of 70 per cent on list prices had been secured (bringing the list percentage additions to the highest point ever reached—215 per cent on list), it was not long after that wage settlement that it became evident all was not well with the industry and that the trade had reached its zenith of prosperity and was on the downgrade. Towards the end of 1920 mills closed down in large numbers and unemployment figures reached the highest point known for years. In February, 1921 an interview was held with the Minister of Labour, with a request that further provision should be made for those workers who had reached the limit of their benefits under the Unemployment Insurance Act. The Act was amended and additional benefits were paid to the unemployed workpeople.

The year 1921 proved to be a disastrous one so far as the welfare of the operatives was concerned. The employers pressed for a 95 per cent reduction in list prices, and joint conferences were held in the Manchester Town Hall, when the employers spoke of their enormous losses. Offers and counter-offers were made, but no settlement was reached; notices were tendered by the operatives, and the mills closed down on June 3rd, 1921. The Minister of Labour met representatives of both sides in London, and on 17th June, 1921 a settlement was tentatively agreed, for a reduction of 70 per cent in list prices, to take effect in two stages (60 per cent at once and 10 per cent in the following December). The workpeople were balloted, with the result that there was a majority of over 27,000 in favour of the proposals. There was great reluctance on the part of some of the Amalgamations to accept the terms, and it was not until June 25th that the settlement was signed.

It was not many months before the employers again made a request for a 75 per cent. reduction in list prices, and this request led to lengthy and almost daily joint meetings in the Victoria Hotel, Manchester, but negotiations broke down in April, 1922, and notices were served for a stoppage of work. Negotiations were, however, resumed between the employers and the Cardroom Workers' Amalgamation, and a tentative sectional agreement had been reached, for a 50 per cent reduction in list prices (to take effect in two stages). The remaining Amalgamations consulted their constituent councils and endeavoured to secure less harsh terms from the employers, but without avail, and the whole of the trade had to agree to a 50 per cent reduction in list prices. This meant that from April, 1921 to October, 1922, there had been total reductions in list percentages of 120 per cent.

This left the Uniform List of Weaving prices payable plus 95 per cent, a figure which remained for a long number of years, and once more brought the actual cash wage level to a figure below the published Cost of Living figures.

Under-Employment

During this period the members of the Amalgamation were seriously affected by another problem, that of Under-employment, caused by looms being stopped waiting for weft, or warps, or other causes over which the weaver had no control. Wages fell by 25 to 50 per cent and more through this cause alone, whilst the weaver was compelled to remain in the mill the whole time. The Northern Counties Textile Trades Federation negotiated with the Employers' Association, with the object of bringing about some joint agreement whereby a fund could be created to compensate the weavers for this under-employment. In April, 1923, the subject was discussed in joint meeting, and the operatives' representatives offered to agree to a scheme which would mean a payment of 2d. per loom per week, 1½d. to be paid by the employer and ½d. by the weaver and benefits to be 6s. 3d. per loom per week. The employers made a counter-proposal for 4d. per loom per week, 3d. of which to be paid by the employer and 1d. by the weaver. No progress was made and it was some years before the establishment of a Minimum Wage was an accomplished fact.

Unemployment Insurance by Industry

On a number of occasions the United Textile Factory Workers had discussed the desirability of Unemployment Insurance being undertaken by the industry, instead of by the State, and a number of the textile unions were very keenly in favour of this. The subject was discussed in some detail at the Annual Conference in 1921, and again in 1922. The Minister of Labour and the Trades Union Congress were also very interested in this matter, and canvassed the opinions of leading trade unions in the country. The Textile Unions replied to questionnaires from the Ministry and the T.U.C., in several general terms: (a) that a Fund should be created to meet unemployment, by joint contributions of employers and employed in the industry; (b) contributions to have a legal status; (c) the Board of Administrators to have power to amend or vary the contributions or benefits;

(d) the Fund to be administered under a joint authority of employers and operatives; (e) a certain sum of money should be provided by Parliament each year towards the cost of benefits and administration; the General Federation of Trade Unions had also been considering this question, and had promoted a Bill in Parliament on similar lines. The Bill did not get any further than the first reading. It was felt by the textile workers' representatives that the principle of Insurance by Industry was a good one, as it would tend to force employers to take some collective responsibility for unemployment, and would encourage them to take steps to obviate it. Much discussion took place on the proposition, but the scheme eventually fell through.

CHAPTER XIII

Post-War Problems: 1918 Onwards

The 48-Hour Working Week.

IN 1919 FURTHER efforts were made to secure a reduction in working hours, when a request was made in February 1919 for a reduction from 55½-hours to 44-hours per week. The employers offered 49½ hours per week, without any compensatory increase in wage rates, but this offer was rejected. General Council Meetings were held and a ballot of members was taken; further joint negotiations were held, without a settlement being reached. The matter was ultimately taken to the Minister of Labour, Sir Robert Horne, who made strong efforts to facilitate a settlement, but without avail. His suggestion for further conferences in Manchester Town Hall was adopted, but these conferences failed to secure a settlement. On 21st June, 1919 the mills closed down, and two days later another joint conference was held, under the chairmanship of Sir Herbert Dixon (chairman of the Cotton Reconstruction Board), when a settlement was reached, fixed the working hours at 48-hours per week, with a 30 per cent advance on list prices to compensate. The recommended settlement was placed before the General Councils of the various textile unions, and met with opposition in several instances. It was not until 9th July, 1919 that it was found possible to reach a final agreement, on the terms stated, to operate from the re-opening of the mills on 14th July, 1919, the strike having lasted three weeks. A second joint agreement made in the same month, fixed the working-hours per day at 8¾-hours for five days and 4¼-hours on Saturdays.

1919 was therefore a milestone in the history of the textile unions, and the benefits of the shorter working day were much appreciated. The 48-hour week remained in operation until 1946, when, as will be related later, the hours were reduced to 45 per week, and later to 42½ hours (and in 1968 to 40 hours for single shift working.)

"Local Disadvantages"

Much dissatisfaction had existed for years against the action of employers in a number of outlying districts making deductions from weavers' wages for what was known as "Local Disadvantages." The Amalgamation finally decided to take the matter before the Industrial Court, which held an Inquiry in the Manchester Town Hall in March and April 1920. The claim affected about 75,000 looms and was very keenly contested by the employers, who had quite an array of legal and financial representatives present, who produced all kinds and forms of evidence to endeavour to prove that by paying full list prices the firms concerned would be ruined. After reviewing all the evidence the Court, with Sir William Mackenzie as chairman, decided that the weavers had not established a case for abolition of all deductions in all the districts. The Court held the view that a number of deductions in certain districts were unwarranted and in other districts were excessive. The award of the Court fixed deductions for certain mills on a definite basis, the deduction being taken from the list percentages.

The Award of the Industrial Court made in 1920 pleased nobody, excepting those Districts where the deductions for local disadvantages had been abolished, and at various times the question had been discussed by the General Council of the Amalgamation. In February 1933 the General Council decided to take steps to collect information from districts affected by the 1920 Award, preparatory to a further onslaught on the remaining deductions. It was found that there were 93 firms which were making deductions, in 14 districts, and every firm was written to, as well as the Cotton Spinners & Manufacturers' Association, requesting their approval of the whole question being placed again before the Industrial Court. Almost without exception the replies were in the negative. The Minister of Labour could not, under the terms of the Industrial Courts Act 1919, proceed to set up a Court unless both parties consented, or the joint rules had been exhausted. This meant that the Amalgamation was faced with the prospect of serving notices at each firm affected, and this procedure was difficult because of the prevailing conditions, due to breaches of agreement, the operation of More Looms systems, and the reluctance of the operatives themselves.

Further developments took place, however, and the Minister of Labour agreed to set up an Industrial Court, which commenced its hearing on 9th March, 1936, in the Manchester Town Hall, under the chairmanship of Sir Harold Morris, K.C., with two independent assessors. Sir John Taylor, (Solicitor) acted for the employers, and the late Mr. Alfred Riley (Solicitor) acted for the Amalgamation, assisted by a sub-committee led by the then General Secretary, Mr. Andrew Naesmith. A tremendous amount of work was put into the preparation of our case, as enormous detail was involved in these inquiries. Our case rested mainly upon the contention that since the hearing in 1920 great developments had taken place in mechanical transport, improved roads, and the fact that the contraction of the industry had given employers generally a selection of operatives which they never had before. Even on the railway there had been great improvements and amalgamations, although the greatest advance had been made in road transport. Large numbers of the firms owned their own motor vehicles, so that they had efficient, immediate, and economical service. Bus-services had improved beyond all recognition, and labour was much more mobile. Furthermore, Manchester was not now the sole market for handling all cloth produced, as the Bradford and London markets had developed, and this assisted such areas as Cowling, Silsden, and Skipton.

After a lengthy hearing the Court ultimately made its Award, No. 1649, dated 7th May, 1936, which perpetuated the deductions for Local Disadvantages in a number of cases, reduced the deduction in others, and abolished the deductions altogether in a number of cases. In consequence of this Award the clause in the legalised List dealing with Local Disadvantages had to be revised and the Minister's approval secured. At a later date these deductions were abolished completely.

The "Half Time" System

The sytem of employing children half-time in mills had been a source of worry to many of our delegates to the General Council for many years, and the subject was discussed at many United Textile Workers' Conferences, and at International Textile Workers' Congresses. At the International Textile Congress held in Blackpool in June 1914 the continental delegates pressed for the abolition of half-time working, and this caused the English textile unions to give further thought to the question.

At the International Congress the Yorkshire Woollen workers had voted in favour of the abolition, whilst the Lancashire textile unions had voted against raising the school-leaving age to 14 years. In the Annual Report of the United Textile Workers for 1914, attention was drawn to the strange attitude of the Lancashire textile workers, and the Secretary asked "Will the position we have taken up on the question bear examination? We are calling for shorter working hours—because we consider the work in a cotton mill to be exhausting and exacting . . . When adult labour cries out against the present hours of work because they are exhausted and depressed after the daily grind amongst high-speed machinery and the uncomfortable heat of the workroom of a cotton mill, the effect on children must be much more disastrous and evil in its consequences."

No further progress was made in this matter until towards the end of 1917, when the Legislative Council of the United Textile Workers' met the Minister of Education, at his request, to hear his explanation of a new Education Bill which he proposed to introduce into the House, which had for one of its objects the abolition of the half-time system, and which also proposed to raise the school-leaving age. Whilst the Bill was being discussed in Parliament early in 1918 the textile unions took a ballot of the membership on the proposal to abolish half-time working. From many points of view the result was disappointing, as only 147,957 members voted out of a total membership of all the unions of 211,680. Amongst the Weavers' Amalgamation there were 38,684 for abolition of the half-time system and 88,596 votes against its abolition, out of an approximate membership of 174,000

In the Amalgamation Annual Report of 1918 there is a reprint of an article published in the *Manchester Guardian* on 20th March, 1918, of which the following is an extract:—

> "The Minister of Education, when he reminded the House of Commons the other day that the cotton industry was erected to a very large extent on workhouse child labour, recalled a practice that once prevailed in Lancashire and must seem almost incredible to the people of the present day. In the early days of the industry the sense of parental authority and the love of the parents for their children proved an effective restraint on the employer's wish for cheap labour. Parents would not permit their children to work in the factories. The very names of "factory boy" and "factory girl" were regarded as terms of opprobrium and disgrace. But circumstances were stronger than parental love.

Rev. Edmund Cartwright
Inventor of the Power Loom

Spinning Room 1860's

Spinning Room 1960's

Drawing-in 1860's

Drawing-in 1960's

Weaving Shed 1860's

Weaving Shed 1960's

Sir Richard Arkwright

Inventor of early carding and spinning machinery

The wages of the parents, owing to the employment of children from outside, were reduced to starvation-point, and so they were slowly and reluctantly compelled to send their children into the factories, that on the combined earnings of all the family might live.

"In the period during which the parents refused to allow their children to enter the factory door the 'Guardians of the Poor' were not troubled by similar scruples. They actually sold children from five years old and upwards to the manufacturers. These children were taken from the workhouses to the manufacturing districts on canal boats in a manner that recalls the horrors of the slave trade. They were kept at work for sixteen hours at a stretch. They were whipped when they either could not or would not work. They fed with the pigs, and they died like flies. The horrors which free trade in the lives and limbs of children brought about in mines and factories were exposed more than a century ago. To those who demanded protection by legislation the answer was given that the responsibility of the parent was the proper and sufficient protection of the child. It was only gradually that the conscience of the nation was aroused, but since the process was begun laws and amending laws relating to the employment of children and young persons in factories, mines, and workshops have been continuously placed upon the statute book."

The Education Act of 1918 was ultimately passed by Parliament, and it provided for the abolition of Half-Time Working of children under 14 years of age, as from January 1921.

Proposed Federation of Textile Workers' Unions.

For many years the Amalgamation, as well as other textile trade unions, had considered the possibility of securing the formation of One Textile Union. The matter was discussed at the Annual Conferences of the United Textile Workers on a number of occasions, and the Legislative Council was asked in 1920 to prepare a scheme for such a Federation. A special meeting of the Textile Factory Workers was held in Bury on November 13th, 1920, when the various schemes which had been suggested in the past were reviewed by the chairman, and a very lengthy discussion ensued. Five societies (including the Amalgamated Weavers' Association) were favourable to the idea, and four were against. It was finally decided that the matter should be referred back to the Annual Meeting of the Textile Factory Workers. The Legislative Council again considered the subject and a sub-committee formulated a draft scheme for a "Cotton Workers' Federation" in 1922, in which it was proposed that the activities of the proposed Federation should include industrial and political questions. The scheme was circulated to the affiliated Amalgamations, and six approved of the recommendations but three Amalgamations were against them.

The Legislative Council again considered the whole position and the 1923 Annual Report of the United Textile Factory Workers contains a very full account of the draft Constitution and Rules which were finally considered. However, there was keen opposition to the proposal, due to the fear of certain Amalgamations that they would have to surrender their rights to take any measures for the advancement of its members. Finally, the Legislative Council had to record its failure to reach an agreement on the question of Federation and the whole matter was referred back to the Annual Meeting.

When the question was ultimately discussed at the Annual Meeting in 1923 a vote was taken resulting in 58 delegates voting in favour of the acceptance of the proposed Federation scheme, whilst 43 delegates voted against it, but there were 85 delegates who abstained from voting, so that the whole position was left in an unsatisfactory state.

The passing of Joseph Cross

On 11th January, 1925 the Amalgamation suffered a grievous loss through the death of its Secretary, Mr. Joseph Cross, J.P. He had been appointed in March 1906 and commenced his official duties on 7th April of that year, so that he had served the Amalgamation for a period of close upon nineteen years. At the time of his appointment the Amalgamation consisted of some 35 District Associations, with a total membership of 88,000, and he had lived to see its zenith in 1921 when the membership reached over 224,000. Since that time conditions of trade had reduced the membership, until at his death the membership was 163,000. It was part of his life trying to secure for the cotton workers improvements in their conditions and wage rates, and many of the improvements he had desired were effected during his term of office. There was no prouder man then he when he attached his signature to the 48-hour working agreement in 1919, and he tried hard to bring about a Cotton Workers' Federation. He had been a hard-working Secretary of the United Textile Factory Workers' Association for a longer period than he had been the Secretary of the Amalgamation, and his influence and contacts in the larger sphere had been of considerable value to the Weavers' Amalgamation. He was succeeded by Mr. John C. Parker, J.P., of Clayton-le-Moors, on 7th March, 1925, Mr. Parker having been Assistant Secretary, and Mr. (later Sir) Andrew Naesmith succeeded Mr. Parker as Assistant Secretary.

J. C. Parker

Mr. J. C. Parker's term of office, however, did not last much more than two years, as he passed away on 5th November, 1927, after a long and honourable career in the trade union movement.

The Weavers' Charter, 1925

Much concern was still being expressed by the Central Committee and the General Council about the wage and conditions of employment of our members. There was a general desire for the institution of a minimum wage, for the abolition of sweeping and cleaning as a duty to be performed by the weaver, and a standard minimum wage for winders, warpers and reelers. There were many complaints of inferior material, inefficient and semi-obsolete machinery, out-of-date weaving sheds, and a variety of causes which handicapped our members from earning satisfactory wages.

Finally, what became known as the "Weavers' Charter" was formulated, and submitted to the two Employers' Associations at a joint meeting held on 24th April, 1925, in the following terms:—

1. An application for the payment of a basis wage of 10s. per loom as a standard for cloth woven in looms up to and including 45 inches, when such cloths are not entitled to any additions above the standard, this basis to increase for other cloths in proportion to the percentage allowed by the various lists.

2. An application for a payment for under-employment at the rate of 2d. per hour for each loom for all stoppages extending over two hours.

3. That weavers should be relieved of all sweeping, cleaning, oiling, cut carrying, &c.

4. An application for the payment to winders and reelers of 5d. per hour, and to beamers 5½d. per hour on each machine plus 95 per cent.

Shortly after the Joint Meeting, the President of the Amalgamation, Mr. J. W. Ogden, J.P., published a lengthy article on the Weavers' Charter in the *Cotton Factory Times*, and when the employers sent a written reply on 2nd May, 1925, rejecting all the items in the Charter, Mr. Ogden published a further article in the *Cotton Factory Times* examining the employers' reply in his usual trenchant style. The Central Committee gave consideration to the unhelpful attitude of the employers and sent a reply on 21st May, 1925, setting out further arguments in favour of the Charter. No progress was made, and later in the year the Amalgamation decided to press the claim before the Minister of Labour, through the medium of an Inquiry under Part 2 of the Industrial Courts Act, 1919. The Minister got in touch with the employers' associations, but they refused to agree to the matter being submitted to arbitration, as they thought the application was unreasonable and impracticable.

Further joint meetings were held, but the employers maintained their attitude of complete rejection of all the propositions, and no progress was made.

General Strike, 1926

A very desperate industrial struggle had been developing in the Mining Industry during 1925 and early 1926, which culminated in the miners being locked-out on 30th April, 1926. There was a tremendous amount of sympathy with the miners throughout the trade union movement, and the General Council of the Trades Union Congress used every means in its power with the Prime Minister to reach a formula which would cope with the situation. The Government did not act in a helpful manner, and the T.U.C. General Council called a General Strike in May. In addition to the miners already locked out there were 1,580,000 workers involved. In circumstances which brought confusion in the ranks of trade unions the General Strike collapsed after eight days, and the miners continued their own bitter struggle for a further six months. The consequences of this General Strike cost the Amalgamation almost £24,000 in grants to Districts; in addition to a grant of £20,000 to the T.U.C. and Miners' Federation funds, as well as a separate grant of £5,000 to the Miners' Federation of Great Britain, and £5,000 to the Lancashire and Cheshire Miners' Federation. In addition, £30,000 was loaned to the Yorkshire Mine-workers' Association, which was repaid the following year.

Trade Disputes and Trade Unions Act, 1927

Although the General Strike had been an industrial weapon used for industrial purposes the Government of the day took advantage of the situation by introducing a new Bill to alter the whole position of trade unions politically. The textile workers became very disturbed in consequence of the new Bill, which sought to restrict strike action, make picketing illegal, and alter the method of collecting funds for the Political Fund. Conferences were held, and the Amalgamation issued a series of handbills which were distributed by the thousand, exposing the retrograde intentions of the Bill. The Bill became law, and the new Act, which exempted all trade unionists from payment of the political levy unless they contracted in, continued to operate until it was repealed in 1946.

Fencing of Machinery, and Prevention of Accidents

Joint Conferences were held between the employers' representatives, the Northern Counties Textile Trades Federation, and the Factory Inspectorate, during November, 1912, with the object of formulating some kind of code or regulations which would improve the fencing of machinery and prevent accidents. This joint committee reached an important agreement on 18th December, 1912, which laid down definite provisions covering the general question of Fencing and Spacing of Machinery, including winding and warping frames, as well as tape-sizing machines. Shuttle guards had to be provided on all looms, and other danger points on a loom were dealt with specifically. Cleaning of looms by women or young persons was not to take place whilst it was in motion. Provision was also made regarding the Lifting of Heavy Weights, and for the Lighting of dark passages and stairways.

This Fencing Agreement was constantly under review during ensuing years, and further tri-partite conferences were held in 1926, 1927, and 1928, as a result of which an amended agreement was reached, which extended the original agreement, with improvements and additions. Provisions were also made for First-Aid facilities in mills.

The 1928 Agreement also provided for the appointment of a Joint Standing Committee, composed of representatives of the two Employers' Associations, the Northern Counties Textile Trades Federation, and the Factory Department, to meet every six months, under the chairmanship of the Superintending Inspector of Factories, to consider the operation of the agreement and any necessary amendments. This Committee has met regularly, and has performed fine service in the direction of prevention of accidents and formulation of methods to safeguard our members.

As will be indicated later, important amendments have been made to the agreement, and the scope of the Joint Standing Committee has been widened as a result of experience gained.

The Rigby-Swift Award

Although the industry had agreed in 1919 upon the adoption of a 48-hour working week, the Amalgamation and other textile unions had to exercise constant vigilance to prevent attempts to violate the agreement. Individual firms had to be tackled on several occasions, and in many cases they pleaded that the breach of agreement was only for a temporary period, to complete an order. In many of the Annual Reports published round about 1925 to 1928 we find repeated references to the subject, and emphasis is laid upon the need for maintenance of the hard-won achievement of a shorter working-week.

The organised employers took another line of attack in 1928, when the two central associations issued "State of Trade Reports," which ultimately came before joint meetings which lasted from 17th January to 5th March, 1928. The employers proposed that working hours should be increased by 4½ per week, (from 48 to 52½ hours) and that there should be a reduction of 25 per cent from list prices. The seriousness of the attack was realised by all, and the executives of the cotton trade unions got together in a spirit of determination and opposition. The operatives' representatives demanded that the two references in the State of Trade Reports should be deleted and that the Government should be asked to set up a Statutory Committee, to hold a public inquiry into all the facts which went to make up the cost of production and to ascertain the reasons for the then existing difficulties in the cotton trade. Joint conference followed joint conference, and dozens of Notes passed from one side to the other, but no definite conclusions were reached, and for the time being the employers' efforts failed.

In the meantime the trade was becoming more and more depressed, and the figures of total and partial unemployment were rising until they reached 14 per cent in September, 1928. Attempts were being made to run overtime at individual mills, whilst other firms were instituting two-shift systems, against the policy of the textile unions. The Annual Report for 1929 states "The continued unemployment of our members in certain districts does, however, make it difficult to exercise that discipline which is essential to ensure the success of our policy. On all occasions our District Committees must refuse to countenance any attempt by any firm to institute either a longer working week or the two-shift system."

During 1929 the organised employers made another attempt to secure a reduction in wages and an extension of the working week, and joint meetings were held during July and August, which culminated in the famous "Rigby-Swift Award." The employers had made a request for a reduction of 25 per cent, but this was refused and notices were served in July 1929. The Ministry of Labour stepped in and a series of joint conferences began, at the Victoria Hotel, Manchester. Sir Horace Wilson was brought down from London, to meet selected representatives of the textile amalgamations, hectic conferences ensued, and many notes passed between the two sides. As the proceedings developed serious differences also crept in between the two sections of operatives' representatives—the spinning section and the manufacturing section, and the manufacturing section met the employers separately, without reaching any settlement. Thus, on 27th July, 1929, there commenced a stoppage of work which lasted for three weeks. Work was resumed on 19th August at the old wage rates pending arbitration proceedings which had been agreed upon, following an employers' deputation sent to meet the Prime Minister in Scotland.

The arbitration proceedings began on 21st August, 1929 in the Manchester Town Hall, with Mr. Justice Rigby-Swift as Chairman, assisted by two assessors each from either side. After a two days' hearing the Board gave its award, which was that there should be a reduction in list rates of 12½ per cent, (bringing the 95 per cent on list down to 82½ per cent) which was equivalent to a reduction of 6.41 per cent from current wages, the reduction to take effect from 7th September, 1929.

This decision of the Arbitration Court caused great resentment amongst our members, and resolutions of protest came in from District Associations. General Council discussions ensued, several meetings being held during August and September, during which it was proposed by one District that the Amalgamation should withdraw from the Northern Counties Textile Trades Federation as well as the United Textile Factory Workers' Association. Another District moved that an immediate application should be made for a 25 per cent increase in list rates, and after two meetings of the General Council this was accepted.

On 12th November, 1929, therefore, a joint meeting was held with the two employers' Associations, when an application was made for an increase of 25 per cent in list rates, and a fall-back wage of 7s. 6d. for stopped looms. The employers gave a negative reply to our requests, and after further meetings of the General Council it was decided to take a ballot of the members, which was taken during the closing days of the year. The ballot vote resulted in 94,142 votes in favour of ceasing work, and 43,531 against. This result was reported to a subsequent General Council Meeting, and in view of all the circumstances, (there were nearly 9,000 blank and spoiled papers, and 20,000 papers had not been returned) it was decided not to proceed with the matter.

Thus ended this unhappy episode in the history of the Amalgamation, which had cost over £178,146 in dispute benefits.

CHAPTER XIV

The "More Looms" System

Burnley Eight-Loom Experiment

IN DECEMBER 1928 representatives of the Burnley Employers' Association approached the Committee of the Burnley Weavers' Association and drew their attention to the severe depression in the industry. Mills were stopping and looms going out of commission in increasing numbers, new methods in production would have to be tried to arrest the decline and place the products of the Burnley mills on the markets of the world at competitive prices. The co-operation of the Burnley Weavers' Committee was sought in an effort to reduce the costs of production, and the employers made certain proposals. On ascertaining the nature of the proposals the Burnley Committee felt they could not be limited in their effects to that district, as they were bound to react on the county. The assistance of the Amalgamation was sought, and the Amalgamation thus became involved in what proved to be a thorny problem.

Ten firms commenced to run 4 per cent of their total looms with eight slowed-down looms to a weaver, on a wage of 50s. per week for 48 hours. Auxiliary labour was provided for oiling, sweeping, cleaning, cut carrying, etc., the weaver devoting the whole time to the immediate process of cloth production. The looms had to be slowed down to a certain percentage, experience determining the figure at each mill. No arrangements were entered into regarding mechanical attachments. At the end of three months further discussions would take place on the data obtained with the object of formulating a piece price list. The experiment began in May 1929, but at the end of three months neither side was ready to discuss piece price lists, because of the work involved in the wages dispute and other questions that were arising at that time. Immediately the Rigby-Swift Award was announced, the firms working the experiment under the temporary agreement applied the reduction to those weavers running the eight slowed-down looms, which made the wage 46s. 10d. Joint meetings were then held to discuss the arbitrary action of the employers, and, in these discussions, efforts were made to formulate a piece price list. Serious differences manifested themselves, in regard to the wages that should be paid, the employers offering a piece price list that would give a wage of 50s. for eight looms running 185 picks per minute, on 85 per cent efficiency. Their suggestion was for a basic price of 16.7 pence per 100,000. Our own proposal was to add such a percentage to the Uniform List as would provide a wage of from 55s. to 56s. for the eight looms on typical standard Burnley cloths, with a fall-back wage of from 52s. to 53s. per week. Large cops and shuttles were to be used. The employers turned our proposals down. The Central Committee became apprehensive of the employers' obvious intention of substituting the Uniform List by some other method of ascertaining wages, and they were also concerned about the problem that would be created by the displacement of labour.

The whole matter was reported to the General Council in March 1930, when a resolution was passed expressing the conviction that the eight-loom system would not bring about the object which the employers had in mind. It was decided that the Central Committee should not enter into any joint agreement, and that District Associations should be requested to oppose the introduction of the new system. The Burnley Employers, with the approval of their central organisation, refused to terminate the experiment, and after fruitless joint meetings and requests by the employers for the Amalgamation to collaborate in the formulation of a new price list to cover an extension of the system the employers themselves appointed a sub-committee to go into the whole matter. The results of their labours were communicated to us on 31st October, 1930, along with their application for the system to operate in all districts wherever an individual employer considered it necessary.

The Amalgamation was seriously perturbed about the new system, which would mean reductions in existing piece price rates on plain grey cloths of 10 per cent on the 6-looms system; 32 per cent on the 8-looms system, and 43 per cent on the 10-looms system. On more intricate cloths the reductions would vary from 50 per cent to 80 per cent. It was true that the individual weaver's wage would be increased, but the aggregate wage bill of the mill would be considerably reduced. The Amalgamation saw many dangers in the new system, and the immediate effect would have been to reduce the numbers of employees engaged in weaving by anything up to 40 per cent. Many aspects of the problem were considered by the Amalgamation, and a series of leaflets were issued to members, emphasising the dangers of the new system. The General Council decided that the experiments on the new system had to stop, and Burnley District reported to the Special Meeting of the General Council on 21st January, 1931 that 4,000 operatives were affected by the stoppage at the mills in their district. The employers had retaliated, by locking out the whole of the operatives in the Burnley mills. In further support of the Burnley employers the county Employers' Association decided to lock the county out. The Ministry of Labour intervened, but they were not successful in preventing the employers from operating a county lock-out. The Amalgamation decided to take a ballot vote of members, as to whether negotiations should be opened up with the employers, but whilst 44,990 voted in favour of negotiations, 90,770 voted against, and the employers embarked upon their lock-out of the county mills. This lock-out lasted for four weeks. During the fourth week it became evident that there was weakness in the employers' camp, and on 13th February, 1931 the employers' representatives met and decided to terminate the lockout as from the 14th February.

Thus one of the most serious industrial disputes in our history up to that time was temporarily patched up. The Burnley strike had started by involving 3,907 operatives, and the number increased later to 16,433 operatives. By the end of the county lockout there were 113,203 members involved, and the dispute cost the Amalgamation over £187,832 in dispute benefits. At the General Council Meeting held on 7th February, 1931, strong disapproval was expressed, through a recommendation by the Central Committee, of the action of delegates from certain north-east Lancashire Districts in attending as an unofficial delegation to the House of Commons. This action was strongly condemned, particularly in view of the fact that the Central Committee had themselves just returned from an interview with members of the Cabinet. The unofficial delegation had interviewed Members of Parliament and had formulated a Notice for the Order Sheet of the House. That action was condemned as formulating policy, and it was contended that no individuals had the right to do that. A card vote showed that the resolution of disapproval was carried by 116 votes for and 18 votes against.

At the next meeting of the General Council the unofficial delegation were further censured for their action in communicating with District Associations offering to hold meetings to report their unofficial delegation results. The general opinion of the General Council was that there should be an end to that kind of business, and the matter was dropped, upon Next Business being moved.

Meanwhile, on the general question of More Looms System an interesting development had been taking place in the Nelson District. Messrs. James Nelson Ltd., Valley Mills, had approached the Nelson District Committee, the Colne District Committee and the Central Committee, to discuss the formulation of a scheme for the running of more-looms to a weaver. Ultimately an agreement was reached, and was approved by the General Council in July 1931. The full text of the agreement is published in the Amalgamation Annual Report for 1932, and it is interesting because the new system at this firm covered high-grade cloths, such as twills, sateens, gaberdines, poplins, venetians, dobbies and jacquards, as well as different classes of silk and rayon goods. A wage of not less than 58s. per week was offered, irrespective of the number of looms run (up to a maximum of eight) on cotton goods, and 60s. on silk and rayon goods. A bonus system was also instituted additional to the basic rates quoted. The speed of the looms would be determined by experience, and outside investigators would be allowed to investigate the working conditions and make independent reports periodically. Large cops on cottons and rewound weft on rayons and silks were to be provided, and yarns generally would be carefully selected. Ancillary labour would be provided, and there would be no fining for alleged unmerchantable cloth.

Later a bonus system was agreed upon, and it was found that the new system considerably improved the earnings of the weavers. The system was investigated by Shirley Institute staff, and full extracts from their reports are quoted in the 1932 Annual Report.

Following upon the conclusion of the county lockout which arose from the Burnley dispute, the position remained fluid for some time, until the question was opened up again by the Cotton Spinners & Manufacturers' Association on 30th July, 1931 inviting a discussion upon some alternative suggestions. Joint Meetings and sub-committee meetings followed, and counter-proposals were suggested, but no progress was made. In December 1931 the General Council gave the Central Committee authority to make arrangements with individual employers, or with the employers' association, when a More-Looms System was proposed, and where the wages and conditions accompanying such system met with the approval of the Central Committee, subject to the ratification of the General Council. Further joint meetings ensued, but the employers rejected our constant insistence upon the recognition of the principle of payment of a Guaranteed Wage. A joint sub-committee again met in January, 1932, with representatives of the Central Board of the Northern Counties Textile Trades Federation present, when the subject was further explored, and in order to get down to minute details a smaller joint sub-committee was appointed, which commenced its deliberations on 25th January, 1932, and day-to-day sittings continued for about 23 meetings. Our representatives fought strongly for the recognition of a certain target wage, but progress was difficult, especially in view of wages being paid in the Hyde district and also at a certain well-known Burnley firm where the system had been continued in spite of our opposition.

Finally, in March 1932 a Draft Scheme for More-Looms to a Weaver System was formulated, a copy of which was printed in full in the Annual Report for 1932, and which contained many clauses of an entirely new character. The tentative agreement was based on the understanding that the weaving conditions would be such that there would be practically no more work involved in the running of more looms than under the present normal system. The proposed price list was based on the understanding that satisfactory conditions would be provided, so as to enable a weaver of average ability, running six-looms, weaving standard cloth, to earn an average wage of 42s. per week of 48 hours. The draft piece price list contained a large number of clauses, restricting the system to cloths with reeds up to 100, and 80 picks when weaving plain cloths, and not more than 180 ends to the square inch on twills, jeans, sateens and drills. The basic price was 18d. per 100,000 picks. Numerous sub-clauses fixed additions for variations from the standard cloth. A fall-back wage was proposed, for the first time in our history, of two-thirds of the normal average wage of weavers on the system. Ancillary labour was to be provided, and displacement of labour to be carried out by the management in such a way that a minimum of hardship was involved. Loom speeds must be reduced, and a 10 per cent reduction was recommended, with not less than 7½ per cent of normal speed. A number of other details were left over for later discussion, such as Reeds and low picks.

A special meeting of District Committees met on 12th March, 1932 to consider the proposals, and a General Council meeting was held on 19th March, 1932, when a card vote showed that the draft agreement was rejected by 83 votes to 73. Thus the negotiations upon the More-Looms System were ended for the time being without any joint agreement being sanctioned, although the Central Committee still retained authority to consider other terms. The More-Looms System did not become regularised until after the conclusion of the "Midland Agreement" in 1932, which is dealt with in a separate chapter.

John William Ogden

During all this turmoil the Amalgamation suffered a serious loss by the death of the President, Mr. John William Ogden, J.P., on 23rd March, 1930. Whilst on his way to attend a meeting at the Central Office in the previous December he had slipped and broken his leg. Later the leg had to be amputated, and this caused undue strain upon a body and mind already weakened by suffering.

He had been President of the Amalgamation since 20th May, 1911, and for more than 39 years he had been connected with our movement. He was appointed first full-time Secretary of the Heywood, Castleton, Norden and District Weavers' Association away back in 1891, and prior to that he had been an auditor and collector for a number of years. He gave outstanding service to the Amalgamation, with his innate shrewdness and good humour, and the Central Committee decided to perpetuate his memory later by providing each District Office with a framed photograph of the late President.

James Hindle

Mr. James Hindle, J.P., of Burnley, who had been Vice-President, was appointed President in place of Mr. Ogden, in May 1930, and he continued to serve until May 1937, when Mr. James Bell, J.P., was appointed in his place. Mr. Hindle died on 31st July, 1942.

CHAPTER XV

"Joseph Cross" Memorial Convalescent Home

PRIOR TO 1927, the General Council had discussed on many occasions the need for assisting members to recover health and strength after absence from work through illness, by the provision of Convalescent Home facilities. The National Health Insurance Acts, as administered by our own Approved Society, had helped in no small measure in the recuperation of ailing members, but difficulties had been experienced in obtaining satisfactory facilities for our members because of the scarcity of the then existing Convalescent Home accommodation. In fact, it was reported to the General Council that up to the end of June, 1927, the Approved Society had subscribed to 434 convalescent cases (112 men and 322 women), which meant an average of 21 cases per week. It was felt that more effective treatment could be given to that class of member by the establishment of a convalescent home of our own. It was also felt that the scheme would be a most fitting way of perpetuating the memory of the late General Secretary, Joseph Cross, who had rendered valuable service from 1906 to 1925.

At the General Council Meeting held on 19th March, 1927, the following resolution was carried:—

> "That this General Council authorises the Central Committee to negotiate and purchase suitable land and/or premises for the establishment of a Convalescent Home for the use of members of this Amalgamation, and that such a Convalescent Home be named 'The Joseph Cross Memorial Home'."

A sub-committee was appointed to go into details and select a suitable site. Several sites were inspected by the sub-committee and by the Central Committee at Lytham St. Annes, Bispham, Blackpool and Poulton. After consultation with Messrs. Alfred Riley & Co., Solicitors, Blackburn, it was decided by the Central Committee on 19th August, 1927, to purchase the private residence and estate known as "The Woodlands," Breck Road, Poulton-le-Fylde, from Mr. F. Halliwell. The proposal was reported to the General Council on the following day, and the action of the Central Committee was endorsed. This estate comprised almost four acres, and the house contained eight bedrooms, bathrooms, dining-room, breakfast-room, drawing-room, lounge, hall, the necessary kitchens and pantries, and other offices. The purchase price was £5,675.

On 30th August, 1927, the following were appointed as Trustees for the property: J. W. Ogden, Jas. Hindle, J. C. Parker, Jas. Helm, Geo. Whittam. These trustees acted as a convalescent home sub-committee and in October the Central Committee appointed Alderman J. B. Thornley, of Darwen, as architect. The architect proceeded to prepare plans for alterations to the existing property and for the erection of new buildings to accommodate about 100 patients.

In January, 1928, the Central Committee considered various alternative plans, and after visiting the site, decided upon final plans which were to be submitted to the Urban District Council. Advertisements were inserted in the newspapers for tenders, and 27 contractors submitted tenders varying in price from £59,988 to £69,000. The contract was ultimately made with Messrs. James Byrom Limited at the price of £61,000. The contract was signed in September, 1928, and excavations and construction work begun. In September, 1929, the Central Committee decided to extend its ownership of land adjacent to the proposed convalescent home, and purchased additional land from the L.M.S. Railway Company for the sum of £850.

In October, 1929, the Central Committee was faced with a serious situation in connection with the Home due to the business failure of the contracting firm of James Byrom & Sons Limited. Meetings were held at the liquidator's office attended by the General Secretary, the Solicitor and Architect. It was finally decided that the constructional work of the Home should be proceeded with by direct contract and labour. Many meetings were held and arrangements made for numerous sub-contracts. Mr. Harry Rigby was appointed Clerk of Works, and by 20th November, 1929, the original contract with Byrom's terminated, when about £25,000 worth of work had been completed. The amount of work thrown on the Architect and the Amalgamation head office staff in connection with the fresh contracts and direct labour was enormous, but the constructional work proceeded apace, so that the convalescent home could be established with as little delay as possible

In April, 1930, the Central Committee decided to negotiate for the purchase of additional land surrounding the convalescent home and finally purchased for £8,000 the Halliwell Estate comprising 36¼ acres which included Croft House (which Mr. Halliwell rented from us) and Breck Farm. During 1930, constructional work was pushed forward and much thought and time were devoted to the purchase of suitable furniture and fittings. These were made to our special order by the Co-operative Wholesale Society, Manchester, and the total cost was over £7,000.

Consideration was given to staffing arrangements and the appointment of a Superintendent and Matron, and on 1st October, 1930, Mr. and Mrs. J. E. Bury, of London, were appointed. Much care and time were spent in the appointment of domestic staff, and it was reported at the time that over 1,100 applications had been received for the various posts, 200 having been received before newspaper advertisements appeared. Eventually a staff was appointed, and commenced duty in March, 1931. Dr. A. R. Murray was appointed Honorary Medical Officer, a post which he retained for a long number of years.

By the middle of March, 1931, the Home was in a sufficiently completed state to receive patients. Accommodation would be available for 120 patients with accommodation for a staff of 30. The scheme was so visualised that in the event of later building extensions being decided upon, a total accommodation could be made available for 250 patients.

Patients were admitted to the Home for the first time on Monday, 30th March, 1931, when 38 patients were admitted. The official opening ceremony took place on Saturday, 9th May, 1931, by the Rt. Hon. Thomas Shaw, M.P. (Secretary of State for War). Over 450 invitations were issued to district associations, textile amalgamations, outside trade union organisations, employers' organisations and prominent civic and administrative personalities. After the opening ceremony, the guests inspected the home, and later were conveyed by specially-chartered buses to Blackpool, where 440 guests sat down to tea at the invitation of the Amalgamation.

The following is an indication of the costs which had been involved in the establishment of the Convalescent Home:

	£	s.	d.	£	s.	d.
Purchase of Land—						
"Woodlands" (original site)	5,675	0	0			
Halliwell Estate	8,000	0	0			
L.M.S. Railway Land	850	0	0			
				14,525	0	0
Legal Charges				708	0	0
Building Costs—						
James Byrom Ltd.	23,600	0	0			
G. B. Murgatroyd (Liquidator)	1,674	16	11			
Cost of completion after liquidation of of J. Byrom Ltd.	52,336	18	9			
				77,611	15	8
Architect's Charges—						
Building Construction	6,000	0	0			
Land and Furnishings	390	19	2			
				6,390	19	2
				99,235	14	10
Cost of Furnishings, Equipment and Incidentals				7,431	13	8½
Total Costs....				£106,667	8	6½

Almost immediately after the convalescent home had been opened, difficulties began to be experienced in securing grants from the Ministry of Health for approved society patients, and the Central Committee attended interviews with the Ministry which resulted in temporary grants up to certain amounts, on condition that the Amalgamation formulated an alternative scheme by September of that year. The Central Committee had to consider the question of imposing a special levy on the district membership, and on 8th August, 1931, a special levy convalescent home levy was placed upon the district associations at the rate of 1d. per member per month for a period of 3 months. When the Home was opened it had been decided to make a maintenance charge of 30s. per patient per week out of which sum the Amalgamation paid the rail fares. In order to administer the new special levy fund as equitably as possible, it was decided to allocate a proportionate number of bed weeks to each district association, and that a portion of the maintenance charge of 30s. should be made from the levy fund. It was also decided to admit members of other textile unions on payment of the maintenance charge of 35s. per week, the patients paying their own rail fares. In order to assist in keeping up the number of admissions during the winter months, it was decided to reduce the qualification of 28 days' sickness to 14 days. At a later date, the period of the special levy was extended, and in March, 1932, the levy was reduced to ½d. per member per month.

During 1934, strong representations were made to the Income Tax authorities that the finances of the Home should be freed from Income Tax. Mr. Alfred Riley, Solicitor, took the matter in hand, and in August, 1934, success was achieved, the Home, like many other similar institutions, being made exempt from payment of income tax. Up to April, 1937, the patients had been contributing 10s. per week towards the maintenance charge of 30s. per week, the remaining 20s. being borne by the special levy fund, but from that date, the patient's portion was increased to 12s. 6d. per week.

On March 8th, 1938, the Superintendent, Mr. James E. Bury, died after a very brief illness at the early age of 48, and Mrs. Dorcas E. Bury, the Matron, was appointed to carry on the work. In 1938 the Solicitors reported that under a new Act of Parliament, land under the Trust Deed could be held by only four trustees, and it was decided on 20th May, 1938, to appoint the following trustees: Messrs. James Bell, W. J. Tout, Cephas Speak, A. Naesmith, and a Deed of Appointment of the new trustees was signed on 24th June, 1938.

The Convalescent Home special levy was increased from ½d. per member per month to ¾d. per member as from 2nd January, 1939, in view of the increasing costs of administration, and the levy remained at that figure until it was discontinued at 31st December, 1939.

In consequence of the declaration of war on 3rd September, 1939, communications were received through the County Medical Officer of Health, Dr. F. Hall, that our Convalescent Home would be required for purposes arising out of the national emergency, and on 11th September, we were notified that the Ministry of Health was making provision for additional accommodation for infectious disease cases in the Fylde area, and that our convalescent home was suitable for that purpose. Steps were taken to discontinue admission of our patients; all patients were discharged by the 16th September, 1939, and the home was requistioned from 18th September, 1939. The Lancashire County Council administered the Home as an Emergency Hospital, and retained our domestic staff. The Lancashire County Council paid an annual rent of £1,250, out of which sum the Amalgamation paid insurances and rates. Our net income was about £750 per annum. These charges were low as we had no desire to exploit the nation during the period of trial, and we considered it as part of our contribution to the national effort.

After the cessation of hostilities in 1945, the Convalescent Home was derequisitioned on 29th September, 1945, and we took steps to restore it for use again by our members. We were able to do this fairly quickly, and patients were admitted from 1st October, 1945. Renewals and renovations were necessary, staffing arrangements had to be reviewed, and wages had increased considerably during the war period. On the advice of the Central Committee, the General Council decided not to re-impose the special levy, as balances in hand were considered sufficient to carry on until experience had indicated needs. It was therefore decided to utilise the balance of £7,000 before considering the restoration of the levy.

Maintenance costs had of course risen enormously as compared with pre-war years, and when we re-opened the Home in 1945, we made a charge of 35s. per week, the member paying the rail fare. The charge for members of other textile unions was fixed at 42s. per week. During 1946, the Home was redecorated throughout, and the Home was put into as good a condition as it had ever been. The Central Committee had been worried, however, about the numbers of patients being admitted, as these were not anywhere near the full capacity of the Home. Costs were rising, and in order to continue administration without recourse to a special levy, it was decided to transfer £5,626 17s. 6d. from the General Fund to the Convalescent Home Fund. In view of the prospects of the Home being taken over by the trade, it was resolved by the General Council on 19th April, 1947, to empower the Central Committee to transfer from the General Fund such amounts as would adequately finance the Home for the time being. On this account alone, it is interesting to note that from the time the Home was derequisitioned in 1945 until its transfer to the Cotton Industry War Memorial Fund, the total sum of £11,626 17s. 6d. had been transferred from the Amalgamation General Fund to the Convalescent Home Fund to keep it going during that period.

During the time the Home had been administered by the Amalgamation, the following numbers of patients had been admitted to the Convalescent Home:—

Year	Patients
1931–32	1,279
1932–33	1,540
1933–34	1,668
1934–35	1,589
1935–36	1,623
1936–37	1,583
1937–38	1,436
1938–39	1,209
1939	868
	12,795
1945–46	126
1946–47	565
1947–48	790
1948 to 8th May	109
Total patients	14,385

During the whole of the above period, the average duration of residence at the Home was 2½ weeks per patient.

Transfer of the Home to the Trade.

Even so far back as May, 1929, the Trustees of the Cotton Trade War Memorial Fund were considering rendering support to a Convalescent Home for textile workers and had in mind the possibility of assisting the Amalgamated Weavers' Association in their scheme for erecting a Convalescent Home, providing the other textile trade union amalgamations would co-operate and make financial contributions. Contacts were made with other textile amalgamations to enlist their support for a larger scheme, and a meeting of all textile amalgamation executives was held in the Geographical Hall, Manchester, on 21st October, 1929, when our General Secretary made a long statement dealing with the Convalescent Home scheme upon which the Amalgamation had embarked and suggested that consideration should be given to an extension of the scope of the scheme to cover the whole of the trade. Mr. J. Hindle (one of the Cotton Trade Memorial Fund Trustees) spoke of the willingness of the trustees to consider an agreed scheme for the trade as a whole, and he went into details of the possibilities of an extended scheme, mentioning a total figure of £200,000 which might be involved. After a very full discussion, the meeting resolved to accept the report presented on behalf of the Amalgamated Weavers' Association and the Trustees of the Cotton Trade War Memorial Fund and to approve the project of a convalescent home for all textile operatives. Various meetings were held during 1930 and 1931, but no actual progress was made in implementing the larger scheme, and the Amalgamated Weavers' Association went on with its own scheme.

In November, 1933, an agreed scheme was adopted on the following lines: £200,000 to be allocated from the funds of the Cotton Reconstruction Board (the name of the Cotton Trade War Memorial Fund Trustees at that time), to be sub-divided as follows: £70,000 to be paid to the Amalgamated Weavers' Association for the purchase of the Home; £30,000 to be held as a reserve fund for future extensions; and £100,000 to be invested as a maintenance fund. In the meantime, the textile amalgamations had discussed amongst themselves the question of re-imbursing £30,000 to the Amalgamated Weavers' Association, which represented the bulk of the difference between the total cost of establishing the Home (over £106,000), and the £70,000 to be paid by the Cotton Trade War Memorial Fund. Legal difficulties were encountered during 1934 and 1935, and no actual progress was made up to the outbreak of war in 1939.

During the war years, the Trustees of the Cotton Trade War Memorial Fund, along with the Solicitors, Messrs. John Taylor & Co., pressed the larger scheme with the Government Departments, but it was not until 1946 that definite progress was made, when a Bill was finally drafted amending the original Trust Deed of the Cotton Trade War Memorial Fund. This Bill was announced to the public through the Press, and was presented to Parliament on 10th February, 1947. During the following month, the General Secretary, along with the Solicitors and another member of the Board of Trustees attended before a committee of the House of Commons to give oral support and supply information. The Bill passed through the various stages in the House of Commons and went to the House of Lords. On 29th April, 1947, the General Secretary and Solicitors, along with another Trustee, made representations to the House of Lords, when separate clauses of the draft Bill were discussed at length. The Bill was finally passed through both Houses and received Royal assent on 21st May, 1947, and is now known as "Cotton Industry War Memorial Trust Act, 1947." Under that Act, the Board of Trade issued a Licence dated 5th January, 1948, authorising the formation of a non-profit company to run the Poulton Convalescent Home under the name of "The Cotton Industry Convalescent Home."

The new Board of Trustees commenced actual administration of the Home on 8th May, 1948, and the direct reponsibility of the Amalgamated Weavers' Association then ceased. The Home is now under the management of a Council of Management. In addition, there are eight selected members of the Council, two selected by the Federation of Master Cotton Spinners' Associations Ltd., two selected by the Cotton Spinners' and Manufacturers' Association, one each by the Operative Spinners' and the Cardroom Workers' Amalgamation, and two representing the Northern Counties Textile Trades Federation.

The purchase price of £70,000 was paid by the new Trustees to the Amalgamation, and a further sum of £2,323 was paid in adjustment of rates, insurances, and in re-imbursement of cost of stocks of food, coal, coke, etc.

In addition, the Amalgamation received payment of a total of £30,000 apportioned amongst the various Textile Amalgamations (of which sum the Amalgamation itself is responsible for £14,440 to cover our own share of the refund). This total sum of £30,000 approximately covers the difference between the purchase price of £70,000 and the original cost of just over £100,000.

On 9th October, 1948, an interesting ceremony took place at the Home, when the Title Deeds of the Convalescent Home land and property were handed over by the Amalgamation to the new Trustees. About 70 persons were present at the ceremony, representatives of the Amalgamated Weavers' Association; Trustees of the Cotton Industry War Memorial Fund; the two Employers' Associations; and various textile amalgamations. The Mayor of Blackpool and the Chairman of the Poulton Urban Distict Council and their ladies attended to extend a hearty welcome to the guests, and Mr. C. H. W. Taylor (representing Sir John Taylor & Co., Solicitors to the Trustees) was also present. The proceedings were presided over by Mr. C. Hargreaves (President of the Amalgamation at that time).

Thus ended another episode in the history of the Amalgamation. The building and furnishing of the Home placed a heavy responsibility on the Head Office staff at the time, and during the subsequent administration of the Home the secretarial and clerical work had been performed by the General Secretary and his staff from the Head Office, without cost to the Amalgamation. It can be proudly claimed that the Convalescent Home afforded first-class facilities for our members to recuperate from illness and indisposition.

Convalescent Home

The Home continued under the new ownership at Poulton-le-Fylde until 1962 when the whole buildings and land were sold with a view to changing the venue.

In January 1963, the Grand Hotel, Marine Road East, Morecambe, was purchased and opened as the "new" Convalescent Home for the Textile Industry. The change has been looked upon as being an improvement in many respects. All who have visited the Home, either as patients or to look round, speak highly of its facilities and the manner in which it is managed.

The Home is administered by a resident Secretary-Superintendent and a Matron—Mr. and Mrs. T. W. Myers.

CHAPTER XVI

The "Midland" Agreement, 1932

Serious Unemployment

PROBABLY THE most momentous year in the history of the Amalgamation was 1932. All during 1930 and 1931 unemployment and partial unemployment had been steadily rising in our trade. In January, 1930, 20 per cent of the total number of insured workers in the industry were unemployed or temporarily stopped, and by December, 1930, the percentage had risen to 47.4 per cent, the highest figure ever officially recorded in our history. During 1931 the position eased but little and in December, 1931 it was still near the 30 per cent mark.

Breaches of Agreement

1932 therefore started with a considerable volume of unemployment; breaches of joint agreement by employers were taking place all over the county, and in a number of mills operatives were being asked to contribute part of their wages as share capital and loans. In April 1932, the Amalgamation, in common with the other organisations comprising the Northern Counties Textile Trades Federation met the representatives of the two Employers' Associations, when the employers requested that we should agree to a reduction in wages, in view of the prevailing industrial situation. The basis of the employers' case largely rested upon the unfair competition that had arisen on a limited market through the selling of cloth which had been produced by firms operating the More-Looms to a Weaver system. This request was discussed by the Central Board of the Federation, and it was decided by all sections that the Board could not enter into any discussions on wage reductions. This decision at once brought from the employers an intimation that after a certain date all joint agreements would be ended. On 11th June 1932, the period expired, and each individual employer was left in the position of being a law unto himself, making approaches direct to his operatives and entering into arrangements with them for the wage rates and hours that should obtain.

This at once gave rise to a most difficult and unprecedented situation, which amounted almost to guerilla warfare. The Amalgamation General Council was disturbed about the whole position, and the Northern Counties Federation decided to take a ballot vote. Our own Amalgamation vote resulted in 70,542 votes in favour of strike action, and 50,917 votes for negotiation with the employers, with 4,852 papers spoiled or blank. The total vote of the Federation showed 78,437 votes for strike action, and 61,742 votes for negotiations. The Central Board met to consider the unsatisfactory nature of the ballot, but stalemate followed and matters were allowed to drift for a while. Circumstances proved too strong, however, and a second ballot was taken, which proved to be as inconclusive as the first ballot.

During July informal conversations took place, which led to a series of joint meetings, at which the employers made definite proposals: a 30 per cent reduction in list percentages; that list percentages taken from the various clauses in the Uniform List be added together and put on in one figure. This proposal was rejected by the operatives' representatives, and for the next few meetings a series of notes containing proposals and counter-proposals sent exchanged, without any progress being made.

In the meantime movement was taking place in our District Associations, and resolutions were being received for a Special General Council Meeting to be held, at which a call should be made for a strike of all our members. This movement apparently affected the employers, as they made fresh proposals at a joint meeting on 5th August, 1932, which the operatives countered. During the discussions the subject of Reinstatement of Operatives (who had withdrawn their labour at mills where breaches of agreement had already occurred) and Sanctity of Agreements was raised.

Very difficult joint meetings took place on 9th August, when the employers refused to reconsider their attitude on Reinstatement and Honouring of Agreements, and the operatives would not, therefore consider the employers amended wage reduction. The impasse was discussed at a Special Meeting of the General Council held on 11th August, 1932, when a recommendation of the Central Committee was carried, that there should be a general stoppage of the industry for the restoration of agreements with regard to list prices, and the reinstatement of operatives brought out on strike. The matter was brought before the Central Board of the Federation, and after hesitancy the Board decided that there should be a withdrawal of labour unless the employers were more reasonable.

It was further decided that in the event of there being no alteration in the situation by Saturday, 20th August, 1932, notices would be served that labour be withdrawn on Saturday, 27th August, 1932.

Meanwhile, in consequence of meetings held in Burnley during July, to consider the position created by the posting of notices at almost every mill throughout the area to reduce wages, action was taken by the Weavers' Association and the Warehousemen and Twisters and Drawers to withdraw their labour, and this became effective on 1st August, 1932.

It will be readily seen that the general situation was causing much uneasiness and behind the scenes certain people were endeavouring to bring the representatives of both sides together, to avoid an open breach of relationships. The Deputy Lord Mayor of Manchester acted as chairman at one joint conference, which lasted three days, but no progress was made and conferences proved abortive.

Four Weeks' Strike

The general withdrawal of labour then took place on 27th August, 1932, and lasted for four weeks, until 27th September, 1932. The response to the appeal for withdrawal of labour was remarkably loyal, particularly in the North-East Lancashire area. So successful was the stoppage that it surprised a very large number of observers who had been watching the trend of events, and who did not think it was possible, in a time of industrial depression, for successful action to be taken by an operatives' organisation. Appeals were made to the trade union movement and the T.U.C. permitted a special statement to be made during the Trades Union Congress then being held at Newcastle. A fund was organised on behalf of the cotton operatives and the administration of the fund was vested in a sub-committee of the T.U.C. General Council along with four representatives of the textile unions. We received from that fund £12,550 in cash, and a total of no less than 256,735 Food Vouchers, each worth 2s. 9d. plus goods valued at 10d., given by the C.W.S., a total value of 3s. 7d. These vouchers were distributed over a period of 16 weeks, and proved of inestimable value to all the recipients. The Boot and Shoe Operatives made a grant of £200 in addition to their grant to the T.U.C. fund, which enabled a supply of more than 2,000 pairs of boots and shoes to be available for many needy children. In consequence of our membership with the General Federation of Trade Unions we received £66,040 9s. 2d. in benefits from them.

Due to this dispute, and the ensuing difficulties due to reinstatement, the Amalgamation itself paid out over £355,853 in dispute benefits, truly a colossal figure at that time.

Midland Hotel Conferences

The withdrawal of labour and the stoppage of practically the whole of the manufacturing side of the industry having been effective, the Ministry of Labour began to take an active interest in the dispute. Behind the scenes movement was taking place in order to ascertain what possibilities there were for any action which the Ministry could successfully undertake to be acceptable. As a result of soundings a conference was arranged between the Northern Counties Federation and the Cotton Spinners & Manufacturers' Association, for 13th September, 1932, at which Mr. F. W. Leggett (later Sir Frederick W. Leggett) the chief conciliation officer of the Ministry of Labour was present, along with two assistants. This conference (and succeeding meetings) were held in the Midland Hotel, Manchester, and became famous as the "Midland Hotel Conferences." Mr. Leggett addressed the conference upon the gravity of the situation and the need for action to be taken that would secure a solution. He suggested that six representatives from each side should be appointed, under his chairmanship, to try to draft an agenda of the various questions that required to be settled. The Central Board of the Federation agreed to the suggestion and our representatives upon that joint sub-committee were:— Messrs. E. Duxbury, J. Lee, L. Bates, A. Naesmith, J. Hopwood, and C. Doodson. The employers' representatives were:— Messrs. J. H. Grey (later Sir John), E. Hamer, Col. A. Birtwistle, J. Nelson, G. Green, and T. Ashurst.

This sub-committee decided that the agenda should consist of the following subjects:—

1. Re-establishment of collective bargaining and restoration of agreements.
2. Machinery to ensure the maintenance of any agreements reached.

3. Wages.
4. Reinstatement.

The main body of Federation representatives were in waiting within the Hotel, for consultation, and they endorsed the agenda quoted above. The sub-committee were able to reach an understanding that provided agreement was reached on the general items on the agenda, it was mutually agreed that all the agreements governing Hours and Wages and Methods of Collective Bargaining, as they existed prior to their abrogation by the employers on 11th June, 1932, should be restored.

These conferences and sub-committee meetings continued, day by day, until Saturday the 24th September, and the most protracted discussions took place. No two problems gave rise to more difficulty than those dealing with Wages and Reinstatement. The Ministry of Labour's representatives undertook to prepare a précis upon the subject of Honouring of Agreements, after the conclusion of the dispute. Very close and sticky negotiations took place on the Wage question, when it was ultimately decided that the wage reduction from price lists should be 15½ per cent or 8.943 per cent from current wages, (1s. 8½d. in the £). This reduction brought the Uniform List percentages down to 67 per cent.

On the problem of Reinstatement, our representatives submitted details of the mills and personnel affected, and urged full unconditional reinstatement of the operatives who left their work at our request, in defence of our policy against breaches of agreements. Eventually Mr. Leggett drew up a document on this subject, which is now Part 4 of the general Midland Agreement.

All the final agreements and decisions of these conferences were embodied in a lengthy document, known as the "Midland Agreement," and its main provisions are:—

(a) The appointment of a Conciliation Committee, to be used after the Joint Rules have been complied with, with the object of more effectively avoiding stoppages of work.

The Conciliation Committee to consist of five representatives from each side, with an Independent Chairman, (Sir Charles Doughty, K.C., was later appointed) and two independent assessors.

The Conciliation Committee shall first endeavour to settle the dispute in hand by agreement, but failing agreement, the Chairman shall make a recommendation (after consulting his two assessors). If invited by both sides the Chairman shall make an Award.

(b) A Joint Prices Committee to be formed, to deal with questions and interpretations of list prices and wage rates.

(c) The Honouring of Agreements was covered by lengthy clauses drafted by the Ministry of Labour.

(d) The wage reduction to be 15½ per cent from list prices.

(e) Firms on the More-Looms System shall not make any reduction on prices they were then paying.

(f) No further extensions of the More-Looms System to be attempted until joint agreement has been reached on wages and conditions under which the system shall continue.

(g) Replacement of Operatives was dealt with in a long document prepared by the Ministry, in which the central body of employers would recommend their member-firms to exercise a spirit of good will and offer employment as speedily as possible to operatives who had been displaced.

(h) Subsequent clauses dealt with the question of a Standing Joint Committee on Economic and Legislative matters, and the Restoration of Collective Agreements as they existed prior to 11th June, 1932, Re-organisation, and an Examination and revision of the Uniform List.

This final document was submitted to a meeting of the General Council on Tuesday, 27th September, 1932, and was endorsed, by 97 votes to 53.

Following these negotiations, efforts were made to reach an agreement upon the spinning side, and an agreement was signed on the 30th December, 1932, which provided for:—

(a) the restoration of the 48-hours normal working week.

(b) wages which rose and fell with the spinners and cardroom workers to be reduced by 14 per cent from list, equal to 7.67 per cent from current, (1s. 6½d. in the £), and at weaving firms in membership with the Spinners' Federation a reduction of 15½ per cent from list, similar to the Midland Agreement reduction.

(c) Honouring of Agreements.

The More-Looms System becomes established

As mentioned earlier, the decision of the General Council in March, 1932, had ended for the time being the possibility of a joint agreement being reached upon the More-Looms per Weaver System, but in spite of our decision the employers were extremely restive and individual attempts were made at many mills throughout the county to introduce the system in some form or another.

The acceptance of the terms of the Midland Agreement, however, imposed an obligation upon the organisation that "every endeavour shall be made within a period of two months, for consideration to be given to the More-Looms System, under the procedure provided by the joint rules as amended."

Joint meetings commenced on 28th October, 1932, and the labours of the sub-committee continued almost without break until the end of December that year. At first the discussions did not run at all smoothly, and common agreement was expressed that the services of Mr. Leggatt should again be called upon. In spite of his guidance there were many occasions when the meetings might easily have broken down, but conscious of the fact that failure to reach agreement would not end the system, the operatives' representatives were compelled to keep pegging away at the task. Apart from the harrassing nature of the negotiations, the workers' representatives were aware of the fact that they were contributing towards aggravating an already serious social problem in our manufacturing towns, through the displacement of labour that would ensue. There was the further doubt that even if the system did become regularised, by agreement, it would not contribute towards a restoration of trade, as the reductions in the production costs would not be sufficient to secure competitive equality in the world.

The operatives' negotiators were conscious of the fact that they were negotiating a new piece price list for a new weaving system in the midst of industrial depression. Disputes on the question had already cost almost three-quarters of a million pounds in benefits, and in spite of the union's opposition the system was establishing itself in places like Burnley, Earby, Rishton, Church, Accrington, Bamber Bridge, Nelson, Blackburn, Great Harwood, Darwen, Preston, Hyde, Chorley and Ashton districts. The economic circumstances then prevailing undoubtedly caused the operatives to lend themselves to the establishment of the system. Eventually the Central Committee and the General Council were compelled to accept the view that a negotiated settlement was preferable to an imposed one.

Consequently, a tentative agreement was drafted and circulated to the District Committees, and at the General Council Meeting held on 17th December, 1932, authority was given to the Central Committee to sign the draft agreement, by 104 votes to 40 against.

Thus the first "More-Looms" system agreement came to be made, known as the "yellow book". The agreement was based on conditions being provided to enable a weaver of average ability to earn approximately 41s. per week on six running looms weaving standard cloths. If earnings fell below 90 per cent of this figure a joint investigation had to be made. Provision was made for preventing "exploitation" of the list (by firms running less than six looms at the new piece rate), and "temporary experiments" were permissible on not more than six per cent of looms on cloths not covered by the new list. (The new List itself was restricted to cloths up to five-lifts, and with not more than 200 threads to the square inch. Heavily reeded cloths were also prohibited). Clauses were inserted dealing with Displacement of Labour, and a Guaranteed Wage was established, (then called the "Retention Wage") of 66⅔ per cent of the weaver's normal earnings, or not less than 28s. per week, whichever was the higher. Ancillary labour was to be provided, and loom speeds had to be reduced by not less than 7½ per cent, and if possible, by 10 per cent.

Immediately the agreement was signed a number of employers rushed in headlong to adopt the new system, which did not ease the problems which existed arising out of the depression in the industry, and in the words of the General Secretary at the time "The outlook for the future is certainly very black."

The Jubilee of the Amalgamation—1884–1934

The Amalgamation reached its Jubilee year in 1934, and the General Secretary took the opportunity in the Annual Report for that year of surveying historically the chequered career of the Amalgamation from its establishment. The experience of the previous year, 1933, had been a repetition of industrial depression and suffering by our members due to unemployment, under-employment and tardiness in securing reinstatement of operatives affected by the 1932 dispute. During 1933 the Amalgamation had paid dispute benefits totalling £48,943.

During the fifty years existence of the Amalgamation the income from Levies paid by Districts had been £1,416,240, whilst Dispute Benefits paid to District Associations during the same period had been £1,381,371, of which £818,546 had been paid since 1920. This showed that practically the whole of the income from Ordinary and Special Levies since the establishment of the Amalgamation had gone back to the District Associations in dispute benefits.

CHAPTER XVII

Legalisation of the Uniform List

THE CENTRAL COMMITTEE had spent much thought upon the problems arising out of breaches of agreements, and how agreements could be enforced at law, by being embodied within the powers of an instrument placed in the hands of the industry by Parliament. Discussions had taken place with the Trades Union Congress and with the Labour Party on the possibility of amending the Factory Acts, or of applying the Trade Boards Act, or other legislative means. It was found that none of these particular lines of action answered our purpose, and in subsequent discussions with representatives of the Cotton Spinners & Manufacturers' Association, and the Ministry of Labour officers, a means was found which eventually led to the promotion of a Bill, entitled the "Cotton Manufacturing Industry (Temporary Provisions) Bill."

The Midland Agreement of September, 1932, in clause 2, had laid emphasis upon the need to consider means by which the conditions agreed upon by the responsible organisations could be made generally operative, and that the subject should be further explored with the Ministry of Labour on the termination of the dispute. It was in pursuance of this intention that the whole question was re-opened and pressed upon the Ministry of Labour. In consequence of representations made by the Ministry, the Cabinet appointed a sub-committee to consider what ways and means could be devised to enable agreements on the manufacturing side of the industry to be honourably carried out.

In consequence this new departure in industrial legislation was undertaken, and although it was taken forward as an experiment, many industries apart from our own were interested and kept a watchful eye on the proposition. The Bill received its first hearing on 3rd May, 1934, and after being discussed in both Houses it became an Act on 28th June, 1934, and would continue in operation until 31st December, 1937.

The 1935 Legalised Uniform List

Under the new Cotton Manufacturing (Temporary Provisions) Act the Minister of Labour had to be satisfied that the organisations making an application for an agreement to be embodied within an "Order" should represent the employers controlling the majority of looms and the Amalgamation should represent a majority of the persons employed in the grades which would be affected by the rates of wages to be legalised. Opportunity was given for objections to be made in writing, or orally before a Board. The Act specified certain areas to be covered by the legalised List, which included Lancashire, portions of the West Riding of Yorkshire, and portions of Derbyshire and Cheshire.

It will be seen therefore that the scene was set for the ultimate legalisation of the Uniform List, after objections had been considered; but before progress could be made in that direction the Central Committee were faced with the enormous problem posed by the employers' organisation: "What agreement shall be legalised?" A series of joint meetings held in June 1934 had revealed that many variations from the Uniform List and the More Looms List were operating, notably in Barnoldswick, Harle Syke, and South Lancashire, whilst large numbers of firms were paying Uniform List less a percentage deduction. In some cases 50 per cent was added to the List instead of 67 per cent, and there were numerous cases of clauses in the List being ignored. At the time it was estimated that 120,000 looms out of 325,000 running looms were working at something less than joint agreements provided.

The employers' representatives were not slow in drawing attention to these facts and making the utmost use of them. They contended that a new Piece Price List was necessary to iron out anomalies and malpractices. In spite of argument and reason the employers remained adamant in their attitude, and were not prepared to agree that a joint request should be made to the Minister of Labour for an Order to be made embodying the existing agreements. No progress could be made with the employers, and the dilemma was reported to the General Council, who considered the situation in July 1934. District Associations were circularised, and the problem was discussed again in August, when the General Council authorised the Central Committee to continue joint discussions in an effort to secure agreement on wage rates to be legalised, the terms of any agreement to be submitted to the General Council for approval or otherwise.

Armed with this authority the Central Committee did not at once proceed to use it, as contact with the employers was known to involve reductions in wages, and probably a revision of the More Looms List, as well as the Uniform List and Coloured Goods List. It was felt, however, that a continuation of the existing situation would be against the best interests of the Amalgamation and its members, and talks were reopened with the employers in September, 1934.

A joint sub-committee was appointed, and proposals and counter-proposals were sent backwards and forwards, without any tentative agreement being reached. The operatives' representatives suggested that the disagreement should be submitted to the Conciliation Committee, but the employers would not agree.

Further joint discussions took place on 27th September, 1934 when a tentative agreement was reached that the Uniform List should be paid plus 57½ per cent in place of the existing 67 per cent, and the More Looms List should be based at 18.2d. per 100,000 picks. It was also agreed that there should be no limitation of cloths for the More Looms system. Consideration was given to numerous clauses in both the Uniform List and the More Looms List, particularly on Reeds, Artificial Silk, and a host of other technical details.

These joint meetings lasted well into October, and a draft document was ultimately submitted to a Special Meeting of the General Council held on 3rd November, 1934, without a decision being reached, and a further meeting of the

General Council on 17th November decided to submit the whole position to a ballot vote of the members. The ballot vote was counted and declared to a General Council Meeting on 15th December, 1934, and showed that out of 104,185 papers issued 89,369 were returned. 56,924 voted in favour of giving the Central Committee full authority to conclude an agreement, and 28,195 voted against.

This decision led to a further series of Joint Meetings which lasted from 18th December until the end of January 1935, and could be termed Revision Joint Meetings. Certain of the original clauses in the draft List had been found very unacceptable at the earlier Council meetings in October and November, and as a result of the revision joint meetings improvements were secured, particularly regarding Heavy Drill cloths, Picks in Sateen cloths, and certain clauses in the Coloured Goods List.

A vexed problem in connection with the coloured section had been that of amalgamating the Radcliffe List and Colne List. The Radcliffe List being the older, was based upon cloth length, and the Colne List was based upon warp length. In order to allay opposition from the Radcliffe section of manufacturers and also to arrive at uniformity, accommodation was found by which cloths calculated by the Coloured section of the new List would in future be based upon 70 yards of warp length where the contraction did not exceed 10 per cent, but where it exceeded 10 per cent the basis would be 63 yards of cloth length.

Under the revised List the conditions governing the Six-Looms system had been entirely re-drafted, and new conditions appertaining to More than Six Looms were formulated, in order to prevent employers, by increasing the number of looms to an operative, evading the Piece Price List that would be generally operating. Thus the principle of paying a base wage plus one-fifth of the earnings that could be produced from the Six-Looms system was adopted.

As a result of these protracted and wearying negotiations the way was now clear for an approach to be made to the Minister of Labour for the machinery to be set in motion under the new Cotton Manufacturing (Temporary Provisions) Act, 1934, and in accordance with the provisions of the Act a Board of Inquiry was set up, under the chairmanship of Dr. Hector J. W. Hetherington, (Vice-Chancellor of Liverpool University), with two other nominated members, and a panel of Assessors from each side of the industry. This Board of Inquiry held preliminary meetings and on 13th May, 1935 the Board received evidence from objectors to the new proposed List. These objectors were cross-examined by the Amalgamation representatives upon the panel of Assessors and by Sir John Taylor, Solicitor with the employers' panel, and the proceedings lasted for a whole week. There were 18 objections, the majority from individual firms, and there were objections from our Nelson and Colne Weavers' Associations. The objections fell into five categories: (1) The geographical limitation of the Act itself; (2) Local Disadvantage allowances which were contained in the new List; (3) Applicability of the agreement to rayon weaving; (4) Reductions in weavers' wages in the Nelson and Colne areas; (5) the agreement would retard progressive methods in weaving.

The Report of the Board of Inquiry was published on 15th June, 1935, and summarised the circumstances leading up to the new agreement, dealt with the points raised by the objectors, and made recommendations to the Minister. The

Board recognised that the new agreement had defects but they had no reason to doubt that it was a notable improvement on what had gone before and upon the then existing chaotic situation in the industry. The Board agreed that the fundamental necessity was to secure a universally enforceable wage basis, and the Minister was recommended to make an Order bringing the new List into force.

The Minister of Labour acted upon this advice, and the first Statutory Order on textile workers' wages was made on 27th June, 1935, by Order No. 602, the new wage agreement to operate from the 15th July, 1935.

The 1937 Legalised List

However, this first edition of the legalised Uniform List did not reign for long, and this narrative will later discuss details of the revision which took place in 1937, when the more permanent legalised Uniform List came into being.

During 1936 it was felt that the time had arrived when a determined effort should be made to secure some improvement in the wage levels of our weavers, and an application was submitted to the Manufacturers' Association for an advance in the basic prices by 15 per cent, and also that a minimum wage of not less than 7½d. per hour be paid to weavers normally running a full complement of looms. Eventually the claim was submitted to the Conciliation Committee, under the terms of the Midland Agreement, and this was the first case to be so submitted to the Committee since its establishment under that agreement. Mr. (later Sir) Charles Doughty, K.C., was the chairman, and his assessors were Mr. A. C. Somervell for the employers and Professor R. H. Tawney for the operatives. The Committee met on 25th and 26th November, 1936, and considered a very lengthy statement of our case, during which copious extracts were quoted from the statistics revealed by the Wage Census taken by the Amalgamation during February, 1936. The average earnings were shown to be £1 11s. 5d. for all persons, and it was contended that this wage level was good cause for disquietude. The employers had also taken a census of wages, which had shown that there was no serious discrepancy between the two sets of returns. It was therefore contended that the Piece Price List, operating under normal working conditions, did not ensure a satisfactory wage, and where under-employment prevailed, the piece list failed to give what could be described modestly as a living wage. The operatives' proposals were therefore designed to relieve that position.

As a result of the Conciliation proceedings an agreement was eventually reached, which raised the basic prices for the four and six-looms systems, and increased the percentage additions on the Coloured List, with subsequent alterations to clauses governing Reeds, Weft, Pickfinding, Stave Work and other factors.

In accordance with the terms of the Cotton Manufacturing Industry (Temporary Provisions) Act, 1934, application had to be made to the Minister of Labour for the revocation of the Order No. 602, and the issuing of a new Order to embody the new agreement. The matter was submitted to a Board of Inquiry, under the chairmanship of Sir Hector J. Hetherington, and the task of the Board was simplified as there had been no objections lodged against the application. The Board recommended the Minister to issue an Order embodying the new agreement, and this was done. The Revocation Order is No. 297 (1937), and the new Legalised Uniform List was embodied in Order No. 298 (1937), and is still in force.

Consequential amendments were made in other wage lists, equal to 10½ per cent on list prices, or 6.38 per cent on current wages. Thus, the Amalgamation secured its first increase in wages since the heavy reductions in 1921, and built a firm foundation for the legalisation of the main Piece Price List. Legalisation proved a boon to our members for it prevented employers from paying less than the proper wages.

The original Act of 1934 was due to expire at the end of 1937, and representations were made to the Minister of Labour by both sides, to ensure the continuation of the Act for a further period. Certain amendments of detail were suggested, and the geographical scope was also in need of expansion, but in consequence of pressure of business before the House at that time the Government was unable to comply with the requests for amendment, but the life of the Act itself was extended through the Expiring Laws Continuance Act, and has been maintained in existence ever since, by that means.

Under-Employment in the Inter-War Years

Looking back upon the years 1928 to 1938 is an unpleasant experience and reading the Annual Reports of that time makes very depressing reading. The numbers employed within the industry had dropped from 621,516 in 1912 to 467,440 in 1934, and the decline continued during the immediately subsequent years. The efforts made to cheapen production by the adoption of the More-Looms System might have reduced production costs on a certain number of cloths but it had been a contributory factor towards increasing the general chaos in production.

The industry had witnessed the rise and fall of the Cotton Control Board. Efforts had been made by the Joint Committee of Cotton Trade Organisations to propose schemes for the benefit of the industry, which did not bring any permanent improvement, although the Joint Committee did some very valuable work through its Statistical Bureau. The Cotton Yarn Association came into being and passed out, in 1927, and there was an experiment through the Eastern Textile Association, to recover bulk trade in the Far East. In 1930 the British Cotton Textile Association was formed but never functioned because of threatened opposition from powerful merchanting interests. An Egyptian Spinners' Convention was attempted in 1930, but failed because a sufficient majority in favour of the scheme was not secured. An American Cotton Spinners' scheme in 1931 was formulated, but failed to secure the necessary majority. The joint Committee of Cotton Trade Organisations' famous scheme for dealing with surplus capacity failed to secure the necessary support from the spinners, and the Cotton Spinners' Convention of 1931, formed for the purpose of purchasing, dismantling or placing in cold storage redundant spinning mills and plant, failed owing to insufficient support, and the scheme was dropped. Then there was the Egyptian Spinners' Production Quota Scheme of 1932, which again failed because of insufficient support. The Royton Agreement of 1933, which was to eliminate weak selling and undercutting, was successful for a time, then collapsed, and was restored in August, 1934. The

Federation of Master Cotton Spinners' Associations brought forward several schemes for relating production to demand, and there was a Dyeing and Finishing Trade Re-organisation Scheme in 1934, designed to consolidate that section of the industry. Then there was the formation of the Lancashire Cotton Corporation, which was registered in 1929 and by December, 1931 had absorbed 106 mills, containing almost 10 million spindles and 20,000 looms. By 1932 they had scrapped some 32 mills, the majority of which were old.

The official figures for Unemployment and temporary stoppages during the period 1933-1935 showed a consistent average of over 22 per cent but this figure did not reveal the tremendous amount of "Under"-employment which existed in the weaving sheds. On 17th August, 1935 the General Council gave special consideration to the seriousness of the problem, and passed the following resolution:

> "That this General Council Meeting, whilst agreeing with the policy of not subsidising wages by public assistance, asks for special consideration to be given to weavers. It is satisfied that no other class of operative is in the position of working a full 48-hour week for less than a full week's wage, although receiving trade union rates of wages.
>
> "It therefore asks the Minister of Health to make a special dispensation in the Relief Regulation Orders 1930, to meet the special type of case, and instructs the Central Committee to implement this request."

The Amalgamation instituted an enquiry into the facts of the position, in October 1935, and evidence was ascertained showing a very widespread problem. The total number of weavers found to be under-employed varied from 60.7 per cent in a Bury mill, to an average of about 30 per cent in the large districts. Messrs. John Jewkes and A. Winterbottom, of Manchester University, attempted to measure scientifically the amount of under-employment in certain weaving sheds, and they had published their conclusions in the Economic Journal of December 1931, copious extracts from the report being reprinted in the Amalgamation Annual Report of 1936. The Unemployment Insurance Act of 1934 did not help matters so far as under-employment was concerned, as the benefits of the Act only applied to persons actually unemployed. The "Determination of Need and Assessment of Needs Regulation 1934" was no more helpful, and precluded a Public Assistance Authority from ordering out-relief. The usual method of the Relieving Officer issuing food tickets if an applicant proved he was destitute, did not meet the situation either.

The whole problem was fully ventilated at an interview between the Central Committee and the then Minister of Labour (Rt. Hon. E. A. Brown, M.P.,) on the 13th December, 1935, in which strong representations were made to him for remedial measures to be taken to ease the very difficult industrial problem, and a promise was given that the matter would receive careful consideration by the Department. This subject is again dealt with later.

The Truck Acts and Fining System

The history of "truck" goes back a very long way in industrial relationships and law. There is evidence that many districts wages were only paid either fortnightly, or every three weeks, and a form of "truck" system was often used, whereby the factory owners or some near relative, kept a grocer's shop, or a public house, either at the mill or nearby, and operatives were expected to make their purchases at such shops. Actual payment of wages in goods was avoided, but the credit, or "strap" system was used extensively. Operatives would keep accounts in a "strap-book", but with the general prevalence of illiteracy, unscrupulous masters could gain more than a fair profit. In addition, credit could accumulate so quickly, thus exceeding earnings, so that workers were for ever in debt to their masters. So long ago as 1831 a Truck Act was enacted to provide that a workman's wage must be paid in cash, and not in kind. This early Act was amended in 1887, and the important Act of 1896 went into more detail in providing against deductions in respect of damaged goods or payment of fines.

Under Section 9 of the Truck Act of 1896 a Home Office Order dated 3rd March, 1897, gave exemption from the provisions of the Act in respect of all branches of the cotton weaving trade of Lancashire, Cheshire, Derbyshire, and the West Riding of Yorkshire. But this exemption has not, however, proved to have been of any service to our members in preventing the objectionable system of Fining. Right throughout the present century the Amalgamation has persistently drawn attention to the pernicious practice, and many joint meetings have been held with the Employers' Associations to secure by mutual agreement its entire elimination from all mills. On untold occasions we have tried to secure the aid of Parliament to bring about its abolition by legislation, but without success. Much litigation has taken place on the subject, and several court cases are now referred to because of their historic interest.

In 1927 action was taken by the Amalgamated Weavers in a Bolton case, known as the Hart v. Riversdale Mill Co., case, where we failed to obtain a favourable decision. In 1928 the whole town of Nelson was stopped because of the objection of a weaver to payment of a fine at Messrs. Mather Brothers Ltd., the stoppage lasting for seven weeks, and costing the District Associations thousands of pounds.

In 1930 the Amalgamation tested the legality in the courts again, and the case of the fine imposed upon Thomas Sagar, of Nelson, by his employers, Messrs. H. Ridehalgh & Sons, Nelson, was taken before the Chancery Court in London, our counsel being Hon. R. Stafford Cripps, K.C., and Mr. Neville J. Laski, K.C. This step was taken in order to avoid any prejudice that might surround the statement of a case in a local court. Numerous witnesses were called, and the case was stated by our counsel, before Mr. Justice Farwell, with considerable skill and acumen. The case was adjourned in order that the defendants could amend their pleadings, and the full hearing of the case took place on 6th May, 1930, when Mr. Justice Farwell decided that we had fully established our claim that the action of the employers in making the deduction was illegal.

The employers at once appealed against the decision, and the case was again heard in the Court of Appeal, from 10th to 14th November, 1930. Unfortunately, between the judgment of Mr. Justice Farwell in the Chancery Court, and the opening of the appeal by the employers, our leading counsel, Mr. Stafford Cripps, K.C., had accepted an appointment in the Government, and was consequently unable to lead the case again. We succeeded in briefing Mr. F. P. M. Schiller, K.C.

The judgment was delivered on 9th December, 1930, and was unanimously against us, leaving the employers in the position of being entitled in law to make deductions from workpeople's wages for producing alleged unmerchantable cloth. It would appear from the judgment that the Amalgamation had been living in a fool's paradise on this question, as the exemption which the Amalgamation obtained from the Truck Act of 1896 had apparently not given us that safeguard which was intended. It would appear from the courts that the weavers are not immune either from the provisions of the 1831 Truck Act or the amending Act of 1896.

Not being satisfied to let the matter stand the Central Committee consulted with the General Council of the T.U.C., with a view to getting the case taken to the House of Lords. The Finance Committee of the General Council were interviewed, and it was decided to take counsel's opinion. A consultation was held with Mr. J. H. Stamp, K.C., in London, and his considered opinion was of such a character that the T.U.C. General Council decided not to pursue the matter. The Central Committee was still not satisfied, and they consulted Mr. Neville Laski, K.C., and on his advice consulted Mr. Wilfred Greene, K.C. In June 1931 the considered opinions of the two counsels were given in which they advised against an appeal to the House of Lords.

Thus the Fining question was left—in an unsatisfactory position. The Amalgamation has always contested the right—and doubted the wisdom—of employers in inflicting fines for alleged unsatisfactory workmanship, or any other causes, and looks forward to the time when an opportunity can be taken to introduce new legislation into the House of Commons that will establish our objection to the Fining System beyond any possible doubt.

Whilst dealing with deductions from wages and the legal position under the Truck Acts it is interesting to recall a very important case which arose in the Darwen district in 1935, in connection with the practice which had taken place in a number of mills during the chaotic conditions which obtained in 1932. In the case of Ada Kenyon v. The Darwen Cotton Manufacturing Co. Ltd., the firm had obtained contributions from the operative's wage each week, authorised by documents which had been signed in 1932, after the conclusion of the 1932 stoppage of work. The plaintiff left the firm's services in January 1935, and the amount she had contributed to share capital from her wages, £9 18s. 3d., was claimed from her late employers. Judge Peel gave a very lengthy written Judgment after the hearing in the Blackburn County Court, in which he found in favour of the employers. This judgment was unsatisfactory, and at once an appeal was lodged, on the advice of Sir William Jowitt, K.C. The appeal was heard in the Court of Appeal on 14th February, 1936, by Lord Justices Slesser and Scott and Mr. Justice Eve. After considerable argument the appeal was allowed, and success therefore crowned our efforts in this case.

Whilst dealing with the question of "Truck" it is interesting to refer to the case Pratt v. Cook, Son & Co. (St. Paul's) Ltd., which was taken to the House of Lords. In this case the firm had paid a wage to the workman and made a deduction from such wage of 10s. per week in respect of meals provided by the firm. This had led to action by the trade union under the Truck Acts, and eventually, the case went to the House of Lords. The effect of the decision given in the House of Lords was to give the Truck Act of 1831 an interpretation which it had not previously been construed to bear, which was likely to imperil good industrial relationships between employers and employed. The practical effect of the Judgment was stated during a discussion in the House of Commons in 1940 to be as follows:

> "It is perfectly legal for an employer to contract with a workman in a written agreement for the payment of a wage say of 63s. per week, and for a deduction from that wage of 10s. a week in respect of meals provided. It is, however, illegal and a breach of the Truck Acts (where these Acts apply) for an employer to agree with his workmen for a wage of 53s. plus meals to the value of 10s. The effect of the two forms of agreement on the workman is precisely the same."

As a result of this case, the Truck Act of 1940 became law, and whilst it restrains proceedings on matters arising before the commencment of the Act from agreements which have been made in the past by reason of a mistaken construction of the 1831 Act, it does not seek to reverse the decision of the House of Lords in the Pratt case, nor does it deal with the general system of Truck Act legislation; but for the future employers and workmen will have to follow the form which the House of Lords has shown to be legal.

The intentions of the Truck Act still remain, which were to prevent the abuses that prevailed in the 18th and 19th centuries, and to ensure that a worker shall obtain the full benefits of the wages to which he is entitled, in current coin of the realm.

Legalisation on the Waste Weaving List

In February, 1935 efforts were made, through joint meetings with the Cotton Spinners & Manufacturers' Association, to secure legalisation of a Weaving List for the Waste trade. A sub-committee was appointed, and considered the formulation of a new Waste Weaving List which was suitable for legalisation. The draft List was submitted to the General Council in October, 1935 and endorsed. In March, 1936 a joint meeting was held with the Cotton Spinners & Manufacturers' Association, with the Waste Manufacturers' Association representatives present, when the whole matter was discussed. It has not been found possible to make any progress at all on this subject, mainly because of the policy of The Cotton Spinners and Manufacturers' Association, which would not permit them to proceed to legalise any weaving list which was based on Yarn Weight, as opposed to payment by Picks put in by the loom.

CHAPTER XVIII

Other Inter-War Period Developments

Standing Joint Committee of Working Women's Organisations

IT WAS in July 1936 when the General Council decided to seek the appointment of a woman representative upon the Standing Joint Committee of Working Women's Organisations, in view of the valuable work which the Standing Committee was performing, and because of the unique contribution which could be made by a textile representative. The application for representation was accepted, and Miss Alice Foley, M.B.E., M.A., J.P., of Bolton was appointed. She served as our representative for a number of years, and later Miss Winifred Gillespie took her place as a member of the Joint Standing Committee, and she also continued to serve well. The position was then taken over by Mrs. C. Gallagher of Nelson and is still serving.

It is not possible to refer in detail to the importance of the work put into the Weavers' organisation by its women members. Hundreds of women have given invaluable service to the District Associations, in the mills, on District Committees, and other public bodies, without thought of reward. It is only fitting that we should put on record appreciation of such services by the women members.

Rewound Weft

Immediately following the introduction of the Legalised List in 1935 under Order No. 602, difficulty was experienced in a number of districts by employers making deductions from the weaving prices for rayon and silk weft. Representations were made to the firms concerned, and the matter reached Manchester in joint meetings, to see if an agreed interpretation could be found. Very little progress was made, and the General Council decided on 21st December, 1935 that legal action should be taken against individual firms making such deductions. Eventually a case was taken against the South Valley Manfg. Co., Colne, and was heard by Judge Burgis at the Burnley County Court on 29th October, 1936. The case was intended to decide whether the deductions from the list prices for rewound weft applied to artificial silk. During the proceedings the Judge intimated that he could not decide the broad principle as the parties desired, but that as a judge he could only decide in the particular case in accordance with the facts. As this would have been a most unsatisfactory position, consultations were held, and as a result it was decided to invite His Honour Judge Burgis to arbitrate, upon terms of reference to be agreed upon by both parties, in order that a general understanding could be reached upon the meaning of the Rewound Weft Clauses as they appeared in both sections of the first edition of the legalised Uniform List. Judge Burgis secured the consent of the Lord Chancellor to act as Arbitrator, and for three days, commencing 17th March, 1937, both sides, who were legally represented, argued their cases at great length. Our case was rendered extremely difficult by virtue of the fact that in the Judge's opinion the Rewound Weft clause was applicable to filament artificial silk, so long as the cop, tube, or bobbin containing the yarn came within the provisions of the length and weight section of the tables in the clause. Moreover, the fact that the List was embodied within an order gave it statutory enforcement. During the course of the three days' hearing, facts emerged which made our position untenable, and eventually on the third day it was agreed that the matter should stand adjourned in order to give Judge Burgis an opportunity of considering the facts and making suggestions for removing the causes of the dispute.

The adjourned hearing was held on 12th April, 1937, in Manchester, and after a full day's hearing an agreement was arrived at, which was embodied in an addendum to the Uniform List. The arbitration agreement in effect authorised deductions for Rewound Weft of 5 per cent and 7½ per cent for prescribed wefts apart from filament rayon, and 4 per cent deduction for filament rayon wefts (2½ per cent on the More-Looms System).

Employment of Women and Young Persons Act, 1936

Although the main Factories Act dealt with the Hours of Labour of women and young persons, separate provision is made in the above Act for such labour when double-shift working is in operation. This Act gives the Home Secretary power, on joint application by the employer and the majority of operatives in any factory, to make orders authorising the employment of women and young persons of the age of 16 and over, to be employed in shifts averaging not more than eight hours per shift, at any time between the hours of 6 a.m. and 10 p.m.

Provision is also made for the taking of a secret ballot of the workpeople, to ascertain their opinions before any application for permission to run a double shift system is granted. In granting any application under this Act the Home Secretary shall impose such conditions as he considers necessary for safeguarding the welfare and interests of the persons employed on the system of shifts. This subject is also dealt with later.

Holidays

There is very little historical record earlier than 1906 on the subject of Holidays, and it was not until 11th December, 1906 that the position was regularised in a county agreement at a meeting of representatives of the Cotton Employers' Parliamentary Association and the United Textile Factory Workers' Association, when it was agreed that Holidays equivalent to 116½ working hours per year be given to the textile workers, to come into force in 1907. These holidays were equivalent to 11½ days per year.

On 21st November, 1913, a joint meeting was held with the two Employers' Associations to discuss a request for an increase in the annual holidays, from 116½ to 136½ hours. The meeting was a failure, and on February 27th, 1914 another meeting was held, at which the employers agreed to take a ballot of their members. This ballot resulted in favour of an extension of the holidays, and in June, 1914, the employers intimated their agreement with the application, and the Holidays were fixed at 136½ hours per annum. As these total holiday-hours were based on a 10-hour working day the effective annual holidays amounted to 13½ days.

When the working hours were reduced from 48 to 45 per week in November, 1946 the total number of holidays per year became 110, equal to 12 working days and two hours. This provided for one week's summer holiday and seven days two hours at other times during the year. This question is also dealt with at length later.

Holidays with Pay

For many years the subject of payment for holidays was discussed by the delegates to the Annual Conference of the United Textile Factory Workers' Association, with a faint hope that some day the textile workers would achieve their object. Towards 1938 it appeared that there was some chance of realisation of the general desire, and that our members would be able to take their holidays without the accompanying dread of the shortage of income which usually followed the annual holiday.

On 8th March, 1938, a joint meeting was held between the representatives of the two Employers' Associations and the Legislative Council of the United Textile Factory Workers' Association, when a strong case was put up by the workers' representatives. In reply the employers pleaded that they were not in the same position as employers in many other industries, as they had to depend upon income from the sale of goods which went overseas and they could not pass the extra cost of such a reform on to the customer. After lengthy discussions the joint meeting stood adjourned for one month.

In the meantime the Minister of Labour had appointed a Committee, which sat under the chairmanship of Lord Amulree, to deal with the question of Holidays with Pay. Their Report was unanimous in its recommendations, and stressed the need for agreements to be reached by negotiation inside the separate industries. The Report also drew attention to the fact that during a future Parliamentary Session, in 1940-41, legislation should be passed making general provisions for Holidays with Pay in industry, the precise nature of the legislation depending upon the progress that had been made.

Further joint meetings ensued with the employers, the outcome of which was the appointment of a joint sub-committee, upon which the Amalgamation had three representatives. This joint sub-committee held numerous meetings, at which a final agreement was reached, and was signed on 15th June, 1939. The agreement covered all firms in the spinning, doubling and manufacturing sections of the trade, and provided for payment for one week's holiday per annum, on the basis of 2 per cent of gross earnings of the previous twelve months.

The achievement of this holiday payment was appreciated by all our members, although it did not cover payment for all holidays in a year. Representations were later made to the employers upon this point, and on 24th December 1942 an agreement was signed between the Cotton Spinners & Manufacturers' Association and the Amalgamation increasing the holiday payment to 4 per cent of gross wages. This benefit was extended to other sections of the manufacturing side at a later date, and similar agreements followed in the spinning section.

The United Textile Factory Workers still continued to press for complete payment for all holidays, and on 26th May, 1942 a joint agreement was signed, covering both spinning and weaving operatives, increasing the holiday payment from 4 per cent to 5 per cent of total gross wages. The manner of disbursement of the holiday pay was left to local arrangement, so far as the manufacturing section was concerned, and the general practice was to make two disbursements per annum, viz: (a) the accumulated amounts from the annual Wakes holiday to Christmas to be disbursed at the Christmas holiday; (b) the accumulated amounts from Christmas to the annual holiday to be disbursed at the annual holiday time.

Since that time the employers had been pressed for increased holidays, but they rejected several applications. This attitude of the employers resulted in the question being referred to the National Arbitration Tribunal in 1950. An application was then made for a total of 144 hours per year, but was turned down by the Tribunal. This rejection caused dismay amongst the textile workers, and further pressure was exerted upon the employers. The subject was again referred to the Industrial Disputes Tribunal (as it was then known) in 1951, when an Award was made granting the application for 144 working hours holiday per week, with a compensatory advance in Holiday Credits to 6½ per cent.

This subject of Holidays with Pay became linked in joint agreements with Working Hours and Wages, and these matters are dealt with in more detail later.

Uniform List for Sheeting Cloths

A fairly large number of firms in certain districts have specialised in the weaving of sheeting and other wide cloths, over a long number of years, and whilst there has been a Uniform List for weaving ordinary-width cloths and coloured cloths, there had not been any uniformity in the county for the payment of weavers engaged in the production of sheeting cloths. Each mill had originally its own list, which had been in use for a lengthy period, or had been negotiated with our local officials, and in some cases these lists were merged into a District List.

Many expressions had been made by delegates to our General Council Meetings that there was need for uniformity in payment for weaving these cloths, but the difficulties were to reconcile the wide variations which existed in types of cloths, types of looms, and conditions as between, say, Nelson mills, Hyde mills, Bacup mills, and other districts.

So long ago as August 1925 the Amalgamation prepared a draft Uniform Sheeting List, and submitted the draft to the Cotton Spinners & Manufacturers' Association. No joint meeting was ever held to consider the draft and the matter had been allowed to drift. During the hearing of objections, in connection with the legalising of the Uniform List under the Cotton Manufacturing Industry (Temporary Provisions) Act, 1934, some firms had objected on the ground that a Uniform Sheeting List should be prepared and embodied within the Order.

During the joint discussions with the Manufacturers' Association in 1936-37 for a wage increase on the Legalised List and other Lists, employers in the South East Lancashire area who were connected with the Federation of Master Cotton Spinners' Associations sent a letter stating that they desired a Uniform Sheeting List before any wage increase could be agreed to.

In 1937 our Nelson Association endeavoured locally to secure some improvement in the wages earned from their local List, which had been long recognised as one of the lowest Sheeting Lists in the trade, but had not succeeded. The matter was brought before the Amalgamation, where it was recognised that it was not an accident that Nelson had become the largest sheeting manufacturing area in the county, and it was feared that in any general discussions at county level upon the terms of a Uniform Sheeting List the employers would make the utmost use of the already low Nelson Sheeting List. Consequently, the Central Committee took the claim for an increase in list prices before the central joint committee, but no progress was made, and the dispute was reported to the Conciliation Committee, in accordance with the Midland Agreement. The Committee met on 16th September, 1937 when the claim was made that the Nelson Sheeting List percentages should be increased from 80 per cent to 105 per cent, which meant an increase in wages of 13.8 per cent.

After lengthy argument the Conciliation Committee made an Award, increasing the list percentage from 80 per cent to 87½ per cent for looms under 80-in. wide, and to 95 per cent for 80-in looms and wider.

Acting on behalf of their members in the Hyde District the Federation of Master Cotton Spinners' Associations pressed for a reduction in the Hyde Sheeting List, from 72½ per cent to 47½ per cent, and although joint discussions proceeded through that winter no settlement was reached, and the dispute was reported to the Conciliation Committee, and the case was heard on 22nd April, 1938. After a very lengthy hearing agreement was reached between the two sides that it was desirable that a Uniform List for Sheeting Cloths should be established for Lancashire and adjoining counties, and both sides agreed to facilitate the formulation of such a List. For this purpose a joint sub-committee, of six representatives from each side, was appointed, the sub-committee to report to the Chairman within four months, although the chairman had power to extend that period. In the meantime the Conciliation hearing stood adjourned.

These recommendations of the Conciliation Committee acted as a spur and the work of formulating some sort of uniform list proceeded. Difficulties were encountered, mainly concerning the Limitation of Cloths and Weft Lengths. Much time and thought was spent in dealing with details, and good work was put into the drafting of clauses in the list by the sub-committee's chairman, Mr. James Whitaker, of Burnley. Finally, a draft was agreed upon, and submitted to a meeting of District Representatives of 23 District Associations interested in the weaving of sheeting cloths, held on 12th September, 1939.

The draft List embodied a number of new principles in ascertaining a weaver's wage, notably in regard to the payment for weft. In the Uniform and other lists the percentage additions or deductions for weft lengths were governed by the counts of the weft, but in the new draft counts were not mentioned, as the deciding factor was the length of weft supplied on the cop or pirn. The limitation of the new list was also defined in detail, in view of the borderline cases with cloths covered by the Uniform List for general weaving.

The special District Conference endorsed the draft list, and recommended its adoption by the General Council. The Council did in fact endorse the draft list on 16th September, 1939. The agreement was duly signed on 2nd November 1939, and began to operate on 1st January, 1940. With the development of larger pirns and shuttle boxes it became possible for weavers to operate six looms in place of the usual four looms. The same piece rate remained but where the weaver could run six looms the rate was reduced by 11 per cent. This enabled the weaver to increase earning by some 30 per cent.

As this agreement was the outcome of recommendations made by the Conciliation Committee the settlement was reported to Sir Charles Doughty, and in November, 1939 he embodied the new Uniform List in an Award. At the time there were thoughts that the new List should be legalised under the Cotton Manufacturing Industry (Temporary Provisions) Act, 1934, but the intervention of the war and the national emergency made this proceeding difficult, and seeing that there was such unanimity amongst all the parties it was considered desirable that the List should be applied on a voluntary basis. This was done, and the List has been in use ever since, and has been faithfully observed.

CHAPTER XIX

The Second World War, 1939-45

Emergency Joint Agreements

THE OUTBREAK of war on 3rd September, 1939 created a number of very difficult problems in our industry, and informal meetings were held with Sir John H. Grey, Chairman of the Cotton Spinners & Manufacturers' Association and his colleagues, when frank discussions took place on such questions as overtime, extra payment, safeguards on a return to normal conditions, working from "light to dusk" and the effect of "black-out" upon the physical condition of the operatives. The result of these preliminary conversations, which we had been instrumental in initiating, was the establishment of an Emergency Joint Committee, consisting of representatives from the Cotton Spinners & Manufacturers' Association and the Northern Counties Textile Trades Federation. The employers in the manufacturing, the spinning, and waste trades, were asked to give facilities for the collection of members' contributions in the mills, because of the difficulties caused by the black-out in the towns, and this was willingly conceded. Many operatives in the North East Lancashire towns normally commenced work at 7 a.m., instead of 7-45 a.m., and a meeting was held in Nelson Weavers' Institute on Sunday, 24th September, 1939, when it was agreed that the starting-time should be altered to 7-45 a.m., until the expiry of the Summer Time Act in November. After that date it was hoped that all the necessary arrangements for conforming to the law as regards the factory black-out would have been made.

The Emergency Joint Committee also reached an agreement that no firm should be allowed to work overtime unless it had taken effective measures for the obscuration of lights. Overtime was only permitted in order to cope with urgent demands for Government cloth requirements, such overtime not to exceed 1½-hours in a day nor 7½-hours in one week. Time and a half rates would be paid.

To cover the exceptional conditions which obtained during the Second World War a number of joint agreements were negotiated with The Cotton Spinners' and Manufacturers' Association, covering Payments for Time Lost during Air Raids; local agreements were made covering the employment of Roof Spotters, and Government Orders dealt with such subjects as the Whitewashing of Shed Roofs, Protection from Flying Glass, the provision of Air-Raid Shelters, and so on. Joint Agreements were also made to govern the working of Overtime, to assist the Government in the national emergency, by the production of more cloth. Permission was granted to certain firms, in conjunction with the Factory

Inspectors, to work up to 55½-hours per week. At the conclusion of hostilities these agreements and Orders gradually lapsed.

Loan to Government

By a decision of the General Council of 20th July, 1940, the Amalgamation loaned to the Government the sum of £25,000 free of interest, during the war emergency. Repayment was made in 1948.

Overtime

The question of Overtime, however, again cropped up in 1947, when the Government pressed for more production to assist in increasing production. Joint Meetings were held and on 7th November, 1947 a joint agreement was made permitting our members to work half an hour overtime per day, payment to be made at Time and a Half rates. Considerable opposition was shown by the operatives to this joint agreement, and hostile ballot votes were taken in Blackburn, Accrington and Oldham districts. The result was that the response to the request for overtime working was patchy. Gradually those operatives who had started to work overtime relaxed their efforts and it appeared that overtime working was practically abandoned when in January, 1948, a meeting was held in London, under the auspices of the Ministry of Labour, when it was decided to make a further appeal for overtime. A mass meeting attended by about 850 delegates was held in the King George's Hall, Blackburn, addressed by Mr. Ness Edwards, M.P., Parliamentary Secretary to the Ministry of Labour, when a lengthy resolution was passed, stressing the urgency of the need for maximum production in the national emergency, and agreeing to recommend that 2½-hours per week overtime be worked. This resolution was only passed by a bare majority (288 votes for and 233 against). As a result of this vote, and happenings on the spinning side, a ballot vote of all the districts within the Northern Counties Textile Trades Federation was decided upon. The ballot paper contained a strong recommendation by the Central Board in favour of overtime working, which was suggested to take place from May to the end of August in 1948.

The result of the ballot vote was announced on 5th May, 1948, and resulted in 20,572 votes for overtime working and 41,545 votes against. An analysis showed that 8 districts were in favour of overtime and 21 districts against. Since the declaration of the vote certain districts continued to operate overtime, and overtime was worked in the spinning and carding sections during that summer, and these efforts certainly greatly assisted in the production drive.

Cost-of-Living Agreement

Not the least of the problems brought about by the outbreak of war in 1939 was that of rising prices. The index figure of the cost-of-living, published by the Ministry of Labour, was 55 points in September, 1939 (over 1914) and by October that year it had risen to 65 points. Even before the war pressure was being exercised by our District Associations, in our General Council meetings, for increases in wages due to the increased activity in the industry. The war gave an impetus to this movement, and the matter was discussed by the Central Board of the Northern Counties Textile Trades Federation, and later by a special conference of all the textile unions. It was decided to claim an increase of 20 per cent in the wages of all textile operatives, and this claim was argued before a meeting with all the employers' representatives (both spinning and manufacturing) on 10th October, 1939. At an adjourned meeting it was agreed that the two sides of the industry—spinning and manufacturing—should proceed separately, and consequently the manufacturing section met on 19th October, 1939, and the following day, when an agreement was reached, providing for an advance in current rates of wages of 12½ per cent, 5 per cent of which would come into operation on 20th November, 1939 and the remaining 7½ per cent on 1st January, 1940.

An important part of this joint agreement was the provision for the first time in our industry for a sliding scale in wage movements, tied to the cost-of-living figure, when it was agreed that a basic figure of 65 per cent over 1914 should be used and taken as the wage rates prevailing in September 1939, any revision necessary under the arrangement to be made at quarterly intervals. This agreement was further interpreted by a subsequent agreement made on 16th January, 1940, when it was agreed that no revision in rates would be made where cost-of-living index figure had not moved by four points. If the figure had moved four points, up to and including seven points, basic rates to be increased by 2½ per cent and so on, up to 16 to 19 points, 10 per cent. Similar agreements were made with the Federation of Master Cotton Spinners' Associations governing the cost-of-living, and with the Waste Manufacturers. There was a slight variation between the spinning and the manufacturing agreements in detail, but the broad principle was the same.

The cost-of-living agreement was abrogated by the Cotton Spinners and Manufacturers' Association in December, 1946.

Minimum Wage

It will be recalled that efforts were made to secure the establishment of a minimum wage, so far back as 1923, but the employers had not shown any great desire to reach accommodation on this matter. The subject was constantly discussed by the General Council, and on many occasions was brought to the notice of the employers in joint meetings and conversations.

In 1937 the Central Committee was determined to press the question again, and in November 1937 a joint meeting with the two employers' associations was held to consider our claim for the establishment of a minimum wage. We had failed to convince the Conciliation Committee in November, 1936, when other improvements in the legalised List were obtained, but were still determined to pursue the matter, and to get the employers to make some change in their traditional outlook towards payment of a guaranteed wage.

Little or no progress was made, however, and the joint discussions dragged on through January and February, to March 1938, when a joint sub-committee was appointed to examine the position and try to hammer out the details of some sort of a scheme.

The Amalgamation enlisted the aid of the Manchester University Research Department to analyse the district returns on the Census of wages taken in 1936 and in 1937, and Mr. George Tomlinson, M.P., for Farnworth Division asked the Minister of Labour in December 1938 when he had completed his enquiries into Under-employment. The Minister replied that he was aware of the position in Lancashire, and he had looked into the matter, but was afraid that it was not possible to find any appropriate method of doing what Mr. Tomlinson had suggested, that is, to make changes in the provisions of the Unemployment Insurance Acts.

Meanwhile, the joint sub-committee had got to work, and some slight progress was apparent, but the employers' representatives got cold feet and decided to consult their constituent district associations. The result of this enquiry was that they felt that they could not continue the joint discussions, and the negotiations ended.

The procedure laid down by the joint rules was followed and joint meetings were held in December 1938, but no settlement was reached. The final joint meeting through the N.C. Textile Trades Federation was held in February 1939, but the meeting was one of formality to comply with the joint rules, and the matter was reported to Sir Charles Doughty, the chairman of the Conciliation Committee. Our claim was heard by the Committee on 5th May, 1939, and during the hearing it became evident that the Court favoured the principle of a Minimum Wage, but that difficulty existed in applying the principle. It was eventually found possible to reach a settlement upon the following terms:—

> "There shall be a fall-back wage of 66⅔ per cent of the individual weaver's earnings averaged over four full weeks' production; but the fall-back wage payable shall not exceed a maximum of 33s. nor be less than 25s. for a weaver normally running four looms."

In announcing the agreement the chairman referred to certain matters of detail which would have to be discussed jointly, and the representatives of the two sides then got together to hammer out details. These proceedings dragged out during the summer of 1939, when the outbreak of War supervened and hampered progress on this particular subject.

In point of fact, no further progress was made untl 1941, when an agreement was finally reached on 19th August, 1941, to take effect as from October, 1941. This Agreement was printed and issued in the form of a "yellow book" and as it was the first *general* agreement in our industry for the payment of a fall-back or minimum wage, the following details are given as a matter of historical interest.

1941 Minimum Wage Agreement

(1) The agreement applied to all weavers on non-automatic looms, but did not apply to automatic loom weavers nor to smallware loom weavers.

(2) The fall-back provisions applied to weavers normally running four-looms, or less than four-looms where the normal complement was less.

(3) For people running less than normal complement, or elderly persons not running a full complement, the fall-back wage to be in proportion.

(4) The agreement did not apply to weavers with less than twelve months' training, nor to "sick" weavers (i.e. temporary weavers).

(5) The amount of the fall-back wage was 66⅔ per cent of the individual weaver's gross normal weekly wages averaged over four full weeks, but subject to a maximum of 33s. and a minimum of 25s. (This was a basic figure, and was subject to the advances gained since September, 1939, i.e. 35 per cent.)

(6) The method of determining entitlement to the fall-back was rather complicated. The average wages over three consecutive weeks had to be taken, i.e., the week preceding, the week itself, and the following week.

(7) The foregoing method applied in the case of a weaver with a full set of running looms. Where any of the looms were stopped (except for normal "gaiting time") and the weaver was kept at work with less than the full normal complement, the fall-back provisions would apply to that particular week alone and there would be no three weeks' averaging.

(8) The employer had the right to lift warps and play off weavers as he deemed necessary.

(9) Separate provisions were made to cover the peculiarities in Quilt weaving and the Towel weaving sections.

The provisions of this Agreement for the payment of a Minimum Wage were a great step forward in our industrial conditions, but this Agreement tended to be overshadowed by what followed, when more comprehensive arrangements had to be made to cope with the conditions created by the "Essential Work Order".

The "Essential Work Orders", 1941 and 1942

The Central Committee were concerned with the form and text of what was known as the "Essential Work (General Provisions) Order, 1941. No. 302," because of its probable application to the cotton industry. Informal discussions took place between the Amalgamation and the Cotton Spinners & Manufacturers' Association, regarding the application of the Order in the manufacturing section. It was considered desirable because of its probable stabilising effect upon the labour position within the mills, as well as through the benefits that would accrue through the payment of a Guaranteed Wage provided for in the Order. Considerable time was spent in securing the operation of the Order in the manufacturing section, as the spinning section was the first to secure. Towards the end of September, 1941, however, the Order began to operate in the manufacturing section, and joint meetings were held to determine the conditions which should obtain so far as wages were concerned. Ultimately an agreement was reached between the Cotton Spinners & Manufacturers' Association and the Northern Counties Textile Trades Federation, dated 18th November, 1941, which operated actually before the Government applied the main General Provisions Order to our trade. The agreement of November, 1941 is very important, and is summarised as follows:-

Agreement under the Essential Work Order.

(1) The agreement provided for the payment of a guaranteed wage to cover under-employment or unemployment.

(2) In the case of weavers paid by a piece price list, an hourly rate per loom to be calculated for each weaver, to be ascertained by taking the individual average wage over the last four full weeks. The hourly rate to be paid for each "stopped" loom. (Note: This hourly rate did not apply to any running looms, where earnings were low, as these were covered by the new Minimum Wage Agreement).

(3) Normal "gaiting-time" not to be paid for.

(4) In the case of velvet and fustian weavers, the four week period to be eight-weeks.

(5) Provision was made for payments to "sick" weavers.

(6) Clauses were inserted to deal with overlookers, and other classes of workers in the manufacturing section.

(7) If work was not available in an operative's usual occupation and he or she was called upon to do other work, he would be paid the recognised rate for that work, or his own standard hourly rate, whichever was the higher.

Following the signing of this agreement approaches were made to the Government to bring the industry within the Essential Work Orders, and this was done in the manufacturing section by a separate Order known as the "Essential Work (Cotton Manufacturing Industry) Order, S.R. & O. 1942. No. 90."

Under the agreement summarised above there were a number of administrative difficulties involved, and joint meetings were necessary before an "Interpretation" agreement was signed on 15th April, 1942, defining the position of Transferred Weavers; defining exactly what constituted "gaiting-time"; Substitute Weavers; General or Partial Stoppages; cases of alleged Inferior Yarn; and the method of Booking stopped time. Later joint agreements defined the position created by Warp smashes and Shuttle smashes.

It will thus be seen that at long last we had secured for our members recognition of some compensatory payment to cover most eventualities concerned with broken production. Unemployment or under-employment was covered by the Essential Work Order Agreements of 1941 and 1942, whilst low earnings arising from running looms (which is neither unemployment, nor under-employment in the sense of stopped machinery) was covered by the Minimum Wage Agreement of 1941 contained in the "yellow book".

The "Starting-point" Wage Principle

In April, 1942 the Conciliation Committee had met to consider our application for an increase of 2d. per hour for all operatives, and had rejected the application; and similarly the spinning operatives had submitted a claim which ultimately was turned down by the National Arbitration Tribunal.

Considerable resentment was caused by these results, and arising from pressure from our District Associations the Central Committee submitted a recommendation to the General Council, on 19th August, 1942, that joint discussions should be undertaken with the object of examining the factors contributing to low earnings of many full-time weavers, winders, etc. The Central Committee's proposal was along the lines of utilising a basic, or "starting-point" wage of 9d. per hour for a weaver running a full complement of looms, plus 50 per cent of the piece price earnings, providing that where existing methods of payment yielded higher wages, no change be made. The same principle to be applied to other sections of our members.

Joint meetings followed, during September, October and November, 1942, but the employers rejected the proposals. The claim was therefore submitted to the Conciliation Committee on 18th December, 1942, when the case was argued very fully, and statistics were used to show the effect of the new proposal on earnings. The proposal was rather startling in its range, as a wage of 30s. per week would have been increased by 70 per cent, the percentage increase being reduced as the existing wage rose, until the figure of 72s. per week was reached, when there would be no increase.

During 1942 the employers had issued reports showing the results of two censuses of wages. In the first census (December, 1941) 5 per cent of the adult weavers earned under 35s. per week, and 78 per cent of weavers earned under 60s. per week. Only 22 per cent earned over £3. The second census of the employers (October, 1942) bore the full percentage additions at the time (35 per cent) and also reflected the operation of the new agreement under the Essential Work Orders. The census revealed that the average wage of adult weavers was 56s. 2d. per week, whilst 67 per cent of the adult weavers earned under 60s.

Flat-Rate Payment Principle and Minimum Wage for Running Looms Established.

The Conciliation Committee hearing did not produce a result along the lines of the application, but two new features were established as a result of the arbitration, i.e. (1) the establishment for the first time of a flat rate payment of 5s. per week for a weaver running a normal complement of looms; (2) the establishment of a minimum wage of 48s. for a weaver running the normal four-looms (41s. for a weaver not running a full complement) and a minimum wage of 55s. for a weaver running on the Six Looms System; (3) New Entrants and Young Persons not on a full complement of looms were to be paid on a graduated "wage for age" scale, varying from 20s. per week at 14 years, to 35s. at 18 years of age; (4) the holidays with Pay allocation of 2 per cent of wages paid by the firm was increased to 4 per cent of the gross wage bill.

This very important joint agreement was signed on 24th December, 1942, and operated from 4th January, 1943.

Guaranteed Wage Agreement, 1946

The joint agreements made under the Essential Work Orders during the war terminated, for the production of cotton and rayon cloths, on 15th May, 1946. Through the Northern Counties Textile Trades Federation, active steps were taken prior to May, 1946 to secure a new industrial agreement which would retain as many of the benefits of the old agreements as possible. There were many difficulties in the way, and lengthy discussions took place during March and April, 1946, when the negotiators worked hard to save as many of the benefits as possible. An agreement was finally reached on 12th April, 1946, by an agreement "to replace all agreements in connection with the Essential Work Order".

Although the new agreement provided for less than the old Essential Work Order gave, it was a substantial improvement on anything which had obtained before those Orders. The principle of a Guaranteed Wage was also agreed upon between the Amalgamation and the Federation of Master Cotton Spinners' Associations, on 1st November, 1946, covering our members employed in the spinning mills. As a result of more satisfactory terms being obtained on the spinning side on certain points, the Cotton Spinners & Manufacturers' Association agreed to an amended agreement on the manufacturing side, dated 30th December, 1946, and these Guaranteed Wage Agreements have continued to give satisfactory protection to our members in cases of unemployment or under-employment.

The Present Position of the Guaranteed Wage and Minimum Wage

It is felt that the foregoing historical statement on this subject may be somewhat confusing, and in order to clarify the position regarding the payment of the Guaranteed Wage and the Minimum Wage, the following is a simple summary of the way in which the various agreements now operate.

Guaranteed Wage

The Guaranteed Wage is payable to our members when totally unemployed or when partially employed (i.e., portion of looms or machinery stopped) under circumstances qualified in the Guaranteed Wage Agreements of April and December, 1946, made with The Cotton Spinners' and Manufacturers' Association. The main provisions of the Agreement are:—

(1) The agreement applies to workpeople employed in cotton manufacturing undertakings.

(2) The agreement only operates in respect of unemployment or under-employment (i.e. Stopped looms).

(3) Seven days' notice to terminate employment shall be given by either side (with certain specified exceptions).

(4) To be entitled to payment the worker shall be (*a*) capable of and available for work; (*b*) willing to perform reasonable alternative work; (*c*) if called upon to perform work other than the worker's usual occupation, the recognised rate for such work, or the gross normal wage for his usual occupation shall be paid, which is higher.

(5) Payment of the Guaranteed Wage to be made for all under-employment or unemployment, with certain exceptions (specified in a number of sub-clauses) such as strikes, stoppages due to improving working conditions; temporary stoppage of a mill or process for a week to adjust output to trade circumstances; stoppage due to waiting-time for normal gaiting-time. Provision is also made as to how payment shall be paid for machinery breakdowns, fuel shortage, &c. The Guaranteed Wage is not payable for recognised holidays, nor for mechanical breakdown in one loom (for the first hour).

(6) The Guaranteed Wage shall consist of 75 per cent of the individual weaver's net normal piece rate earnings, averaged over the previous four full weeks,

plus the full flat rate payment, similar provisions for other workers than weavers.

(7) The agreement clearly defines the procedure governing Transfer of Weavers, Weavers on the More than Six-Looms System, Efficiency Bonus System, and so on.

Minimum Wage

On the other hand the Minimum Wage is payable to our members when employed upon their machinery but the piece rate earnings fall below a given figure. In other words, the Minimum Wage is payable on Running Looms, and the Guaranteed Wage is payable for Stopped Looms.

The Minimum Wage Agreement of 24th December, 1942 (as amended in succeeding agreements) provided that weavers should be paid the usual piece price rates, or the following minimum rates, whichever were the higher:—

(1) On the Ordinary System (normally four-looms per weaver) a minimum wage of 74s. 2d. (1950 figure). (In 1968 this figure is 151s. 6d).
(2) On the Ordinary System, for a weaver running less than a full complement, on account of age, disability or other personal reasons, the minimum wage was 61s. per week (in 1950). In 1968 this figure became 125s. 3d.
(3) In the case of the More than Six-Looms System the basic figure of 51s. 6d. (per clause 2(*a*) of the 1937 legalised Uniform List) was 102s. 8d. in 1950. In 1968 this figure became 199s. 11d.
(4) Where the hours worked by the weaver were less than 48 (in 1942) in any week the minimum rates payable should be in proportion.

Demarcation of Membership with other Unions

From time to time agreements have been reached with other Unions—both textile and non-textile—with the object of defining clearly the class of members which should properly be organised and catered for by each. In 1937 an agreement was reached with the Amalgamated Textile Warehousemen that they should be responsible for organising such operatives as clothlookers, bundlers and hookers, cloth pickers, cloth bookers, cloth and weft carriers, cloth trimmers, and hemmers, folders, packers, etc., as well as winding masters, and labourers in winding and taping rooms. On the other hand the Amalgamated Weavers' Association were recognised as the appropriate union for all classes of weavers, winders, warpers, as well as spare weavers and helper-weavers, hopper and battery fillers, loom sweepers and oilers.

The failure of our District Associations in the past to organise certain types of operatives in the doubling section had created a number of problems which had caused trouble. The Stockport Yarn Doublers' Association were allowed to link up with the National Union of General and Municipal Workers, and other Yarn Doublers were organised by the Women Workers' Trade Union, in the Manchester area, and these ultimately affiliated with the General and Municipal Workers. A number of isolated Doubling firms in areas where we were comparatively strong were organised by our own District Associations, and this diversion of interests created rivalry for membership. In 1928 serious efforts were made to end the internecine struggle between our District Associations and the General and Municipal Workers, but without success. Arising out of incidents which occurred at Rochdale in 1940 a joint committee was established with the object of reconciling the varying interests involved, and an agreement was ultimately reached, dated 23rd December, 1940, whereby definite lines of demarcation were laid down, and the mills which the Amalgamated Weavers' Association and the National Union of General and Municipal Workers were entitled to organise were specified, and reciprocal arrangements made for transfers from one union to the other. The agreement has worked well, in difficult circumstances, and has made for harmony between two important working-class organisations.

Similarly, a mutual agreement was signed on 31st July, 1943, between the Amalgamation and the General Union of Lancashire and Yorkshire Warp Dressers' Associations, whereby the Amalgamation had the right to retain in membership those operatives working as Chain Beamers who were in membership at the date of the agreement. After July 1943 any members of the Amalgamation changing their occupations to Chain Beaming, Dry Taping or Warp Dressing would be transferred to the Warp Dressers' General Union, and if those operatives should change back again to weaving, winding, reeling or beaming, they would be re-transferred to the Amalgamation. The General Union of Warp Dressers was recognised as the appropriate Trade Union for organising Chain Beamers, Dry Tapers or Warp Dressers, with the exception mentioned, and for negotiating wages and conditions for all such operatives.

At a much later date, difficulties arose in the Narrow Fabrics industry, due to the incursion of the Amalgamated Society of Textile Workers and Kindred Trades, of Leek, in Staffordshire, and on 28th April, 1948, an agreement was made between the Amalgamation and that Union, whereby mutual discussions would take place before the Leek Union undertook organising activities at certain specified mills.

In 1951 the Leek Society joined the Amalgamation as a separate District Association, and remained with the Amalgamation until 1956, its Secretary, Mr. H. Lisle, serving as a member of the Central Committee during the period of affiliation.

Concentration of the Industry During the War

In April, 1940 an Order was introduced, with the specific object of limiting the amount of woven textiles (cotton, rayon, and linen) reaching the home market. Wholesale dealers in these goods had to register with the Board of Trade; and manufacturers had to make a return specifying their name and place of business. The supply of controlled goods for the home market was restricted for the period of April to September, 1940, to 75 per cent of the yardage supplied during a similar period in 1939.

The Board of Trade made a further order in June, 1940 which in effect gave buyers or sellers of cotton and rayon cloths the right to cancel their contracts.

The immediate effect of these Orders was extremely serious, and many cancellations of orders took place. Deputations from the trade waited upon the President of the Board of Trade asking for the withdrawal of the Order, but without securing satisfaction.

Meanwhile, in view of the need to conserve raw material as much as possible, because of the growing difficulties of finding shipping space, and to keep available shipping facilities for exports, the Government further reduced the amount of cotton and rayon goods that could be made available for the home market so that by September, 1941, only 20 per cent of 1939 supplies of cotton, linen and silk goods could be available for the home market, and 40 per cent of rayon goods.

The situation was further complicated by the imposition of a Purchase Tax upon home market textiles in October, 1940, with the object of (*a*) increasing revenue; (*b*) limiting consumption of goods in the home market, and both these objects had serious repercussions upon the productivity and employment in our industry.

In January, 1941 further intimations were made by the Cotton Controller (an officer who had been appointed by the Government) that the consumption of raw materials had to be restricted, due to shipping difficulties, air-raids on our seaports, and the abnormal consumption of raw cotton in producing cloths needed by the armed forces. There was also the additional problem of finding man-power (and woman-power) to staff the new armament and shell-filling factories being built all over the country.

It was finally decided to be in the best interests of the trade that a system should be adopted by which a certain amount of machinery within each mill would be definitely stopped, and to concentrate necessary production on the remaining machinery and operatives. In this system it was contemplated that the employment of 60 per cent of the machinery running during November–December, 1940 would be the basis, and that under no circumstances would the system lend itself to under-employment of workpeople or the establishment of a rota system. Details of this proposal were placed before Sir Percy Ashley (The Cotton Controller) and the Ministers of Departments involved, but this method did not meet with the approval of the Government Production Defence Committee, and on 4th March, 1941 a statement was made in the House of Commons by the President of the Board of Trade (Captain Oliver Lyttelton) that the aim of the Government's economic policy in wartime was to facilitate the fullest possible transfer of resources to war production. This demanded the severe cutting down of civil consumption, the release of labour, materials and factory space for more essential purposes. Amongst the industries affected by this pronouncement were Textiles, Boot and Shoe, Pottery, Textiles being by far the largest.

This pronouncement of Government policy caused grave concern inside our General Council, and the Cotton Board itself had kept in close touch with the industry. The Chairman (Sir Raymond Streat) convened a meeting of the producing sections on 5th March, 1941, along with the Cotton Controller and the Divisional Controller of the Ministry of Labour and National Service, when a memorandum was adopted embodying the policy of the industry for submission to the respective Ministers concerned. This policy was one of concentrating the production of yarns and cloths in fewer mills, and, in order to restore confidence amongst all sections, to co-ordinate future activity of the industry and transfer labour to the munitions industries with a minimum of individual hardship. The mills which were kept in production had to make some contribution to the "care and maintenance" of the closed mills. The mills kept running would be protected to the extent that raw material would be available for them, and their operatives would not be allowed to leave their employment, and the employer would not be allowed to discharge an operative (except for grave dereliction of duty).

It will thus be apparent that conditions were developed which were safeguarded and governed by the "Essential Work Orders" referred to elsewhere in this survey.

In view of the transfers of labour which were taking place under this concentration scheme, temporary agreements were made with other Unions, such as the National Union of General and Municipal Workers, the Amalgamated Engineering Union, and so on, for recognition of cards, or to govern the re-transference of membership at the end of hostilities.

It will be obvious that during these changing conditions within industry there was large-scale interference with trade practices and trade union restrictions. On 3rd February, 1942, the Minister of Labour introduced in the House of Commons a Bill which was designed to honour the pledge that had been made by the Government to restore pre-war trade practices, at the end of the war. The Bill became an Act of Parliament on 26th February, 1942, and was the result of consultation with the representatives of the British Employers' Federation and the Trades Union Congress.

"Concentration" closed several hundred cotton mills of one kind and another. The closed premises were used for storing foodstuffs, raw materials and war stores, or else were converted into war factories. By the end of 1941 there were about 210,000 operatives in the spinning, doubling and weaving industry, as against 360,000 in 1937, and by the end of 1944 the number had contracted by a further 20,000 or so. The proportions of females, and of persons of both sexes in the higher age groups, moreover, rose steadily through the period, and the output reflected these trends. As most of the "concentration" had occurred before the Essential Work Orders were applied, when many younger operatives had gone to war industries or had joined the Forces, by the time the E.W.O.s had taken effect in 1942 the concentrated industry was short of workers and output fell consistently short of the targets, which tended to increase as new essential war demands expanded with the growth of the fighting forces and the development of new techniques in attack and defence.

Overtime working was adopted in several of the sections during the summer months in 1942, 1943 and again in 1944, but according to one authority, this proved to be more of a gesture of willingness on the part of the operatives to "do their bit" than a means of raising total output. The high average age of the workers, the black-out, the part-time duties in Civil Defence, fire-watching, and the Home Guard, and the difficulty of combining mill-work with queueing for food and with housekeeping, when every commodity was in short supply, restricted the effect which the longer working hours could have on production.

From 1941 onwards, therefore, the task of meeting the demand for cotton goods, carefully pruned at all stages though it was, became more and more that of getting a quart out of a pint pot. The demand was not only for overalls, uniform linings, shirts, underwear, socks, haversacks, kit-bags, webbing, etc., for the individual fighting man, but also for tyre-fabric, insulating tape, barrage balloon fabric, anti-gas clothing, window-replacement fabric, anti-shatter cloth, powder bags, bandages, life-saving suits, tents, camouflage cloth, air-crew dinghies, parachute harness, plastics, sand-fly netting, etc., as well as civilian requirements at home and abroad, such as apparel, household textiles, furnishings, food-bags, typewriter ribbons, tracing cloth, filter cloth, mechanical cloths, boot and shoe linings and laces, black-out curtains, leathercloth, nursery squares, dusters, and so on. A big step was the production of the "Ventile" fabrics, which excluded cold and damp, but whose pores nevertheless "breathed" so that they were self-ventilating.

On the side of production, a new system was introduced in August, 1941, when preference directions were superseded by a comprehensive scheme of licences for the delivery of yarn. Licences were issued only in respect of approved orders, and bore symbols indicating the purpose to which the yarn was to be put when delivered. Each individual order for goods, where cotton yarns were used, had to be sponsored by some competent authority and approved by the Cotton Control before it could be executed. The production of towels, sheets, and other household textiles was severely restricted, both in quantity and in range and quality.

Austerity regulations were introduced during 1942, in the interests of economy in the use of material and labour, limiting the amount of labour, the number of buttons, and the degree of ornamentation to be employed in the making-up of particular garments.

Rationing of cloth and clothing (and footwear) was introduced on June 1st, 1941, and the flow of goods to the shops was regulated to meet the rationed demands, and to ensure the full use of "utility" goods.

Gradually the Ministry of Supply, operating through the Cotton Controller and his staff, had assumed full responsibility for the importation and distribution of the industry's requirements of raw cotton, a position which was reached by slow stages. For a period after March, 1941 all cotton coming into the country was requisitioned and distributed by a company, Cotton Importers and Distributors Ltd., set up by the Liverpool and Manchester Cotton Associations. This method encountered grave difficulties, and the company ceased to operate after March, 1942, after which date the Control itself undertook the importation, storage, and allocation of all cotton. From that time Lend-Lease shipments came to account for all imports of American cotton. East Indian was bought by the negotiation of offers from Indian shippers through merchant houses, whilst Egyptian imports consisted mainly of purchases by the Buying Commissions in that country at first.

In 1941 the Cotton Control fixed raw cotton prices, and spinners were insulated against losses through changes in the prices. Waste yarns came under Control from March, 1942, and many forms of grey cloth were controlled from April, 1942. Control ultimately became extended to cover a very wide range of cloths.

In the early stages of the war the industry's export trade was virtually unregulated, but when the Cotton Board was separated from the Cotton Control in the early summer of 1940, it immediately organised export promotion measures. Spinners' prices were manipulated to encourage the export trade; *ad hoc* voluntary associations were formed to develop export trade with particular markets, and a new company, British Overseas Cottons Ltd., was formed to organise the production of cloth in special cases where neither independent firms nor syndicates could cope with the difficulties of providing it in quantities and at prices considered to be necessary.

Space does not permit the giving of more details of these war-time measures, but the foregoing survey indicates the careful steps which were taken to ensure that what was allowed of the industry to remain running and producing was utilised to the best possible ends, and that unnecessary fluctuations in prices were prevented by the rigid systems of control.

The Board of Trade scheme for clothes rationing during the war caused a good deal of uneasiness amongst industrial workers. It was felt, particularly by our women workers, that to surrender clothing coupons for working clothes was an unfair imposition as against the allocation of the same number of coupons to those who did not earn their livelihood in the mills.

The Central Committee made representations to the Board of Trade and the Superintending Inspector of Factories, and the Cotton Spinners and Manufacturers' Association also rendered useful assistance in the prosecution of the subject. We endeavoured to secure the provision of aprons, overalls, boiler suits, and so on, coupon free, but we did not succeed in this, although concessions were granted, and ultimately the scheme for granting "Industrial Ten" coupons was instituted, and was of great help to our members.

Restoration of Pre-War Trade Practices Act, 1942

On 26th February, 1942, an Act of Parliament was passed, at the instigation of the Minister of Labour, designed to honour the pledge that had been made by the Government, to restore pre-war trade practices at the end of the war. The turning of industry from that of peace to war-time activity involved tremendous changes. Labour had been diverted into many channels, and the necessity for rapid adjustment in the character and methods of production had involved complete revision of piece price systems and alterations in working hours. The Act provided that after a period of eighteen months from a specified date, pre-war practices had to be restored, and was of great assistance at the conclusion of hostilities in helping to stabilise trade practices and agreements in many industries.

CHAPTER XX

Post-War Problems: 1945 onwards

The Cotton Board

Running through the references in this historical survey to the inter-war years will be noticed constant references to the decline in trade and consequent unemployment. This phase in cotton's history is referred to in some detail in the Working Party Report which was issued in 1946, where, in the earlier chapters, a keen review is made of the developments which have taken place in the trade. The Report stated that the special significance to Lancashire of the recession which began in 1920 was not appreciated at the time, mainly due to the general fall in commodity prices and world purchasing power; but these effects were over by 1924, and a phase of contraction was entered which was greatly intensified after 1930, and continued until the 1939 World War. Lancashire had to face its own special difficulties caused by the development of textile industries in other countries, made still greater by the worst world economic crisis ever known. Exports to India dropped from 3,000 million yards to 300 million yards between 1913 and 1938, and we were driven out of other markets by a fierce competitive onslaught from Japan. But it was not so generally recognised that other countries too, adopted policies which had damaging effects on Lancashire on a smaller but still very substantial scale. For example, as a result of a tremendous tariff increase British exports of piece goods to America fell from 163 million sq. yds. in 1924 to 11 million in 1931. Brazil's tariff policy killed our trade. Roughly speaking, two-thirds of Lancashire's export losses were due to development by her former customers of their own industries, and one-third was captured by Japan. Right up to 1939 the industry was fighting a rearguard action, and when the second World War came the industry was still unbalanced, unstable, and unprofitable.

This background of economic depression and frustration, allied with the loss of capital resources and human suffering, led the industry, on the initiative of the Joint Committee of Cotton Trade Organisations, to promote the Cotton Industry (Re-organisation) Bill in 1939. The provisions of the Bill were considerably altered during the discussions in the House of Commons. The Bill itself represented the greatest common measure of approval amongst the representatives of the industry, for they were now realising that a sound position could not be attained unless the producers were protected against uneconomic internal competition and weak selling. The Act which emerged accordingly provided machinery for establishing compulsory minimum prices. On the insistence of the Board of

Trade a ballot vote of the producing sections was taken, and 65 per cent of the firms voted in favour of the legislation.

Before it was possible to implement this legislation War broke out in September, 1939, and the whole course of events was suddenly changed, and it was realised that the Act could not be put into effect because price controls had to be exercised directly by the Government as part of the war measures in a national economy. One highly important point must be mentioned in connection with the 1939 Act. In the movement which led to it, the industry recognised that in the condition to which it was then reduced it could not secure its own regeneration by the normal methods of free competitive enterprise, and it was forced to ask Parliament to create statutory powers for ensuring orderly competition.

Though the Act was placed in cold storage the idea of a Cotton Board had taken root, and one was immediately set up a few days after the opening of hostilities in 1939. It was at first purely an advisory body to the Government, without any powers at all. Subsequently, in March, 1940, it was established as a statutory body by the Cotton Industry Act, 1940, for the duration of the war.

The new Cotton Board was financed by a levy on raw cotton purchased by the spinners. Its object was to encourage the consumption and export of the products of the industry, to promote technical and economic research, and generally to further the interests of the industry. The Board was composed of three full-time officers, a Chairman and two executive members, and nine other members, all of whom were appointed by the President of the Board of Trade. The nine part-time members represented the raw cotton market, spinning, weaving, finishing, and merchanting sections, and included three trade union representatives, one each from the spinning, weaving, and finishing sections. The General Secretary of the Amalgamation, Andrew Naesmith, served as a member of the Cotton Board from its inception.

Whilst they were representative of their respective sections the members served as independent individuals, arriving at decisions entirely on their own responsibility. They were entitled to maintain the fullest contact with and to keep themselves fully acquainted with the views of their sectional organisations, but they were not expected to report back for instructions. It was considered that it would have been disastrous in the interests of leadership and decision.

The Cotton Board as thus constituted actually continued in existence until May, 1948, when its activities were given a fresh lease of life by virtue of further legislation.

As the war developed the place taken by the Cotton Board within the structure of the industry became very important indeed, and the Board of Trade imposed greater responsibilities upon the Board, in the direction of control of imports, the administration of "care and maintenance schemes" necessary due to the "concentration" of the industry, and the Board generally became a sort of Headquarters of the industry, where it worked in consultation and collaboration with the various sections and interests in the industry. The Board established a Recruiting and Training Department, which not only focussed attention on the acute shortage of labour, has linked up many educational activities. The Board also established a Colour, Design and Style Centre, to stimulate the imagination and encourage the determination to achieve the highest standards of production. The Board gave support to the industry's technical research station, the Shirley Institute (run by the British Cotton Industry Research Association, and upon the Council of which Association the Amalgamation is represented).

In 1967 the character and name of the Cotton Board was changed. The scope was widened from being a Board which dealt exclusively with cotton matters to one which incorporated man-made fibres. The name was changed at the same time to THE TEXTILE COUNCIL.

The Cotton Industry "Working Party" Report

The General Election in July, 1945 gave the Labour Party power to form a Government, and the Government took steps to inform the country of its policy. In certain industries which were specified, policies based on Nationalisation would be followed, but the majority of industries would still be left in the hands of private enterprise. It was well-known that many of our major industries had fallen behind in mechanical development and productive efficiency, and the opportunity was taken to examine certain industries, with a view to making constructive proposals for their competitive efficiency.

One of the first industries to be so recognised was the Cotton Industry, and the President of the Board of Trade established a "Working Party" representative of employers, operatives, and consumer interests, with an Independent Chairman (Sir George Schuster). The terms of reference were "to examine and enquire into the various schemes and suggestions put forward for improvements of organisation, production, and distribution, methods and processes in the industry, and to report as to the steps which should be taken in the national interest to strengthen the industry and render it more stable and more capable of meeting competition in the home and foreign markets." The Working Party began its work in November, 1945, and a very large volume of evidence was received and sifted.

The Schuster Working Party Report was issued early in 1946, which was a most comprehensive and penetrating analysis of our industry yet made. Its recommendations very wide in their scope, would, if adopted, have a profound effect upon the cotton textile industry. The trade union representatives on the Working Party (including the then General Secretary, A. Naesmith) issued a Memorandum in reply to a Memorandum of Dissent made by the six employers representatives.

Following the publication of the Working Party Report, a joint meeting of representatives of all sections of the cotton industry was held in Albert Hall, Manchester, on 5th June, 1946, under the chairmanship of Sir Raymond Streat, the Chairman of the Cotton Board. Sir Raymond urged a co-operative effort to resolve the industry's problems, in the light of the Schuster Report, and he made certain recommendations for the industry to consider.

The Legislative Council of the United Textile Factory Workers' Association appointed a sub-committee to examine the Working Party Report, and this sub-committee subsequently made recommendations to the Legislative Council, which were accepted. On 26th August, 1946, the Legislative Council met a delegation of Labour Members of Parliament, representing Lancashire and Yorkshire constituencies, for an exchange of views on the Working Party Report. Useful discussions ensued on the Shift System, More Looms System, Labour Supply, Re-equipment, Replacement of Mules by Rings, Vertical Integration, and Trade Union Structure.

On 3rd December, 1946, Sir Stafford Cripps (President of the Board of Trade) addressed a meeting of the main organisations (employers and trade union), when he reviewed at length the problems confronting the industry, and put before the meeting the Government's policy of financial assistance, as a special case, to the cotton industry. The Government were prepared to make a grant of 25 per cent towards the cost of mechanical re-equipment of the spinning mills provided the re-equipment was carried out within a fixed period, on certain conditions, such as, the grouping of mills into manoeuvreable units of not less than 500,000 spindles each; the introduction of two-shift working as and when the mills were progressively modernised; the acceptance and encouragement of new methods of labour deployment and utilisation by both sides.

The Stafford Cripps scheme was considered by a special Delegate Conference of the U.T.F.W.A., on 8th February, 1947, when the following recommendation by the Legislative Council was submitted.

"The Legislative Council agree to co-operate wholeheartedly in the implementation of the Scheme put forward by Sir Stafford Cripps, President of the Board of Trade, on the condition that Grouping of Mills and Re-equipment and Modernisation precede shift-working, and that redeployment of labour on old machinery is not allowed to become a substitute for re-equipment."

The various Amalgamations accepted this recommendation, but only by narrow majorities in some instances, and it was decided to ask Sir Stafford Cripps to address a meeting of Amalgamation and District Executive Committees, which he did, in Bolton, on 22nd February, 1947, when Sir Stafford answered a number of questions, chiefly on the shift-working proposals.

At a further Conference on 22nd March, 1947, the Legislative Council recommendation was accepted by 99 votes to 51, and the result conveyed to Sir Stafford Cripps. This subject is also dealt with later.

Winders, Beamers, Doublers and Other Preparatory Workers

Almost from the inception of the present Amalgamation, in 1884, the operatives employed in the winding and beaming departments have been organised in membership with the Amalgamation. Reelers were admitted by General Council resolution in 1887, but in that year the General Council rejected an application for membership by the Stockport Yarn Doublers' Association. It was not until much later that Doublers were taken into membership.

Efforts were made by the Central Committee so far back as 1896 to formulate and negotiate a Uniform List for Ring Winding, but there was no success, and the General Council decided in 1899 to make further efforts to obtain a Uniform List for Winding and Beaming, but no progress was made. Winders were paid by individual mill lists, and that position has persisted until the present time, so far as the spinning mills are concerned. In the weaving mills efforts were made to secure a District List for Cop Winding, and the 1918 edition of the Uniform List for Weaving Prices contains a copy of the Blackburn and District Price List for Winding Mule Yarns. This List was later adapted and formed the "Uniform List of Prices for Mule Cop Winding," which was adopted in June, 1921, and is still observed in mills covered by the Cotton Spinners' and Manufacturers' Association, with appropriate additions provided by later general wage increase agreements.

In 1943 a Minimum Wage Agreement for fully competent Winders in the Manufacturing section was negotiated, which at that time provided for a minimum wage of 10½d. per hour (in 1968 this figure became 42.29 pence per hour, or 141s. per week). A "wage for age" scale was also negotiated in 1943, to cover new entrants and young persons.

In Beaming, or Warping, there has always been individual mill lists, except that in the manufacturing section the Burnley Beaming List has been in operation for a very long time, the latest copy of which was printed in the 1924 edition of the Uniform List of Weaving Prices. In 1943 a Minimum Wage was negotiated for Beamers in the manufacturing section, being at the rate of 1s. per hour (in 1968 the figure became 45.34 pence per hour, or 151s. 2d. per week).

In the spinning section of the trade many efforts have been made to secure some uniformity in wage rates for winders, reelers, and beamers, but without success, and the most that has been attained is a form of minimum wage and average wage agreement. The first of these agreements was made on 2nd June, 1919, when a temporary agreement was made, to cover all classes of winding, for an average standard wage on piecework of 21s. per week (plus 110 per cent. general wage advance then in operation). This wage was for a 55½-hour week, and when working hours were reduced to 48 per week later in 1919 it meant that the average wage basis became 18s. 2d. for a 48-hour week, plus 140 per cent. The agreement provided that in arriving at the average wage the lowest one-fourth of the wage earners should be eliminated from the calculation, to cover learners and inefficients. This method of elimination of a portion of the earnings to ascertain the average has been in operation ever since, although the proportion has been altered from time to time and is now one-tenth. The original agreement contained a clause exempting the firms in the area covered by the Bolton Employers' Association.

This temporary agreement of 1919, made with the Federation of Master Cotton Spinners' Associations, continued in operation until 1926, when the agreement was reviewed, amended, and made permanent. This winding agreement was again reviewed, in December, 1939, when the average wage figure of 35s. 6d. per week was provided for, and reelers were brought within the agreement, at a similar figure. Provision was also made for an average wage for beamers, of not less than 39s. on one beam and for 45s. for 1½ beams. This agreement also fixed day wage rates for all three classes of operatives.

This amended agreement of 1939 continued to operate until 1944, when a dispute with the Federation of Master Spinners was referred to the Conciliation Committee, and Sir Charles Doughty, K.C., the chairman, made an Award, which fixed various rates for winders, reelers, beamers, and crossballers, which have operated ever since, with suitable amendments to cover the general wage increases in the trade. This 1944 Award fixed three different wage rates for winding and reeling operatives, i.e., the average wage, the minimum wage, and the day wage; and for beamers and crossballers the Award fixed average wage rates and day wage rates. A "wage for age" scale for learners was also included in the Award. In the case of Winders and Reelers the average wage was ascertained after eliminating one-tenth of the lowest wage earners, and the minimum wage was applicable to the remaining nine-tenths.

For reference purposes a full statistical survey of the progress made in improving wage levels in the winding and beaming departments is given in the Appendix.

The Sweeping and Cleaning of Looms

Although the inception of the More Looms System arrangements had been made for the provision of ancillary labour to perform what could be termed the unskilled jobs associated with weaving, such ancillary labour to be provided without deduction from the weavers' wages, when the later position developed after the 1932 strike and the establishment of a legalised Uniform List, the provision of this ancillary labour became an accepted and universal practice. Under the legalised Uniform List, however, the employers were entitled to make deductions from the weavers' wages in the case of weavers not engaged on the More Looms System, varying from a 2½ per cent deduction for sweeping and cleaning, to 4 per cent where oiling, cloth and weft carrying was also performed by other labour, whilst in the case of weavers employed on the Six-Looms System, a deduction of 1 per cent. was permitted where the cloth and weft was carried for them.

These deductions had never been accepted with good grace by the weavers, and it has always been felt that the weaver's job was to weave, and that the ancillary jobs surrounding the weaving of cloth could better be done by ancillary labour. In point of fact so long ago as April, 1925 the subject was discussed at a joint meeting between the Amalgamation and the two Employers' Associations at the time when the "Weavers' Charter" was submitted to them, clause 3 of which read: "that weavers should be relieved of all sweeping, cleaning, oiling, cut carrying, etc."

On 16th March, 1940, on a Notice of Motion by Rishton district, a resolution was passed, that representations should be made to the Employers' Association to make the provision of this ancillary labour a charge upon the employer, and that the permitted deductions from weavers' wages should be abolished.

The objections to deductions had been particularly keenly felt in the waste weaving trade, for reasons which will be fairly obvious, and joint meetings had been held in 1938, but had proved abortive. In 1943, as a result of a series of incidents in the Bacup and Haslingden districts, further efforts were made to resolve this vexed question, and joint meetings were held with the Waste Manufacturers' Association. The meetings were held in an atmosphere of stress, due to action which the operatives at certain mills were contemplating taking.

As a result of this further effort, an agreement was reached and signed on 18th October, 1943, whereby the employers in the Waste weaving trade would provide Loom Sweepers to sweep and clean the looms free from any deduction from weavers' wages, although the weavers would continue to clean the boxes and oil certain parts of their own looms. Owing to difficulties in labour supply the weavers would continue to sweep their own looms until firms could obtain the necessary ancillary labour.

For the first time in the history of our industry, therefore, so far as weavers are concerned, it was established that sweeping and cleaning looms was work that should be done by other labour, at any rate as regards the Waste weaving industry. Meantime, the Central Committee continued to press the subject with the Cotton Spinners and Manufacturers' Association so far as the general weaving industry was concerned, and that Association appointed a sub-committee to consider the matter, along with cognate matters relating to the physical conditions of the mills and the welfare of the operatives.

The matter was again discussed in the General Council in September, 1944, on a resolution from Burnley district, and discontent developed in the main section of the weaving industry due to the lack of progress. On 8th June, 1945, a joint meeting was held to discuss a dispute which had arisen at a Blackburn mill, due to the action of the firm in making deductions for sweeping and cleaning when certain looms had not, in fact, been swept due to the absence of a number of sweepers. Further joint meetings were held on this case, without reaching agreement on principle, although accommodation was found, without prejudice, by the firm refunding to the weavers concerned a sum of money covering a two-weeks' period.

A further discussion at the General Council Meeting in October, 1945, led to a joint meeting with the employers on the subject, but they replied in writing that it was almost impossible to obtain adequate supplies of labour for the ancillary work, but they were prepared to discuss the matter when an adequate supply was available. On the other hand the Amalgamation representatives said that labour could be secured if the wage and conditions were made attractive enough. Demobilisation was taking place and more labour was becoming available for industry. No progress was made, however, but the employers subsequently sent a letter stating that they were prepared to advise their members to introduce loom sweepers and cleaners as and when suitable ancillary labour became available, but on the understanding that the prescribed deductions would continue to be made from weavers' wages until there was a general revision of the weavers' wage structure.

The Central Committee considered this reply to be most unsatisfactory, and informed the employers that the weavers were not going to settle down to the pre-war practice on this matter, as there were strong feelings that these ancillary tasks should be taken away from them.

This question remained in the realm of joint discussion until 1950, when the matter was again raised in joint meeting but no agreement could be reached. It was finally decided to submit our claim for the abolition of deductions for sweeping &c., to the Conciliation Committee, and the hearing took place on 17th

August, 1950, before Lord Terrington, C.B.E., with two Assessors. Lord Terrington was asked to give his Award, which he did a few days later, which was to the effect that our claim succeeded in principle, but Lord Terrington appreciated that his decision might affect certain clauses in the Uniform List, so that he remitted the question to the parties, for settlement by negotiation what other amendments, if necessary, were desirable in the Uniform List, as a result of his decision.

The subject therefore went back to joint meetings for discussion of details, but it is gratifying to record that at long last the claim had been met, that the weaver should be permitted to spend the whole of his or her time attending to the job of cloth production, and that the unskilled work of sweeping, cleaning, and oiling should be performed by other labour, paid for by the employer.

Combined Fustian and Velvet Weaving List

During 1945 serious efforts were made to secure a uniform list for the weaving of Fustian and Velvet Cloths, to take the place of the two separate lists which had existed for a long number of years. Success was achieved on 16th April, 1945, when a tentative agreement was reached, which would operate on a basis which was different from the methods in use in either of the previous lists. A "standard hank rate" figure was fixed for each inch of yarn width (from 30 up to 112 inches) and percentages were to be added or deducted for weft lengths, lost picks, shaft work, stripes and checks, jacquards, spun rayon yarns, etc., large cops, high pick and heavy cloth. The new uniform list would provide in the main for higher earnings for many of the weavers and it was felt by both sides that efforts should be made to secure legalisation of the list. Under the Cotton Manufacturing Industry (Temporary Provisions) Act, 1934, legalisation of a weaving list could only be obtained by joint action through the Amalgamation and the Cotton Spinners and Manufacturers' Association, and it was decided to submit the new draft uniform list to them for their consideration and endorsement. It soon became apparent, however, that there was strong opposition to the proposals, from manufacturers in certain districts not covered by the British Fustian Manufacturers' Association or the Velvet Manufacturers' Association, and the matter was not resolved until May, 1947, when, by agreement with the Cotton Spinners and Manufacturers, certain firms in the Preston and Heywood districts were exempted from the provisions of the new uniform list for fustians and velvets. A Burnley firm was later added to the list of exempted firms.

The Five-Day Working Week (40-hour week)

During 1946 further pressure was placed upon the cotton employers, in the struggle to achieve a 40-hour working week, and in August, 1946, the United Textile Factory Workers' Association made a definite application to the two employers' organisations for a 40-hour week, to be achieved by stages, the first stage to be the early introduction of a five-day working week of 43¾ hours, with *pro rata* increases in day wage and piece rates. The application was discussed in joint meetings held during the following months, and agreement was finally reached on 4th November, 1946, to reduce the working hours from 48 per week to 45 hours per week, nine hours per day on a five-day week. The agreement also provided for an increase in day and piece rates by 6½ per cent to compensate for loss in earnings. The allocation of the nine hours per day presented some difficulty, and a degree of flexibility was permitted to accommodate local desires. This new agreement meant that the total number of hours per year for holidays was altered from 117 to 110, which was equivalent to twelve working days of nine hours each, plus two hours to be allocated by local agreement. An appendix to the agreement was made with the Northern Counties Textile Trades Federation, which urged the workpeople to observe the recognised times for starting and finishing on each day, besides urging the importance of avoiding unnecessary absenteeism. The appendix also stressed the vital importance of maximum productive output in the national interest.

The whole question of Working Hours was constantly under review in the ensuing years and in 1961 joint discussions led to an agreement to reduce working hours for single shift working to 42½ per week, with a compensatory increase in wage rates. The total paid Holidays were to be equivalent to 16 working days per year.

In 1963 the subject of Working Hours became linked with efforts to improve wages, holidays with pay, and compensation for Redundancy. Meetings were held with employers during December, 1963 and early 1964 with a view to securing a comprehensive joint agreement to cover a period of three years.

In June, 1964 agreement was finally reached providing for such a comprehensive three year arrangement covering wage increases of 4 per cent per year for the three years; an extra day's holiday per year (making three extra days over the three years) with progressive increases in Holiday Pay Credits.

On the subject of Working Hours it was agreed that the working week of 42½ hours (single shifts) be progressively reduced to 42 per week in January, 1965, to 41½ hours in January, 1966, and to 41 hours in January, 1967. If, during that period, a 40-hour week were to become generally applicable throughout British industry, the whole question would be reviewed.

Towards the end of 1966, however, Government White Papers on Incomes and Prices postponed the final application of the joint agreement covering the reduction in hours to 41, until June, 1967. As the 40-hour week was becoming general practice throughout industry pressure was put upon the Government, culminating in a deputation to the Ministry of Labour in February, 1967, and correspondence ensued between the Textile Unions and the Ministry on the subject.

As a result of further joint meetings with the employers agreement was reached in June, 1967 for working hours to be reduced for single shift working, to 40 per week, as from January, 1968. The attainment of a five-day week was a notable achievement for the textile organisations, and the free Saturday mornings were greatly appreciated by the workpeople, especially the women members.

Political Rules and Parliamentary Representation

As reported earlier in this history the question of Parliamentary Representation and Political Rules had been left in an unsatisfactory position ever since the

General Strike of 1926 and the Trades Disputes Act of 1927. After the conclusion of the Second World War, and upon the accession of the Labour Government to power, steps were taken to clarify the position of Political Representation, and under the Trades Disputes and Trade Unions Act of 1946 (in conjunction with the Trade Union Act of 1913) a new set of Political Rules were adopted by the Amalgamation in August, 1946, under which a political levy was payable by all members, except those who contracted-out, of 1s. per year, 75 per cent of which was remitted to the Amalgamation and 25 per cent retained by the District Associations for local purposes. These Rules remained in operation until 1950, when the General Council decided in December, 1949, to increase the political levy from 1d. per month to 3d. per month, or 3s. per year, the same proportions being applicable as before, (i.e. 75 per cent of the levy being paid to the Amalgamation and 25 per cent retained by the Districts).

During the past thirty-five years a number of our officers have served at different periods in the House of Commons. The late Rt. Hon. Thomas Shaw represented Preston constituency for a long number of years, and Mr. Robinson Graham, ex-Secretary of Burnley Weavers' Association, represented Nelson and Colne Division, Mr. George Tomlinson represented the Farnworth Division for a very long time, and became a member of the Cabinet as Minister for Education. Mr. James Bell represented the Ormskirk Division from 1918 until 1922. Mr. W. J. Tout represented Oldham Division in 1922 until 1924, and Sowerby Division from 1929 to 1931. Mr. Zeph Hutchinson, Secretary of Bacup Weavers' Association fought the Chorley Division in 1924, but was not successful, and Mr. Joseph Nuttall, ex-Secretary of Rochdale Weavers' Association fought the Middleton and Prestwich Division in 1935, but was unsuccessful. In 1936-37 Mr. Stephen Shaw, of Nelson, was the candidate in the Clitheroe Division, and the late John Wm. Sunderland, of Great Harwood, was adopted as candidate for the Preston constituency, when his sudden death in November, 1945, brought to an end a promising political career.

Mr. Lewis Wright (now Lord Wright) made a gallant fight at Withington, when he was Amalgamation President, but was unsuccessful.

Mr. Ernest Thornton, our Rochdale Secretary, followed George Tomlinson as Member for Farnworth (after the death of Mr. Tomlinson) and has continued to represent that Division ever since. In the 1964 Labour Government he was appointed Parliamentary Secretary to the Ministry of Labour (now Ministry of Employment and Productivity).

Mr. Harold Bradley (lately President of the Amalgamation) also contested the Clitheroe Division as one of our nominees, but he was unsuccessful. The present panel of parliamentary candidates includes Raymond W. Hill, (Barnoldswick Weavers' Secretary).

Staff Superannuation

On 19th February, 1944, the Central Committee recommended the General Council to affirm the principle of superannuation for Head Office and District Office staffs, and asked for authority to prepare a scheme for later consideration. This recommendation had originated in a request made by the chairman of the

United Textile Factory Workers' Association at the annual conference held in 1943, when each Amalgamation was asked to consider the preparation of such a scheme for the whole trade or for sections.

The recommendation submitted by the Central Committee, concerning our own staff, was carried by a very large majority. Steps were immediately taken to consult a leading firm of London actuaries, Messrs. Bacon & Woodrow, who had prepared similar schemes for the Labour Party staff. On 20th October, 1945, a lengthy report was submitted to the General Council upon the efforts made to formulate a satisfactory scheme for our own officers. The actuaries had furnished details of a scheme, which was intended to cover all officers, both trade union and national health insurance, and would affect a total of 125 persons. The Central Committee was not very satisfied with the scheme submitted, and felt that more generous treatment should be shown to the older long-service officers. It was thought that an initial sum of £75,000 would be required to finance an acceptable scheme, and it was further decided that the proposed scheme should apply only to officers employed wholly or mainly on trade union work. The General Council was therefore again consulted, and in their turn the General Council agreed to consult the District Committees.

At a later meeting of the General Council held on 17th November, 1945, a recommendation submitted by the Central Committee was carried by 98 votes to 63, the recommendation consisting of four propositions: (a) agreement to establish a scheme covering officers employed wholly on trade union work by the Amalgamation or District Associations, and those other officers whose salaries were substantially met out of trade union funds; (b) that the capital sum of £75,000 be set aside to meet the initial liability of immediate retirements and to finance the scheme generally; (c) that the Amalgamation and District Associations make a contribution of similar amounts to those paid by individual employees; (d) that the Central Committee be empowered to prepare a scheme along with the actuaries.

Questionnaires were issued to District Associations, and the information furnished in reply showed that the average age of the 68 persons then affected was 54.64 years, and the actuaries proceeded to prepare an amended scheme, which led the Central Committee, in the early part of 1946 to recommend the General Council to set aside a capital sum of £50,000 (instead of the previous figure of £75,000) to finance the revised scheme, which would provide for retirement of male staff at 65 years of age and female staff at 60 years. Contributions would be 5 per cent from the persons employed, up to 50 years of age, and 6 per cent from those over 50 years, with equal contributions payable by the Societies. Two scales of pensions were proposed, one to cover current contributions, and one to cover pension payments for past service. The estimated capital cost of the initiation and maintenance of the scheme was £44,941, and the balance of £5,059 would be used to ensure that a minimum pension of £52 per year would be paid.

This scheme was submitted to the General Council on 18th May, 1946, when it was decided by a large majority to proceed with the preparation of model rules and Trust Deed, on the revised capital figure of £50,000. A proposal made at the

June meeting of the General Council, from Colne District, to submit the proposal to a ballot vote of the members was defeated by 86 votes to 75, and the scheme was proceeded with.

The General Council finally approved the scheme on 21st September, 1946, and the Central Committee proceeded with the intention of commencing operation of the plan from 1st January, 1947. By the end of December, 1946 nothing had been heard from the Inland Revenue Authorities, and after consultation with the actuaries, it was decided to bring the scheme into actual operation on 27th January, 1947, pending the approval of the Inland Revenue department. This approval was later secured, and the scheme started with a membership of 73 persons. Seven members retired almost immediately, and the number of pensioners gradually increased until in 1967 there were 21 persons in receipt of pensions from the Fund.

European Volunteer Workers

In view of the overall shortage of labour in our industry efforts have been made to recruit operatives from amongst the displaced persons of Europe. The spinning section has received the largest number of such persons, and it was decided during 1947 that the manufacturing section should balance its labour personnel by receiving additions to its ranks. The employment of these foreign workers was conditional upon consultation with the District Associations and that joint agreements now operating should be applied to the employment of the foreign workers. They should become members of the appropriate trade unions, and in the event of economic circumstances in the industry changing and unemployment or under-employment becoming prevalent the position of the foreign workers would have to be reviewed. A fixed wage was paid to the foreign workers during their period of training, and certain precautions were taken to satisfy ourselves upon the methods of "screening" and selecting such labour, and their medical supervision. In April, 1951 a joint agreement was concluded with the Federation of Master Cotton Spinners' Associations Ltd., limiting the percentage of Foreign Workers who could be employed in the departments of spinning mills covered by this Amalgamation.

Educational Activities

Mention is made earlier of the establishment of three full-time scholarships at Ruskin College, tenable for two years, in memory of three pioneers of the Amalgamation. These scholarships were established in 1906, and the Amalgamation continued to select and send three students each two-yearly period for intensive training at Ruskin College, Oxford, until 1922, when the last three students finished their courses at the College.

During 1923 the General Council considered the advisability of renewing the scholarships, and circularised Districts to ascertain opinions on the matter. As a result the General Council, on 16th September, 1922, decided that, "in view of the unsatisfactory results achieved as indicated by the replies received from the districts," the Central Committee should give consideration to the whole subject and submit recommendations for an alternative scheme. This the Committee did, and interviewed representatives of the Workers' Educational Association, as well as making enquiries from other large trade union organisations who operated educational schemes.

On 19th May, 1923 the General Council accepted a recommendation of the Central Committee to institute a scheme for sending twelve students to the W.E.A. Summer School held at Bangor University College, and made a total initial grant of £6 per student to cover costs and personal allowances, and paid rail fares.

In March, 1925 Colne District endeavoured to persuade the General Council to revive the Ruskin College scholarship scheme, but they did not get any support.

Bangor Summer School

As a consequence of the General Council decision of 19th May, 1923, students were sent by the Amalgamation to the Bangor Summer School each year until 1960 (with the exception of 1940, when no school was held). Since 1924 a member of the Central Committee has attended the School along with the students. The cost of the scholarship scheme at Bangor has varied with the years. In 1950 the cost was £11 16s. 1d., per student to cover the charge for accommodation, tuition, socials and excursions and photographs. In addition each student was paid £5 to cover personal expenses, and their rail fares were also paid by the Amalgamation. From 1923 up to 1960 the Amalgamation sent over 470 students to the 37 Summer Schools, and the total cost since the inception of the scheme has been over £6,700. The course of study lasted two weeks, and in the earlier years the special subject was "The Economics of the Cotton Industry." The tutors were Wm. Bruce, B.Sc., Dr. A. Roberts, Arthur Riley, M.A.(Com.), and Arthur Crook, M.A. In the later Schools the course was divided into two; in the first week the subject was the Economics of the Cotton Industry, and in the second week Trade Union History was dealt with. The tutors were extremely helpful to our students, and from reports received each year the students appreciated the facilities provided, both for study and the recreational and social activities.

In addition to the Amalgamation Scholarships six students were also selected to attend the Schools through the General Federation of Trade Unions.

In 1960, however, in view of lack of interest, it was decided to discontinue awarding these Scholarships.

Week-End Schools

In 1947 there was a further extension of the educational activities of the Amalgamation by the institution of Week-End Schools run exclusively for our members. A number of these schools were held at Lyme Hall, Cheshire, and in Blackpool, the Ribble Valley, Morecambe, Skegness, and so on. Interest in these week-end schools has been maintained, and students have also been selected to attend other Week-End Schools, run by the Trades Union Congress, the Labour Party, and the General Federation of Trade Unions.

The selection of students for these schools is not determined by any high educational standards, the main qualifications asked for are average common sense and the taking of an active interest in the work of our organisation. Many hundreds of students have attended the schools.

The "C.M.C." Wage System

On 4th November, 1946 Mr. George Isaacs, M.P., the Minister of Labour and National Service held representatives of employers' and operatives associations at the Midland Hotel, Manchester, with the object of ascertaining how far both sides were prepared to collaborate in examining one of the recommendations made by the "Schuster" Working Party, to devise a method of "redeployment" of weaving operatives and other sections in the manufacturing industry.

As a result of the joint conference the Minister established a Commission, which became known as the "Cotton Manufacturing Commission" and consisted of five members from each side, with two independent members, and sat under the Chairmanship of Mr. R. Moelwyn Hughes, K.C. The first meeting of the Commission was held on 19th December, 1946, and a considerable volume of oral and written evidence was submitted to the Commission, by witnesses from both sides of the trade and from industrial consultants, statisticians, and other experts.

The policy on the Commission was to deal first with the piece price lists of weavers; and the Uniform List of Weaving Prices, because it covered a substantial section of weaving operatives, was given prior consideration. Gradually a new system of payment was devised to remunerate weavers who were "redeployed." The new proposal was outlined in the Commission's Interim Report issued on 6th March, 1948. The Report condemned the existing Uniform List, and in paragraph 59, the emphatic words "the Uniform List must go," were used. We need not be alarmed today at the definiteness of this statement by the Commission, for in numerous discussions throughout the years at our General Council meetings, the Uniform List as a method by which wages are paid was condemned times without number. The Commission, however, in condemning the continuing existence of the Uniform List made definite recommendations for a more scientific method of wage assessment based upon workload and skill. This principle of approach, whilst new to us, is not unknown in other countries. In countries like Holland, Belgium, France, Italy, Sweden and Denmark, the principle has been applied on an extending scale for a number of years. It was early recognised by the Commission that the new system should not be applied at once throughout our industry, and it was agreed that a "notional" test should be taken at 39 firms who were willing to try out the scheme. By agreement, these tests were taken over a period of eight consecutive weeks when wages paid under the Uniform List, and wages that would have been paid under the Commission's scheme, were recorded. The tests covered 1,032 weavers, operating 5,268 looms. The results were tabulated and issued as part of the Final Report, Part I, on 28th March, 1949.

At a General Council meeting held on 21st May, 1949, this Report was fully discussed, and the Central Committee was authorised to "examine all the implications and recommendations jointly with the representatives of The Cotton

Spinners' and Manufacturers' Association, and report subsequently to the General Council." Joint discussions took place with the employers' representatives, and it was agreed that a joint sub-committee should be appointed to consider details. The joint discussions revealed progress towards clarification of certain aspects of the new system, and a special meeting of district committees was held on 13th August, 1949, in order that a full report could be presented, and to provide an opportunity for a free and frank discussion on the whole of the Commission's recommendations.

Meantime, a number of firms invoked the assistance of Associated Industrial Consultants Limited, and by and with the consent of the operatives, the new system was tried out. By July, 1949, there were 28 weaving sheds with 5,327 looms, where the new system was being tried out with certain modifications. At a meeting of the General Council held on 20th August, 1949, the Central Committee were authorised to negotiate a joint agreement with the representatives of The Cotton Spinners' and Manufacturers' Association, and the Central Committee, through its representatives on the joint sub-committee, undertook a closer examination of the whole proposals with the employers' representatives. By 19th November, 1949, a handbook embodying the proposed terms and conditions, and methods for the C.M.C. Wage System had been negotiated. This final draft was submitted to the General Council, and after a long discussion, the Central Committee was authorised to conclude an agreement on the basis of the proposals submitted. Varying amendments had been suggested by our General Council during these discussions, and further joint discussions were held when points raised in our General Council meetings were discussed jointly with the employers' representatives. Such progress was made, that on 13th December, 1949, the final agreement was signed by both sides, the new terms to operate as and from 2nd January, 1950. Meantime, more firms had taken steps to try out the new system, and it was reported that 33 weaving concerns, covering from 9,000–10,000 looms had the system in operation, whilst a still larger number was making surveys of its practicability. During the reports presented to our General Council, it was stated that the new wage structure was based on a number of propositions.

1.—Careful measurement of workload, which in turn implies:—

2.—Improved preparation and higher qualities of yarns.

3.—Improved machine conditions and lay-out.

4.—Division of labour between the skilled and unskilled operatives.

The final scheme followed the broad outlines recommended by the Commission, but important additions and modifications were made. For instance, the original base wage of 71s. 3d. was increased to 75s. An allowance was made in the weavability factor to cover weft breaks, and a definite improvement was made in the clause dealing with colour. Provision was also made for the wages of the learner weavers and helper weavers. Many matters of policy, as well as the application of technical details were under discussion, and the final agreement consisted of four sections:—

1.—A joint letter to firms and trade unions emphasising the permissive nature of the new system, whereby the C.M.C. scheme could be introduced at a mill by joint desire and consent. For a time there would be two wage systems operating side by side—the Uniform List and the C.M.C. System, but it was felt that ultimately only one of the systems would operate in any one mill. It is understood that the permissive legislation by which the Uniform List was enforceable at law, should continue, but the C.M.C. was open, and its implementation rested upon the goodwill and moral sanction of both organisations.

2.—The main agreement stipulated the conditions under which firms might introduce and operate the new system. Provision was made for prior consultation with the employers' associations and our local associations; for obtaining the consent of management and operatives; and making available relevant information. A Joint Standing Committee was set up to keep the new system under constant review, and to deal with technical points as they arose.

3.—This section continued the operation of the Guaranteed Wage Agreement, already in use, suitably amended to fit the new conditions. This new section made provision only for payment of compensation in certain cases of total unemployment as the new C.M.C. System covered under-employment by paying for lost time.

4.—This section dealt with the technical basis of the whole system, and consisted of detailed exposition of the mechanics of applying the new rates and methods of payment.

In connection with this new system, the amalgamation endeavoured, by lectures, week-end schools and area meetings, to give the district officials the utmost information possible. The General Council undertook financial responsibility for paying extra costs involved in district officers attending special schools established by the Cotton Board for the study of workload systems.

Time and Motion Study

The introduction of the C.M.C. method of wage payment, and the increasing activities of various firms of Industrial Consultants, made it imperative that our full-time officials should receive special training in the technique and methods of of time and motion study. It was not an easy task for the Central Committee to provide students to undertake the training. Nominations have been received from district associations, but not enough to enable the organisation to be in a position to meet all the calls for assistance which districts are likely to make in the coming years.

Two methods of training have been employed. The first, which commenced in March, 1949, was conducted by the Associated Industrial Consultants Limited, when a small number of our officers attended two days per week inside a mill, where a system of redeployment was actually being introduced. The second method was conducted by Messrs. Urwick, Orr & Partners Ltd., on behalf of the Cotton Board. This training was on a full-time basis, and covered a period of three months. A number of our officers have attended three such schools, two in the manufacturing section, and one in the spinning section. A third method has been utilised in conjunction with the Cotton Board, whereby eight full-time trade union officers from the Districts have attended a part-time course of studies at the Bury Technical College.

Developments in Shift Workings: Double-Day Shifts

In the early part of 1950 The Cotton Spinners' and Manufacturers' Association made an application for the Northern Counties Textile Trades' Federation to consider the need for a joint agreement, to govern the running of double-day shifts in manufacturing mills. This was a subject of serious concern to the Amalgamated Weavers' Association, and a further census was taken (an earlier census had been taken in 1949) to ascertain the extent to which automatic looms were in use, and the shift systems employed. This census of June, 1950 revealed that there were 102 firms in the trade operating 25,322 automatic looms, and the number of operatives employed was 2,400. Of these automatic looms 18,779 were Northrops; 1,978 were Crompton & Knowles' looms; 961 looms had Whittaker attachments, and 910 had the Fischer attachment, for replenishing the weft package. There were 644 Toyoda automatic looms, and 208 Harling & Todd automatic looms.

The census also showed that 53 firms (out of 102 firms) ran their automatic looms on a single shift of 45 hours per week; 32 firms ran double-day shifts of 37½ hours each per week; the remaining firms running double-day shifts with varying hours. The average wages being earned were £6 10s. 3d. (single shift); £7 6s. 9d. (double-day shifts of 37½ hours) and £7 7s. 8d. (double-day shifts of varying hours).

The employers' application was discussed by the joint committee, and eventually a joint sub-committee met on numerous occasions, when a draft agreement was tentatively reached, to provide for the operation of a double-day shift within the five-day working week (Monday to Friday) of 38¾ hours each shift; an alternative was provided, to institute a maximum of 40-hour shifts if after a ballot vote and by consultation the operatives agreed. This alternative involved Saturday morning work, which the employers were prepared to remunerate at Time-and-a-Half rates. The draft agreement was submitted to the various amalgamations affiliated with the Northern Counties Textile Trades' Federation, when the Amalgamated Weavers' Association and two other small amalgamations voted in favour of accepting the draft agreement, but the remaining five amalgamations voted against the draft. This decision to reject the draft agreement was communicated to the employers, and it was thereupon decided that the dispute should be referred to the Conciliation Committee.

The Conciliation Committee met on the 17th and 18th August, 1950 for the hearing, when the arguments on both sides were fully stated, and the Chairman was asked in writing to give his Award. The Chairman gave his Award later in writing, which in effect implemented the draft agreement arrived at earlier, with the proviso that certain wording should be strengthened in regard to the need for a ballot vote. Lord Terrington also expressed the opinion that it was in the national interest that wherever practicable a 40-hour shift should be introduced by joint agreement and consent.

Further joint meetings were held between the two sides to consider the implications of the Award, when the details of a final joint agreement on this subject were hammered out and embodied in a document dated 20th September, 1950. The principal provisions of this joint agreement were:—

(1) Both parties recommended the operation of a double-day shift on automatic looms.

(2) Prior to the introduction of a double-day shift there should be local consultation.

(3) If the shifts were run within a five-day week the working hours per shift to be not less than $38\frac{3}{4}$ per week nor more than 40 hours, excluding meal breaks of 30 minutes per shift.

(4) The hours not to be increased beyond $38\frac{3}{4}$ per week unless a ballot vote had been taken, and consent of operatives given.

(5) If the operatives consent by ballot vote, an employer may run double-day shifts over a $5\frac{1}{2}$-day week, with higher hours than $38\frac{3}{4}$ but not exceeding 40 hours (exclusive of meal breaks).

(6) No first shift to start before 6 a.m., and second shifts must end not later than 11 p.m.

(7) Time-and-a-half rates to be paid for all Saturday morning work.

For many years the policy of the Amalgamated Weavers' Association had always been one of opposition to shift working although one or two firms had succeeded in establishing two shift working.

In October, 1955 further changes in policy took place. Following meetings between the Cotton Spinners and Manufacturers' Association and the Central Board of the Northern Counties Textile Trades Federation two resolutions were adopted at the Annual Meeting of the Northern Counties Textile Trades Federation as follows:—

Double-Day Shifts on Non-Automatic Looms

"The Central Board shall investigate each application from a firm to operate double-day shifts where the firm had installed new looms and/or new machinery in the preparatory or weaving departments, or where high capital expenditure has been incurred in improving existing machinery or in reconditioning looms to make them, in the opinion of the management, the workpeople concerned, and the Central Board Investigating Committee, comparable with new looms, and provides adequate welfare facilities and satisfactory wages and working conditions.

"Permission to operate double-day shifts or not shall be decided by the Central Board after investigations have been made at mill level. The approval of the local trade unions concerned must be obtained, and two-thirds of the workpeople involved must have voted in favour of accepting double-day shift working before such double-day shifts may be operated."

Three-Shift Working

"That the action of the Central Board be confirmed in recommending to the respective affiliated amalgamations that, having regard to the economic state of our industry, they should agree to permit three-shift working in such cases where they are satisfied that the circumstances at any mill making application are such as economically justify three-shift working, and where the employer is willing to provide wages, working conditions, and welfare facilities acceptable to the workers and the trade unions".

Negotiations broke down because of the refusal of the employers to agree that any agreement on night shift working should include a clause making trade union membership a condition of employment.

Despite failure to reach any general agreement the unions made agreements with individual employers, all agreements being uniform, and up to the end of 1962 110 firms were operating three shifts and accepting trade union membership as a condition of employment on the night shift, and 77 firms were given permission to operate double-day shifts on non-automatic looms.

Double Day Shifts

As from January, 1961 the Double Day Shift System became based on a 37½ hour working week, with provision for overtime payment at Time and Half Rates where 40-hours were worked over a 5½-day week.

Multi Shift Working

During subsequent years the whole question of Multi-Shift Working was under consideration, and the following joint agreement was signed in May, 1968, but at the time of writing much argument between the employers and the unions is taking place regarding the actual number of operative hours to be worked in the week.

THE EXTENSION OF MULTI-SHIFT SYSTEMS AT FIRMS IN THE SPINNING, DOUBLING AND WEAVING INDUSTRY

Preamble:

This Agreement is to provide great flexibility in multiple shift working by permitting firms complying with the specified terms and conditions to operate modern or modernised machinery on shift systems that could include seven days a week according to circumstances. It is agreed that:—

1. It is additional to present agreements and arrangements for shift working (e.g. double-day shifts, evening shifts, treble shifts and other special variations operating by joint approval); these will continue to apply where appropriate as at present.
2. In furtherance of flexibility, a firm may operate more than one system of shift working on one or more units provided it complies with the relevant requirements for each system.
3. Under this Agreement, the normal procedure for a firm wishing to introduce a multiple shift system on new or existing plant shall be for it to prepare proposals and initially discuss them with the local employers association secretary and the appropriate local union officials, making available to them all relevant information reasonably necessary, and providing facilities for a joint inspection of plant, premises and conditions associated with the machinery to be worked on the proposed system. Workers who it is suggested should go on the system over and

above existing systems (in so far as they are already employed) must be informed and consulted by ballot vote: newly-engaged workers shall be made aware of the appropriate terms proposed for their future shift employment.

4. There shall not be any standard multiple shift system under this Agreement, and proposals may be framed to suit circumstances. All proposals shall, however, conform with the following general terms and conditions:

(a) They shall relate only to modern or modernised machinery operating (or to be operated) on modern methods under modern conditions.

(The parties to this agreement, either locally or centrally, must agree that this clause is satisfied before shift working within this agreement is permitted).

(b) Shifts which involve night work or Sunday work shall normally be staffed by males but this shall not preclude female staffing of other shifts within a composite proposal.

(c) Workers newly engaged to take part in a multiple shiftwork system coming under this Agreement and present employees who have to change their existing shiftwork arrangements to do so shall be required to be, or become as soon as possible, members of their appropriate trade union. Provided that a worker who raises objection on genuine conscientious grounds shall be entitled to have his/her case jointly considered and, if upheld, to be exempted on such terms as are jointly decided. The normal Joint Rules procedure shall apply in dealing with such cases.

(d) There shall be provision for proper supervision of each shift so that machinery and labour is utilised to the full.

5. A proposal complying with the requirements of Clauses 3 and 4 above, and which is jointly agreed locally can be implemented forthwith. Failing local joint agreement, the proposal (along with a full report of local discussions) shall be remitted for settlement to a standing Joint Central Supervisory Committee which shall be established to deal with and decide such disputes and generally exercise overall supervision of the Agreement.

Normal Joint Rules shall be observed before any case is referred to the Joint Central Supervisory Committee.

NOTES:

1. The main purpose of this agreement is to encourage high capital investment in new and modern machinery. To recover high capital and overhead charges, expensive machinery should run as nearly continuously as possible. It is not intended to apply to such firms which have not been involved in high capital expenditure. With this in mind, schemes under this Agreement should be so devised as to ensure up to or as nearly as possible 168 machine hours per week, including staggered meal break running.

2. The Agreement deliberately permits flexibility in the devising and operation of schemes as the needs of different firms, the availability and type of labour, etc. will vary.

3. Schemes under this Agreement can only be effective and acceptable to the parties and serve the national interest if they utilise machinery and labour

efficiently, provide modern and satisfactory working conditions and ensure adequate remuneration at a level appropriate to the work performed on multiple shift systems. A successful scheme should therefore make a substantial contribution to the competitive costing of the product, and also provide that the workers should share in the benefits of increased productivity achieved.

Each party should benefit, but none excessively at the expense of the others.

4. Whilst it is not possible, within the principle of flexibility of schemes, to lay down rigid formulae of shiftwork hours and wages, it is vitally important to realise that excessive recompense for untraditional working spells, or the fixing of unduly low individual shift hours will kill the industrial benefits expected from this Agreement.

5. Where the multiple shift system is one in which it may not be practicable for the hours lost during the whole or part of the final shift before certain holidays to be made up by work at another time, in such cases, the multiple shift scheme concerned shall make provision for a compensatory payment approximately equal to wages lost on such shifts.

Movements in Wage Rates

From the date of the establishment of the "Uniform List" for the ascertainment of the weaver's wage there have been very many movements in the wage rates, which means that at various dates since 1892 the List has been paid "minus so-much per cent" or "plus so-much per cent". As this story of the work of the Amalgamation has proceeded it has not been thought advisable to overload the narrative with chronological details of such movements in wages, but future historians of our movement will be interested if some brief summary is made at this point, to indicate the many changes that have taken place in the weaver's wage rates and wage levels.

When the List itself was first adopted and operated from 1st August, 1892, it was subject to a reduction of 10 per cent. This reduction continued to operate until July, 1899, when there was an advance of 2½ per cent, or, in other words, the reduction was lessened, to 7½ per cent. A further easement of the reduction was made in March, 1905, when the reduction was altered to 2½ per cent, and it was not until April, 1906 when this reduction was abolished and the List was paid nett.

The first advance of 5 per cent on List was gained in March, 1912, and this wage-rate level remained, even during the early part of the First World War, until January, 1916, when the first "war advance" was made, and the List was paid plus 10 per cent. These advances on List rates slowly increased during the period of that war, and when hostilities ceased in 1918 the List was paid plus 115 per cent. (December, 1919).

In 1919, when the Working Hours were reduced from 55½ to 48 a compensatory advance of 30 per cent. was granted, which brought the List basis to "plus 145 per cent," although the earnings remained approximately untouched. The highest point in "List percentages" was reached in May, 1920, when an advance of 70 per cent brought the List percentages to 215 per cent.

This peak did not remain for long, however, and in June, 1921 began a series of shattering reductions, which continued until September, 1932, when the reduction imposed by the "Midland Agreement" of 15½ per cent brought List percentages down to 67 per cent. This rate continued until July, 1935, when the first Legalised Uniform List was adopted, and this involved a reduction of almost 5¾ per cent in the four-looms basis, which brought the equivalent list percentage down to 57·44 per cent. As related elsewhere in this history, negotiations took place for improvements in the Legalised Uniform List, and in April, 1937, the revised edition of the Legalised Uniform List was adopted (and is still in use), which increased the old four-looms basis by 10½ per cent, and brought List percentages up to 77½ per cent. The "Worsted Clause" of the old Uniform List has still continued in use, and this percentage of 77½ per cent was used in calculating from that Clause.

The new Legalised List of 1935, and the revised edition of 1937, adopted a new basis for the weaving of Grey Cloths, and it will not be found possible to make direct comparisons between wage rates before 1935–37 and subsequent dates, because of many alterations which took place in the clauses of the List itself. The Coloured Section, however, retained its original basis of payment of 1½d. per pick per quarter inch (for Stripes) and 2d. (for "Checks"), and by the agreement of 1937 the List percentages in those cases stood at 81½ per cent for Stripes and 76½ per cent for Checks.

From 1937 onwards the wage rate movements took place upon all Lists, by certain amounts, adding up to a total of 54½ per cent in 1950, plus a total of 28s. per week "flat rate payments". So that whilst the Grey Section of the Uniform List would, in 1950, be paid plus 54½ per cent. plus 28s., the Stripe section of the Coloured List would be paid plus 81 per cent, plus a separate 54½ per cent., plus 28s. flat rates; and so on. A full statistical summary of all these various wage movements will be found in the Appendix.

Most of these wage rate movements took place during the Second World War, 1939–45, and were operated through the joint agreement referred to earlier, which pegged wage rates to the Board of Trade Index figure for Cost of Living. This joint agreement, made in October, 1939, operated until abrogated by the Cotton Spinners and Manufacturers' Association in December, 1946. The agreement operated on a sliding scale as from January, 1940, but prior to that date two percentage increases, totalling 12½ per cent were granted.

As the war proceeded, therefore, and as the official figure for cost of living advanced, the percentages increased by varying amounts, from 2½ to 7½ per cent, until in January, 1942, the total percentage increase upon the 1937 Legalised List basis (and upon the varying bases of the other Lists) was 35 per cent.

This level remained until February, 1946, when a further advance, due to an award of the Conciliation Committee, brought the figure to 45 per cent. This figure of 45 per cent remained in operation for day-rate workers, as the further advance of 9½ per cent, making a total of 54½ per cent was a compensatory percentage to cover the reduction in working hours to 45, as from December, 1946.

When the Cost of Living Agreement ceased to operate in 1946, the "percentage" position had become complicated by the granting of "flat rate" advances of 5s. per week (1943), 4s. (1944) and 7s. (1945), making a total of 16s. per week flat rate advances. This method was adopted in order to give discriminatory advances in the wages of the lower-paid workers. These flat rate advances were still further increased, by 7s. 6d. in 1948 and a further 4s. 6d. in 1949, making a total of 28s. flat rate payments.

After 1949 percentage increases were made, and these percentage increases also applied to the 28s. flat rate figure. The percentage method of increase continued until 1963, when a further flat rate payment was made of 5s. 9d. per week, and this brought the flat rate figure up to 49s. 8d. per week.

Since 1963 wage movements have been on a percentage basis, and a full survey of the various Wage Movements, from 1912 up to 1968, is given in the appendix.

Movements in Wage Levels

The previous chapter refers to movements in wage-rates, and it is interesting to attempt to estimate what have been the varying wage levels attained by weaving and other operatives since the early days of the industry. The principal authority on wages in the cotton industry in its earliest days is undoubtedly George Henry Wood, who issued in book form in 1910 a series of papers he had written and were printed in the Journal of the Royal Statistical Society. He was very painstaking in the ascertainment of his facts, and his book is therefore very reliable, each authority being quoted in support of his figures.

Hand loom weavers' wages have already been referred to in the early part of this History.

Early Wages of Factory Weavers, Winders, &c.

In dealing with earnings of factory operatives, as distinct from Handloom Weavers' wages dealt with earlier, G. H. Wood quotes figures of wages earned in the Manchester district for a number of years, showing Reelers earnings from 12s. to 14s. in 1809, this rate varying until it reached about 15s. per week in 1815. The earliest information concerning factory weavers relates to 1826, when the average was from 10s. to 12s. per week, and for winders, 9s. to 10s. 6d. per week. Warpers' earnings are given as 10s. to 12s. per week in that year. By 1834 the average earnings of weavers had remained about 12s. 6d., and showed no improvement for a considerable time, in fact in 1845 the average is shown as 9s. 9d., per week. It was not until 1877 that they began to rise to about 18s. per week, and not until 1890 is the round figure of 20s. per week recorded.

Average wages quoted from Oldham and other districts are not greatly at variance with the above statements, the average wages of weavers in Preston in 1906 being 19s. 5d.; in Blackburn, 22s. 1d. Even in 1908 the average wages of weavers in the North-East Lancashire area as a whole varied from 23s. 8d. to 24s. per week.

In 1913 the Amalgamation itself undertook a census of weavers' earnings, and the returns showed an average wage of 6s. 6⅞d. per loom, or 26s. 3½d. per week for a four-loom weaver.

Again, in 1936, the Amalgamation took a census of weavers' earnings, showing an average of 31s. 5d., and a year later a further census showed an average of 36s. 8d. During later years the Cotton Spinners' and Manufacturers' Association took a number of censuses which are shown in the Appendix.

Proposed Centralisation schemes

The Central Committee proceeded in 1932 to formulate a new scheme, involving proposals for centralisation, with new draft Rules, and the new scheme was published in booklet form in January, 1933. The new name of the Amalgamation was to be "The National Union of Weavers and Allied Workers"; mill committees were to be formed at each mill, and local or area committees were to be established, to act under the authority of the central executive. Secretaries, Organisers and necessary staff to be appointed by the Executive. The contribution was to be 1s. per week, with benefits of 25s. and 20s. per week, and a funeral benefit of £6. Unemployment benefit would be 15s. per week. The central office would be departmentalised in the following departments: Finance, Correspondence and General, Legal, Organisation, Statistical, Trade and Technical.

The new scheme was discussed by the General Council, but in March, 1933, on a Motion by Preston District it was decided not to proceed with the project, and an original Notice of Motion by Wigan district was rescinded.

The subject was again introduced into the General Council discussions by Colne district on 17th June, 1939, when the following Notice of Motion was submitted:

> "That this General Council instructs the Central Committee to devise some scheme whereby continual attention shall be given to maintaining and improving the organisation of all weaving, winding, and beaming operatives within the area covered by the Legalised List, such scheme to be submitted to the next General Council Meeting."

The Notice of Motion was withdrawn on the understanding that the Central Committee would give the subject serious consideration. This they did, and on 19th August, 1939 the Central Committee submitted a series of proposals, which recognised at the outset the difficulty of making suggestions for concerted effort when districts enjoyed local autonomy. The Central Committee recommended that as an experiment for a period of months a temporary Organiser or Organisers be appointed, their duties to consist of initiating and directing organisational work, in conjunction with the officials of the District Associations. A weekly report to be submitted to the Central Committee, and periodical reports to be made to the General Council Meetings. District Associations to bear the cost of distribution of handbills, leaflets and such other forms of local publicity. The Central Committee to have the necessary authority to send the Organisers into any District to make investigations.

These recommendations were adopted by the General Council by a large majority and the Central Committee proceeded to put the scheme into operation. Applications were invited from District Associations, and Mr. Edmund Hothersall, of Great Harwood, was appointed as Temporary Organiser. He commenced his duties on 20th May, 1940, and carried on with the work until November that year. More than half of our District Associations availed themselves of his services, and much good work was done. This temporary organising effort again brought into sharp relief the whole question of the Amalgamation structure and method of organisation. By history and tradition District Associations had themselves in the past been mainly concerned with the recruitment of members into their separate organisations. When the Temporary Organiser finished his work the District Associations were urged by the Amalgamation to devote keen attention to the maintenance of their organisations and recruitment of membership, and the services of members of the Central Committee were offered to assist in organising work at all times.

Structure of the Amalgamation

In the 1967 Amalgamation Report an examination was made of the existing structure of our trade union organisation. It outlined the defects of our present federal structure and suggested that the time had come to take a close look at ourselves.

This is what was said:

Membership.—Our membership is contracting as swiftly as the industry itself. Over the past five years the figures read:—

1962	50,398
1963	45,483
1964	44,463
1965	43,113
1966	41,701

March of 1967 saw a further reduction to 36,586.

Our peak membership in 1921 was 224,219, with one District alone having 27,000 members. Today we have fewer members than we had at the formation of the Amalgamated Weavers' Association in 1884 when we were 37,000 strong.

Districts which once numbered their members in thousands now do so in hundreds and the need to examine our trade union structure becomes more pressing with each passing year. Eleven of our Districts each have fewer than 1,000 members. Six have 900 or less and three are in the 800 mark. Six have fewer than 800. Eight districts form four pairs, each pair covered by a joint secretary leaving each district with their own Committee and local automony. Burnley and Nelson, for instance, with a combined membership of 6,199 are served by one District Secretary.

It became apparent some years ago that the time had come to consider whether a federal system with local autonomy could stand up to modern conditions and a rapidly contracting membership. The situation is rapidly becoming chaotic and more than half of our districts need only one or perhaps in some cases two, more mills or factories in the district to close and make a separate district completely unjustified. The reluctance to merge or associate with adjacent districts is not motivated by common sense but by a form of narrow parochialism reminiscent of the last century. It is sad to reflect that whilst all of us are crying out for a more efficient industry and more Government planning for the benefit of the industry, we toddle along making do with a trade union structure which defies common sense and, if it were not so serious, would be laughable. If our present structure continues the next few years will witness a trade union tragedy with many districts struggling to pay their full-time officials a very low salary to serve a mere handful of members. This is not what trade unionism is all about and ought not to continue when in large measure it can be dealt with. That is why, in 1964, Rule 73 was adopted to try to create some order out of approaching chaos. It is no substitute for a complete re-appraisal of our structure but, if the Rule is observed, and it must be observed, it will help to mitigate the worse effects of rapid contraction. Nelson and Burnley have been mentioned with a total membership of more than 6,000 being served by one joint secretary, one assistant secretary, one full-time work-study officer and two clerks—a total of five. On the other hand one can find seven districts with a little over 5,000 members with six full-time secretaries, two assistants, and one part-time clerk. Eight full-time officers and one part-time for 5,000 members. How ludicrous can we become?

Under Rule 73 the problem can be met without hardship and no full-time officer would lose a job. Mergers must be encouraged whilst there is time before disintegration sets in. But it must be recognised that after all this is done it will be a long, slow process and time is not on our side.

The whole structure needs recasting so that an efficient organisation can be built without waiting for districts to disappear and their secretaries with them. The members' interests are paramount and there can be no doubt that a properly deployed staff of five can serve five or six thousand members better than one all-purpose District Secretary can serve a few hundreds.

Parochial interests must be subordinate to members' interests and the time is fast coming when the members themselves or possibly some other Union will bring this home to us.

At the General Council Meeting on 25th November 1967, a resolution was adopted, with only one district dissenting, instructing the Executive Council to prepare for submission to a future General Council Meeting a draft scheme of centralisation in place of our present federal structure and to make approaches to the Cardroom Amalgamation with a view ultimately to the merging of the two Amalgamations. A sub-committee has been appointed and has had several meetings.

Districts have co-operated in supplying the Office with information requested and more meetings will be necessary before the broad principles of a plan can be submitted to a General Council Meeting.

The Cardroom Amalgamation has been asked to consider the desirability of a merger with us and after they had considered the matter a Joint Sub-Committee was set up.

It was pointed out in the 1967 Report that time was not on our side and that we needed to act before disintegration sets in. But we cannot afford to rush districts into a hasty and ill-contrived scheme and the preparation of something well understood and meaningful will take time. In the meantime the situation worsens. In the current year since our last report we have lost a further 3,500 members. At this rate of contraction our Amalgamation and its districts have only ten years of life left! This is, of course, an oversimplification of the situation but it does bring home the urgent need to recast our organisation. If things are left alone it will mean some districts collapsing far sooner than we think. It is doubtful whether any district in ten years' time will be able to make ends meet and give a satisfactory service to its members. It is to be hoped that District Committees and their leaders will have the courage to grasp the nettle and save what remains of our once powerful Union. The Amalgamation, as we know it, has grown old and it shows. I believe that most of our members know this and are ready for changes.

Cotton Industry Act (1959)

The subject of providing some financial assistance to the cotton industry was first raised at the Cotton Board Conference held at HARROGATE in October, 1958, when the Prime Minister was present.

The question was put to the Prime Minister as to whether the Government would give some financial assistance to the Cotton Industry as had been given to other industries. He replied to the effect that if representations were made to the Chancellor of the Exchequer he, no doubt, would consider the matter sympathetically.

Almost at once the Cotton Board set up a Development Committee comprising all sections, including the trade unions, to examine the subject. This was swiftly followed by the Committee dividing itself into sections representing Spinning, Weaving, Doubling and Finishing. The Unions were not included in these sub-committees and at no stage despite our protests, were they brought into the discussions nor were any reports of sectional discussions with the Board of Trade reported to the Development Committee.

The trade unions were kept in the dark as to what was going on.

At the end of March 1959, the sub-committees of the trade unions and the employers' organisations got together again, when the employers were asked to indicate the nature of proposals which they had made to the Government relating to the removal of surplus capacity and re-equipment. The employers said they were in no position to give details, but they had asked the Government for financial help, as the industry had suffered much due to Government policy in allowing unlimited imports from the Commonwealth countries. The operatives' representatives pressed that in any scheme submitted to the government there should be provision for compensation for operatives rendered redundant, and we again submitted a plan along the lines of the original proposals agreed to by the three Amalgamation Executives in January 1958.

Further developments took place when the President of the Board of Trade made a statement in the House of Commons on 23rd April 1959, outlining the definite proposals of the Government for bringing in a Bill to provide for direct financial assistance from public funds. The first step in the Government's plans was to remove surplus capacity, and the Government would contribute from public funds two-thirds of the cost of bringing this about, under schemes to be approved by the Board of Trade. The balance of the cost would be met by the industry itself, by statutory levy. The Government made it a condition that the industry itself would compensate operatives faced with loss of employment as a result of the schemes, and this was a matter for the employers to settle directly with the trade unions concerned. After the elimination of surplus capacity the next step in the Government plan was to encourage re-equipment, and the Government would be prepared, provided that the Board of Trade was satisfied that enough surplus capacity in the industry would be eliminated, to pay a grant of one-quarter of the cost of modernising existing machinery and providing new machinery. It was intended that this modernisation and re-equipment should be completed within the next five years. The President of the Board of Trade said it was impossible to give exact figures as to what the total of such Government grants would amount to, but the Government would, if a favourable response was shown by the industry, be prepared to grant up to a total of about £30 million over five years.

Details of this Government plan were contained in a White Paper, issued in May 1959, and the terms of a Parliamentary Bill were published at the same time.

Parliamentary consideration of the Bill began on 4th June, 1959 and after being thoroughly discussed in the House, received Royal Assent and became an Act of Parliament on 9th July 1959.

In the meantime joint talks took place within the industry on the question of compensation for redundant workers, added impetus being given by the clause in the Cotton Industry Bill which laid down a condition of acceptance of a scheme for Government aid that satisfactory arrangements had been made with the industry "for the payment of compensation in respect of loss of employment due to the elimination of the excess capacity".

On 28th April 1959, there was a very lengthy meeting of the joint sub-committees, when the employers made tentative proposals for compensation payments, based on a complicated formula which included *(a)* the age factor, and *(b)* years of service with the present employer. Such formula would produce "points value" and these points values were related to a scale of payments, varying from one week's wage to a maximum of 14 weeks. This proposal was thoroughly discussed and ultimately rejected by our representatives as being totally inadequate and unsatisfactory. Various counter-proposals were made by our representatives during a series of joint meetings. It was generally recognised by both sides that it would be almost impossible to utilise any method of calculation which took into account the total years of service within the industry. Past experience had shown in connection with Workmen's Compensation claims for industrial diseases that it was impracticable to assess accurately the total years of service of many workers, who might have worked at a number of mills during their lifetime, many of the firms having gone out of existence in the meantime and their records destroyed or lost.

The trade union representatives therefore concentrated on formulating a scale of payments based on age alone (with a minimum period of service, to be agreed,) and in the end this method of calculation was accepted by both sides. The main negotiations therefore concentrated on the amount of compensation which could be extracted from the employers. It must be borne in mind that none of the proposed compensatory payments could be met out of the Government grants, but must be borne by the firms who remained in the industry, who would have to contribute to an industrial levy.

These negotiations continued until 15th May 1959, when tentative agreement was reached in the form of recommendations to be made by the joint sub-committees to their respective larger executive committees. These recommendations were reported to the larger meetings on each side, held on 19th May 1959, and ultimately accepted, as the basis for further joint negotiations with the object of reaching a conclusive and acceptable agreement to cover the many complicated situations which were bound to arise in administering any scheme of compensation.

Up to this point in the negotiations the employers had only visualised the payment of weekly sums of compensation, over a period of time, whereas our representatives still pressed for the payment of a lump sum, if not the whole amount in one sum then a proportion at the commencement of redundancy and the balance in weekly payments. During later discussions the employers expressed dismay at the attitude of our representatives and complained that we were going back on our original propositions. They contended that their calculations had been based on the payment of weekly sums, and that to make total lump sum payments would involve them in considerably increased costs. Our representatives, however, pressed hard for the principle of some lump sum payment, and the employers ultimately offered to pay 25 per cent of the entitlement in such a lump sum. This was not acceptable to our larger committee (who were in attendance) and the joint talks were adjourned.

At a later joint meeting, on 18th June, the employers indicated that they were prepared to agree to our claim for payment of half of the entitlement in a lump sum, but they asked as a *quid pro quo* that the subsequent weekly payments should operate after a two weeks moratorium. One or two other details were discussed, and it was agreed to present a full report of the negotiations to the joint executives of the trade unions, on the following day. At that meeting of the full executives a lengthy report was presented, and the meeting ultimately accepted the principle of lump sum payment plus a remaining weekly payment, and authorised our sub-committee to negotiate further with the employers on the terms and conditions which would govern the operation of an agreed scheme.

Accordingly the joint Working Party met on several occasions during the remaining weeks of June, and ultimately reached final agreement on Thursday, 2nd July 1959.

The final draft joint agreement was reported to the Central Board on the following day. The Central Board accepted the tentative agreement and agreed to support its acceptance at the meeting of the tripartite executives held later that day. At the later meeting the draft agreement was fully explained, and questions were dealt with, the meeting finally endorsing the agreement.

The agreement was signed on the 9th of July 1959, and the following is a copy:

COMPENSATION FOR REDUNDANT OPERATIVES AGREEMENT

1. IT IS JOINTLY AGREED AS FOLLOWS:

2. DEFINITIONS

A "redundant operative" is a worker in the cotton spinning, doubling, or weaving industry

(*a*) who has lost his or her employment due to the elimination of surplus machinery or the introduction of new machinery under the Government-aided scheme for disposal of redundant plant and re-equipment of spinning, doubling, and weaving mills and

(*b*) who was employed up to the time of losing his or her employment by a mill entitled to compensation under the said scheme and whose contract of employment had not been terminated prior to 23rd April 1959.

For the purposes of Clause 3 below, employment in the "same firm" is employment by the same firm in the same mill, or in another mill owned by the same firm and within the same curtilage or in the immediate vicinity and close enough to form a single entity; provided that the definition is extended to cover any mill owned by the same firm or combine in the case of classes of persons who normally move or may be expected to move from one mill to another within a bigger group.

3. QUALIFICATION OF PAYMENT OF COMPENSATION

Compensation at the rates hereinunder set out shall be paid for loss of employment or for loss of earnings or status to redundant operatives provided that

(*a*) payment of compensation shall be dependent upon the operative concerned having worked out the proper notice given by the employer or having been given permission to leave;

(*b*) no compensation shall be payable to an operative for whom suitable alternative employment is immediately available in the same firm at approximately the same level of earnings;

(*c*) where suitable employment later becomes available to a redundant operative, his or her entitlement shall be adjusted to the amount he or she has already received at the date when new employment is taken up.

Example:

Operative aged 42 entitled to compensation based on eight weeks. Full entitlement for average earnings of £10 per week—lump sum of 4 x £10=£40, plus £40 in weekly payments of two-thirds of £10 minus £2 10s. 0d. =£4 3s. 4d. Total £80. If work obtained after four weekly payments, entitlement adjusted to:

£40+(4 x £4 3s. 4d.) = £56 13s. 4d.

(*d*) compensation shall be paid to an operative for whom work is or becomes available in a suitable but lower paid employment of equal status (i.e. an employment in which the average earnings are more than $2\frac{1}{2}\%$ below previous earnings) at a rate in the same proportion to the full rate as is the reduction in his earnings to his previous average earnings.

Example: (i)

Operative aged 42. Previous earnings £10 per week. Suitable new job available with same firm at £9 10s. 0d. per week. Full entitlement: 8 x £10=£80. Entitlement for loss of earnings amounting to 0.5/10 of £80=£4.

Example: (ii)

Operative aged 42. No job available with firm. Previous earnings £10 per week. Full entitlement: 8 x £10=£80. New job at lower rate obtained after 4 weeks at £8 per week. Half entitlement payable on loss of employment: £40. Compensation during unemployment: £4 3s. 4d. for four weeks=£16 13s. 4d. Residual entitlement on taking new job at £8 per week: 2/10 of £23 6s. 8d.=£4 13s. 4d.

provided that where work becomes available in suitable lower-paid employment in another occupation with lower status in the same firm, an operative shall receive as full compensation a lump sum amounting to half his full entitlement.

Example: (iii)

Operative aged 42. Previous earnings £10 per week. Suitable new job available with same firm at £8 per week, involving a change to an occupation with lower status. Full entitlement: 8 x £10 = £80. Entitlement for loss of earnings and status: ½ x £80 = £40.

Note: Provided the employment is suitable, examples of equal status are:

(i) In the spinning section:
Female tenters on any machines in card rooms or ring rooms.
Female assistants in card rooms and doffers in ring rooms.
Bobbin carriers and oilers and banders.

(ii) In the Weaving section:
Overlooking as an occupation. Weaving as an occupation. Winding as an occupation.

(*e*) No compensation shall be payable to any operative who has served for less than a total of five years in the cotton spinning, doubling or weaving industry since 8th May 1945.

(*f*) no operative shall receive a total amount of compensation from the central fund greater than his or her maximum entitlement under Clause 4;

(*g*) no operative shall be entitled to receive compensation other than a lump sum equal to half his or her full entitlement unless he or she has registered as being available for employment at the appropriate employment exchange immediately on becoming redundant, and has given permission for the Ministry of Labour to report to the administrating authority if he or she ceased to register.

4. RATES OF COMPENSATION

Subject to Clause 3 above, the maximum entitlement to compensation shall be as follows:

REDUNDANT OPERATIVES—COMPENSATION

Age	*Number of weeks' compensation payable*	*Age*	*Number of weeks' compensation payable*
Under 21	—	49–50	14
21–23	1	51–52	15
24–26	2	53–54	16
27–29	3	55	17
30–32	4	56	18
33–35	5	57	19
36–38	6	58	20
39–40	7	59	21
41–42	8	60	22
43	9	61	23
44	10	62	24
45	11	63	26
46	12	64	28
47–48	13	65 and over	30

Average earnings shall be taken to mean the average weekly earnings excluding overtime of the operative concerned for the most recent available four-week period during which the mill worked full-time in his or her normal job at that mill.

The age for this purpose shall be taken as the age as on the date on which the operative became redundant.

5. METHOD OF PAYMENT OF COMPENSATION

Subject to the above clauses and to such adjustments as are therein provided the entitlement to compensation for loss of employment shall be paid

(*a*) as to one half in the form of an unconditional lump sum;

(*b*) as to one half in weekly instalments amounting to not more than two-thirds of normal weekly earnings less the standard rate of unemployment benefit, provided that:

(i) the first of such instalments shall become payable on the second Friday after loss of employment has occurred and

(ii) in cases where the total entitlement due does not exceed one week's earnings, it shall be paid as a lump sum.

Compensation shall be paid from the central funds of the cotton spinning/doubling/weaving industry established for that purpose and through such agent or agency as the administering authority of the fund shall appoint. The administering authority shall be set up after consultation between the parties to this Agreement.

6. LISTS OF REDUNDANT OPERATIVES

Any firm where operatives become redundant under the terms of this Agreement shall prepare a list of such operatives giving details of sex, age and service in the industry since 8th May 1945, together with the average earnings figure for each and such other details as may be appropriate, and shall submit it to the appropriate Local Union and Employers' Association secretaries who shall agree the list. Proof of age by birth certificate may be required.

The administering authority or its agent may require any or all operatives on the list.

(*a*) to give an initial written assurance that he or she has been employed for more than 5 years in the cotton industry since 8th May 1945, is not currently employed and is available for employment.

(*b*) to sign an appropriate receipt before receiving the lump sum payment,

(*c*) to sign appropriate receipts before receiving the weekly instalments certifying that he or she is not employed and is still available for employment, provided that certified sickness shall not prejudice compensation.

Redundant operatives who refuse suitable alternative employment prior to expiration of the weekly instalments shall thereby forfeit all further entitlement to compensation. Disallowance of unemployment benefit may in general be taken as grounds for forfeiture of entitlement to compensation but any doubtful case including those where there has never been entitlement to unemployment benefit will be considered locally and if necessary centrally by the usual joint procedure or by special procedure set up to deal with such cases. Both parties will consider all such cases from the point of view of equity and taking into consideration any special factors arising.

7. ALTERNATIVE EMPLOYMENT

Employers and Unions shall co-operate in every way possible to find suitable alternative employment for operatives likely to become redundant or who have become redundant.

8. DISPUTES, INTERPRETATIONS AND DOUBTFUL CASES

The normal local and central procedure will apply but suitable cases will be referred to a central body with representatives nominated by the Employers and Unions, sitting under an independent Chairman.

Signed on behalf of:

THE FEDERATION OF MASTER COTTON SPINNERS' ASSOCIATIONS LIMITED
Philip Lees, *President*
C. Henniker-Heaton, *Director*
A. H. Rigby, *Secretary*

THE COTTON SPINNERS' AND MANUFACTURERS' ASSOCIATION
J. M. H. Grey, *Chairman*
Geo. B. Fielding, *Director*
Arnold K. Roberts, *Secretary*

THE CONDENSER AND ALLIED SPINNERS AND MANUFACTURERS' ASSOCIATION (*for Weaving Interests*)
J. W. S. Utley, *Chairman*
Peat Marwick Mitchell & Company, *Secretaries*

THE AMALGAMATED ASSOCIATION OF OPERATIVE COTTON SPINNERS & TWINERS
James W. Whitworth, *President*
Charles Schofield, *Secretary*

THE NATIONAL ASSOCIATION OF CARD, BLOWING & RING ROOM OPERATIVES
H. Chorlton, *President*
Alfred Roberts, *Secretary*

THE NORTHERN COUNTIES' TEXTILE TRADES' FEDERATION
Harry Earnshaw, *President*
Lewis Wright, *Secretary*

Dated this 9th day of July, 1959.

Since the foregoing joint agreement was negotiated there have been several meetings of the joint negotiating committee, when questions of interpretation and difficult cases have been discussed, and "Interpretations" have been formulated and issued to all concerned.

In the Government's scheme for the elimination of surplus machinery it was visualised that at least six million mule equivalent spindles would have to be scrapped, 400,000 doubling spindles, and at least 45,000 looms. If the applications were not received in respect of at least that number of spindles and looms the scheme would not become operative. Each scheme was independent of the others, and it was possible for one, two, or all three of them to come into operation. To qualify for the Government grant surplus machinery must be scrapped between 24th April 1959, and 31st March 1960. Applications by firms for the Government grant had to be made before 30th September, 1959. and those firms which made application before 31st August 1959, would qualify for a premium of five per cent. Up to 31st August, applications had been received in respect of 11,969,386 mule equivalent spindles: 14,407 carding engines; 492,994 doubling spindles, and 95,491 looms. This meant that the three schemes were proceeded with.

After the last date for applications (30th September 1959) it was announced that 12,444,000 mule equivalent spindles had been registered for scrapping, leaving 12,901,000 mule equivalent spindles (6,619,000 rings and 2,973,000 mules) still in use. In the doubling section a total of 571,000 spindles were scheduled for scrapping, leaving 1,038,000 spindles in use. In the weaving section 104,747 looms were scheduled for scrapping, (68,597 up to 48 inches wide, and 31,997 between 48 and 71 inches). After scrapping was completed 154,497 looms would remain, before re-equipment under the second part of the Cotton Industry Act.

The effects of the Cotton Industry Act and the worsening situation in the industry since can be seen in the drastic reduction of cotton workers on the books of firms as illustrated below:

Number on books at end of 1958 — 196,360
„ „ „ „ „ „ 1962 — 139,970
A reduction in the labour force of 56,390—or nearly 29%

Of the total of 56,390 only 37,000 received compensation for redundancy, the other 19,390 who have been thrown out of work have had no compensation.

By the beginning of March 1961, 36,726 claims had been received by the Administrators for the industry as a whole. Of these, 15,653 concerned the manufacturing section. Out of these totals, 2,399 had been rejected for the whole industry and 929 for the manufacturing section. The amount of cash paid out, where redundancy had occurred as a result of scrapped machinery, was £3,254,249 for the Industry and £1,494,726 for the manufacturing section. The amount of cash paid out at the same date for redundancy caused by re-equipment was £12,016 for the Industry and £5,033 for the Manufacturing Section.

Appeals Board

Cases were submitted to the Appeals Board only after they had been rejected, in the first place by the Administrators and then by the Employers' Organisation. The preparation of cases and their presentation to the Appeals Board was, therefore, a detailed and meticulous task and very time-consuming. But the work has been of great value to the members of the District Associations as will be seen by the following table of granted and rejected cases by the Appeals Board.

	Granted	*Rejected*	*Adjourned*
Up to August 1962	109	57	5

In addition to these, the Head Office staff were able to secure payments, either through the Administrators or the Employers, in a further 140 cases. Many thousands of pounds were obtained for our members in these two ways.

Recent Presidents

James Bell

After lengthy service as a member of the Central Committee and for a number of years as Vice-President, James Bell was appointed President in 1937, and served in that capacity until his retirement in May, 1947. He was a member of Parliament for the Ormskirk Division from 1918 to 1922, and had served on a number of Government Commissions, He had been a member of the General Council of the Trades Union Congress, and for a number of years was Secretary of the United Textile Factory Workers' Association. Mr. Bell died on 27th December, 1955, aged 83 years.

Carey Hargreaves

When Mr. Bell retired in 1947 his place was filled as President by Carey Hargreaves, Secretary of the Nelson Association. Mr. Hargreaves had been vice-President, having followed Mr. Bell in that office. Carey Hargreaves retired in May, 1949, having served on the Central Committee since 1930. He passed away on 11th October, 1954.

Lewis Wright

In May, 1949 Mr. Wright, Secretary of the Ashton-under-Lyne & District Weavers' Association, and who had acted as Vice-President, was elected the President of the Amalgamation.

Harold Bradley

In May, 1960 Harold Bradley retired as President, having succeeded Lewis Wright in 1953. Mr. Bradley had been Secretary of the Darwen Weavers' Association since 1933, after having served as a member of the Nelson District Committee for a long number of years.

Ernest Thornton, M.P., M.B.E.

On the retirement of Harold Bradley, Mr. Thornton became President of the Amalgamation in 1960, and served until 1964, when he relinquished the office to become Joint Parliamentary Secretary to the Ministry of Labour.

Fred G. Hague

Mr. Hague, who was serving as Vice-President, became President in 1964, upon Mr. Thornton's Government appointment, and Mr. Hague was still serving in 1968.

Recent General Secretaries

Sir Andrew Naesmith, C.B.E., M.A., J.P.

Andrew Naesmith was appointed Assistant Secretary of the Amalgamated Weavers' Association in 1925, and on the death of Mr. J. C. Parker he became General Secretary on 17th December, 1927, a position he held until his retirement at pension age in August, 1953. His connection with the Weavers' Organisation dated back to 1912, when he was in full-time employment with the Oldham Weavers' Association in the Middleton area. He later became Assistant Secretary to the Todmorden District Association, working in conjunction with the late William J. Tout. Mr. Naesmith served on the Todmorden Town Council for a number of years.

Some of the most momentous happenings in the earlier history of the Amalgamation took place during Andrew Naesmith's period of office. The building of the Convalescent Home by direct labour, under the direction of the General Secretary and the Architect was a very onerous task, and no sooner had that venture been completed than the trade ran into unprecedented difficulties in 1931 on account of unemployment. The employers abrogated all joint agreements in 1932, and there followed the four weeks' county stoppage, which culminated in the protracted negotiations which produced the "Midland Agreement" in September, 1932. There followed lengthy negotiations concerning extensions of the More Looms per Weaver System, and, during the war years, all the emergency Orders and Regulations. He took a prominent part in the deliberations of the Moelwyn Hughes Commission, which produced what has become known as the "C.M.C." System, involving work study methods and a new system of wage assessment. He was a member of the Cotton Board for many years, and also of the General Council of the Trades Union Congress. After receiving the awards of O.B.E. in 1942 and C.B.E. in 1948 he was made a Knight of the Order of the British Empire in 1953. Manchester University also honoured him in 1948 by conferring upon him the degree of Master of Arts (*honoris causa*). He was appointed to the Court of Directors of the Bank of England in 1949, he was still a member when he retired from our service. On his retirement he received the good wishes of the Amalgamation at a presentation ceremony on 19th September, 1953, held at the Grand Hotel, Manchester. Sir Andrew passed away on 23rd October, 1961.

Lewis Wright

Appointed General Secretary on 22nd June, 1953, upon the retirement of Sir Andrew Naesmith. In 1968 Lewis Wright was awarded a life Peerage, and was also Centenary President of the Trades Union Congress. Owing to the age limit Lord Wright retired as General Secretary of the Amalgamation in October, 1968.

Harry C. Kershaw

Mr. Harry C. Kershaw, elected Assistant Secretary, Colne Weavers Association in 1944. Appointed to Head Office in 1947. Elected General Secretary 1968 on the retirement of Lord Wright.

* * *

Recognition for Lengthy Service

On Saturday afternoon, 4th May, 1946, about 230 members of District Committees attended as guests of the Central Committee at a Dinner and Presentation Ceremony held at the Casino Restaurant, Blackpool, when the President at that time, Mr. James Bell, J.P., and Mr. Cephas Speak, J.P. (member of the Central Committee) were presented with a cheque for 100 guineas each, as a token of appreciation of their long service to the Amalgamated Weavers' Association. Mr. Bell was appointed Secretary of the Oldham Weavers' Association in 1905, and became a member of the Central Committee in 1907, became President in 1937. Mr. Speak had joined Mr. Bell at Oldham, as Assistant Secretary, in 1906, and in 1907 he went to Bolton, where he became Secretary in 1911.

A similar ceremony took place at the Co-operative Cafe, Bury, on Saturday, 18th June, 1949, when the then present General Secretary, Mr. Andrew Naesmith, was presented with a cheque for £100 to commemorate his long service with the Amalgamation.

It is interesting to record various other instances of recognition by the Amalgamation of valued and lengthy service in the case of past officers. On 3rd February, 1889, the General Council granted the sum of £100 to Mr. T. Birtwistle for his work in connection with the compilation of the Uniform List which was ultimately adopted in 1892. On 20th October, 1906, the General Council, as recorded earlier, decided upon the Memorial Scholarships at Ruskin College known as the "Holmes, Wilkinson & Barrows" Scholarships, and framed photographs of the three officials were presented to each District Association.

On 18th November, 1916, the General Council appointed Mr. Luke Park as an honorary member of the Central Committee, in appreciation of his service to the Amalgamation. He had been Secretary of the Preston Association since 1875, and had been a member of the Central Committee since the formation of the Amalgamation. The following Resolution was adopted:—

> "That this Council hereby express their approval and appreciation of the good services rendered to this Amalgamation by Mr. Luke Park, and approve of the recommendation to make him an extra member of the Central Committee without the necessity of the annual election so long as he continues his connection with the Preston District Association."

Mr. Park continued to serve until 1919, when he retired. On 20th September,

1919 the General Council granted the sum of 100 guineas to Mr. Park for his useful and valuable services to the Weavers' Amalgamation, and the presentation took place on 18th October, 1919.

On 16th September, 1922 the General Council placed on record a resolution of appreciation of the Parliamentary services rendered by Mr. Thomas Shaw, M.P., and in October of that year the General Council agreed to empower the Central Committee to mark appreciation of Mr. Shaw's services, to the extent of £50.

Mr. William Ward, who had a lengthy record of service as Secretary of the Nelson Association and as a member of the Central Committee, retired in 1923, and on 19th May, 1923 the General Council passed a resolution expressing appreciation of his services. In June of that year the General Council made a grant of 100 guineas to Mr. Ward in commemoration of his lengthy services.

At the General Council Meeting held on 17th November, 1928, Mr. W. A. Appleton, Secretary of the General Federation of Trade Unions, presented to Mrs. J. C. Parker the Gold Medallion of the General Federation of Trade Unions, in recognition of the faithful service of her late husband, Mr. J. C. Parker.

On 9th May, 1931, when the Convalescent Home at Poulton-le-Fylde was opened by the Rt. Hon. Thomas Shaw, M.P., as a Memorial to the late Secretary, Mr. Joseph Cross, the Central Committee presented each District Association with a framed photograph of Mr. Cross.

The Central Committee also supplied to each District a framed photograph of the late Mr. John Wm. Ogden, who had been Secretary of the Heywood Association and President of the Amalgamation for a long number of years.

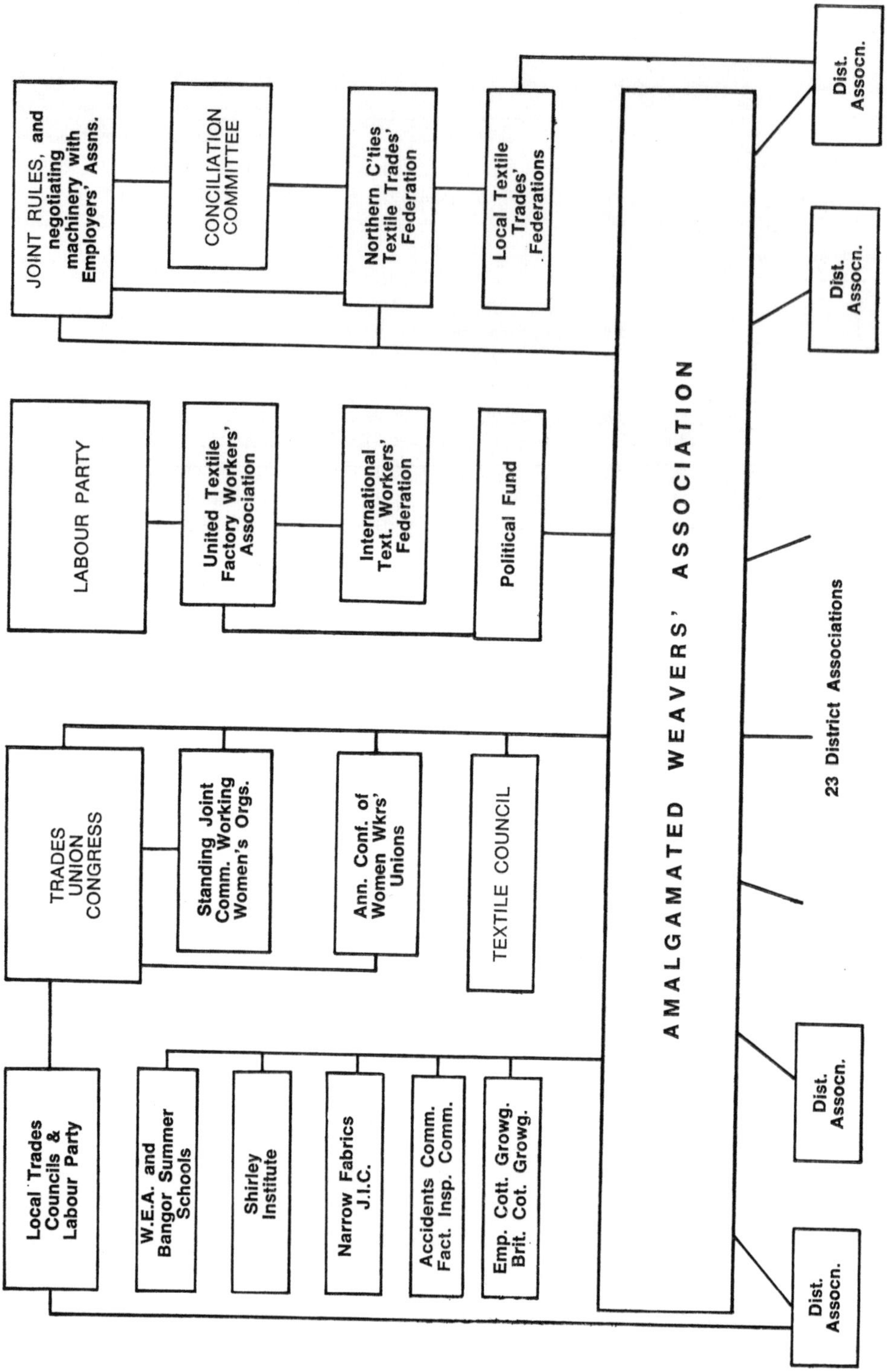
JOINT RULES, and negotiating machinery with Employers' Assns.
CONCILIATION COMMITTEE
Northern C'ties Textile Trades' Federation
Local Textile Trades' Federations
Dist. Assocn.
Dist. Assocn.
LABOUR PARTY
United Textile Factory Workers' Association
International Text. Workers' Federation
Political Fund
AMALGAMATED WEAVERS' ASSOCIATION
23 District Associations
TRADES UNION CONGRESS
Standing Joint Comm. Working Women's Orgs.
Ann. Conf. of Women Wkrs' Unions
TEXTILE COUNCIL
Local Trades Councils & Labour Party
W.E.A. and Bangor Summer Schools
Shirley Institute
Narrow Fabrics J.I.C.
Accidents Comm. Fact. Insp. Comm.
Emp. Cott. Growg. Brit. Cot. Growg.
Dist. Assocn.
Dist. Assocn.

Appendices

THE UNITED KINGDOM TEXTILE MANUFACTURERS' ASSOCIATION
and
THE NORTHERN COUNTIES TEXTILE TRADES FEDERATION
JOINT RULES
FOR THE SETTLEMENT OF TRADE DISPUTES

Comprising Agreement dated 21st February, 1913 and extract from Agreement dated 27th September, 1932, between the Cotton Spinners' and Manufacturers' Association and the Northern Counties Textile Trades Federation.

The Cotton Spinners' and Manufacturers' Association changed its name in 1961 to the United Kingdom Textile Manufacturers' Association; and references in the Agreements to the C.S.M.A. are to be taken as references to the U.K.T.M.A.

AGREEMENT OF 21st FEBRUARY, 1913

The object to these Rules is to secure the consideration and settlement of trade disputes in their early stages, and thereby to preserve good feeling between Employers and Operatives. For the purpose of carrying out this object it is agreed as follows:

1. In the event of a trade dispute arising between any Member of an Association comprised in The Cotton Spinners' and Manufacturers' Association, and any Operative Member or Members of an Association comprised in The Northern Counties Textile Trades Federation, the following course shall be taken:

(a) Before any notices shall be given by either party to terminate employment for the purpose of a lock-out or strike, the dispute shall be brought forthwith before a Local Joint Meeting of Representatives of Employers appointed by the Local Employers' Association and of Operatives appointed by the Local Operatives' Association, in the particular section of trade affected, and such meeting shall be held within four days (exclusive of Sunday) from the date of an application by either party for such meeting; and if a settlement of the dispute be not come to at that meeting, or at an adjournment thereof, then

(b) Before any notices shall be given by either party to terminate employment, for the purpose of a lock-out or strike, the dispute shall be brought before a Joint Meeting of Representatives of The Cotton Spinners' and Manufacturers' Association and of The Amalgamated Association of the Trade Unions formed in that section of the trade to which the dispute relates, and such meeting shall be held within seven days from the date of an application by either party for such meeting; and if a settlement of the dispute be not come to at that meeting, or at an adjournment thereof, then

(c) Before any notices shall be given by either party to terminate employment for the purpose of a lock-out or strike, the dispute shall be brought before a Joint Meeting of Representatives of the Cotton Spinners' and Manufacturers' Association and of The Northern Counties Textile Trades Federation, and such Meeting shall be held within seven days from the date of an application by either party for such meeting; and if a settlement be not come to at such meeting, or at an adjournment thereof, then either party shall be at liberty to take whatever course it thinks fit.

2. In the event of a complaint of bad material in the weaving section which the Local Secretaries of the respective Associations have been unable to settle, the Local Secretary of the Operatives' Association shall have power to claim a joint inspection by Representatives of Employers and of Operatives of the material complained of at the mill where such material had been given out for work, in which case each Association shall appoint Representatives to make such a joint inspection within three days (Sundays excepted) from the making of such claim, and failing a satisfactory settlement at such joint inspection or at an agreed adjournment thereof, or if facilities be not given for a joint inspection within such period as aforesaid, or within such extended time as may be mutually agreed upon between the Secretaries of the two Local Associations, the complaint shall then be regarded as a trade dispute and be subject to the procedure provided by Rule 1 hereof in relation to trade disputes, except that the procedure under Rule 1 (b) shall be disregarded, and the procedure under Rule 1 (c) shall be followed with this modification; that at the Joint Meeting held thereunder, the Representatives of The Amalgamated Weavers' Association shall attend with the Representatives of The Northern Counties Textile Trades Federation.

3. Whenever a settlement of any trade dispute shall not have been come to and operatives are on strike or locked-out of employment in consequence thereof, then meetings shall be held periodically between Representatives of The Cotton Spinners' and Manufacturers' Association and of

The Northern Counties Textile Trades Federation; the first of such meetings shall be held in Manchester four weeks after and at the same place and hour as the last meeting of representatives in the same dispute, and subsequent meetings shall be held at the same place and hour periodically every four weeks until the dispute be settled, and without any formal application by either party for any such meeting; provided, however, that in a trade dispute relating to bad material in the weaving section, the Meetings to be held under this Rule shall be between the Representative of The Cotton Spinners' and Manufacturers' Association and of The Amalgamated Weavers' Association and The Northern Counties Textile Trades Federation.

4. If the attendance of any person or persons is desired by either party at any meeting to be held for the consideration of a trade dispute, and notice in writing is given to the other party of such desire, each party will, when so desired, request such person or persons to attend the meeting.

5. In the event of an application being made by the operatives in any section for an advance of wages, or by the employers in any section for a reduction of wages, such application, if not granted, shall, before any notices are given by either party to terminate employment for the purpose of a strike or lock-out, be brought before a Joint Meeting of Representatives of The Cotton Spinners' and Manufacturers' Association and of The Amalgamated Association of the Trades Unions formed in that section of the trade to which the application relates, and such meeting shall be held within seven days from the date of an application by either party for such meeting, and if a settlement be not come to at such meeting, or at an adjournment thereof, then, before any notices shall be given by either party to terminate employment for the purpose of a strike or lock-out, the matter shall be brought before a Joint Meeting of Representatives of The Cotton Spinners' and Manufacturers' Association and of The Northern Counties Textile Trades Federation, and such meeting shall be held in Manchester within seven days from the date of an applicaton by either party for such meeting, and if a settlement be not come to at such meeting, or at an adjournment thereof, then either party shall be at liberty to take whatever course it thinks fit.

6. All meetings shall be held at such time and place as may be mutually agreed upon between the officials of the Employers' and Operatives Associations.

7. The proceedings at Joint Meetings shall be regarded as strictly private and confidential. Every question discussed, every statement made and every opinion expressed shall be treated by each person present as strictly private and confidental, and shall not be communicated to any outside person, or to the Press, except by direction or permission of the meeting, and the particular part taken by any person in any of the discussions, shall not be quoted at any public meeting.

8. An application by the employers for a meeting with Representatives of The Northern Counties Textile Trades Federation may be addressed to the Secretary for the time being. An application by the operatives for a meeting with Representatives of The Cotton Spinners' and Manufacturers' Association may be addressed to the Secretary for the time being.

9. In the event of an Association, either of Employers or Operatives, failing to appoint a time for and to give notice to the Secretary of the other Association affected by a dispute, of a Joint Meeting to deal with such dispute, in accordance with these rules and within the period limited for such purpose, or within such extended period as may be mutually agreed upon between the Secretaries of the two Associations, then either party shall be at liberty to take whatever course it thinks fit.

EXTRACT FROM AGREEMENT OF 27th SEPTEMBER, 1932.

I. It is agreed that the following additions shall be made to the Joint Rules for the settlement of Trade Disputes:—

A. *Conciliation Committee*

(1) The Scheme under the Joint Rules shall remain unchanged, but certain provisions shall be added for the purpose of the more effective avoidance of stoppages of work.

(2) When a question in dispute has been dealt with in accordance with the provisions made in the Joint Rules and a settlement has not been reached, a Conciliation Committee consisting of not less than three or more than five from each side of the Central Committee of the Cotton Spinners' and Manufacturers' Association and the Central Board of the Northern Counties Textile Trades Federation shall be appointed, the members being chosen according to the nature of the subject in dispute.

*(3) The Chairman of the Conciliation Committee shall be an independent person to be nominated by agreement between the parties, or alternatively, by the Minister of Labour. He shall be chosen for a period of not less than three but not exceeding five years as Standing Chairman.

(4) There shall be associated for consultation with the Standing Chairman two independent members (one to be appointed by each side) who shall also be Standing Members and appointed for a specified period.

(5) There shall be Joint Secretaries who shall be the Secretaries of the Employers' and Operatives' main organisations.

(6) The Joint Secretaries shall inform the Standing Chairman as soon as the matter has passed through the normal procedure without a settlement being reached, and he will thereupon make arrangements for the convening of the Conciliation Committee.

(7) The Conciliation Committee shall first endeavour to settle the matter by agreement but failing settlement, the Standing Chairman, after consultation with the independent members, shall make a recommendation. If invited to do so by both sides the Chairman shall have authority to make an Award.

(8) From the time at which he begins to sit with the Committee the Chairman shall have the right to have such technical, statistical, or other assistance as he may consider to be necessary.

(9) These Rules shall remain in operation for a period of three years from the date of signature, and thereafter shall be terminable on six months' notice being given on either side.

*As amended 20th June, 1950

TOTAL MEMBERSHIP OF THE AMALGAMATION
since its inception

Year	*Membership*	*Year*	*Membership*
1884	37,539	1928	157,113
1885	40,028	1929	155,741
1886	40,000	1930	162,601
1887	37,333	1931	158,660
1888	36,460	1932	150,380
1889	34,556	1933	128,219
1890	46,102	1934	109,093
1891	49,414	1935	100,911
1892	65,147	1936	95,739
1893	71,180	1937	93,959
1894	75,510	1938	95,455
1895	84,160	1939	86,665
1896	83,195	1940	86,843
1899	74,420	1941	89,544
1900	81,500	1942	74,473
1901	81,175	1943	72,668
1902	82,267	1944	72,556
1903	82,597	1945	72,458
1904	80,877	1946	72,854
1905	80,385	1947	70,966
1906	88,175	1948	72,273
1907	101,842	1949	73,717
1908	115,314	1950	75,849
1909	118,626	1951	86,259
1910	114,434	1952	89,465
1911	112,462	1953	87,617
1912	137,196	1954	85,288
1913	179,391	1955	84,073
1914	197,957	1956	80,748
1915	179,691	1957	66,030
1916	175,845	1958	64,592
1917	165,204	1959	59,719
1918	169,314	1960	55,647
1919	178,825	1961	53,709
1920	211,621	1962	50,398
1921	224,219	1963	45,483
1922	219,329	1964	44,463
1923	174,585	1965	43,113
1924	169,172	1966	41,701
1925	162,611	1967	36,586
1926	162,391	1968	33,066
1927	163,929		

SURVEY OF WEAVING MACHINERY IN GREAT BRITAIN, 1948.

(Extracts from Survey taken by the Cotton Board, as at September, 1948)

	No. of Firms	*No. of Looms*
Cotton, Rayon and Mixture Fabrics	793	394,220
Silk and Rayon Fabrics	45	7,487
	838	403,707
Other Fabrics	48	1,847
*Narrow Fabrics	6	726
*excluding 1,010 looms narrower than 23in. R.S.	892	406,280
Northern Ireland	70	6,528
„ „ (Other Fabrics)	—	18,096

Analysis by type of loom:

	Ordinary Lancashire Looms	*Automatic Attachments*	*Fully Automatic*	TOTAL
Tappet—				
Plain	144,814	1,997	8,341	155,152
3 to 5 shafts	84,515	363	8,759	93,637
Over 5 shafts	52,409	125	1,499	54,033
Dobby	68,500	293	5,570	74,363
Jacquard	16,524	133	738	17,395
Towel	6,846	—	801	7,647
Quilt	1,029	—	—	1,029
Other	3,013	—	11	3,024
	377,650	2,911	25,719	406,280
(Single Shuttle)	320,342	2,908	21,224	344,474
(Multiple Box)	57,308	3	4,495	61,806

Analysis by loom widths:

Reed Space (inches)	*Ordinary Looms*	*Automatic Attachments*	*Fully Automatic*	TOTAL
24 — 30	633	—	153	786
31 — 36	29,589	49	3,400	33,038
37 — 42	93,036	201	3,780	97,017
43 — 48	116,240	1,432	8,753	126,425
49 — 54	42,251	134	2,556	44,941
55 — 60	44,976	312	1,768	47,056
61 — 66	23,729	202	1,504	25,435
67 — 72	10,802	23	935	11,760
73 — 84	8,463	138	1,054	9,655
85 — 100	6,148	306	1,391	7,845
Over 100	1,783	114	425	2,322
	377,650	2,911	2,5719	406,280

AMALGAMATION OFFICERS

Presidents

David Holmes,	elected	4th May, 1884, died 14th January, 1906.
D. J. Shackleton,	,,	19th May, 1906, resigned December, 1910.
J. W. Ogden,	,,	20th May, 1911, died 23rd March, 1930.
James Hindle,	,,	17th May, 1930, resigned May, 1937.
James Bell,	,,	15th May, 1937, resigned May, 1947.
Carey Hargreaves,	,,	17th May, 1947, retired May, 1949.
Lewis T. Wright,	,,	21st May, 1949, appointed General Secretary, June, 1953.
Harold Bradley,	,,	15th May, 1954, retired May, 1960.
Ernest Thornton,	,,	21st May, 1960, resigned May, 1965.
Fred G. Hague,	,,	18th May, 1968, resigned December, 1968. (Appointed Industrial Assistant).

Secretaries

Thomas Birtwistle, appointed 4th May, 1884, resigned October, 1885.

Alderman Wm. Hy. Wilkinson, appointed 18th October, 1885, resigned 6th April, 1906, died 25th April, 1906.

Joseph Cross,	elected	10th March, 1906, died 11th January, 1925.
J. C. Parker,	,,	7th March, 1925, died 5th November, 1927.
A. Naesmith,	,,	17th December, 1927. Retired August, 1953.
Lewis Wright,	,,	22nd June, 1953. Retired 11th October, 1968.
Harry C. Kershaw,	,,	21st September, 1968.

Agent

Joshua Barrows, appointed 17th May, 1884, died 18th July, 1905.

POSITION OF VARIOUS WAGES LISTS—DECEMBER, 1968

Legalised Uniform List—		Plus separate 195%, and plus 73/1 flat rate increase (Day Shift). Plus separate 232¼%, and plus 77/3 flat rate (Multi Shifts).
Grey Section	Nett.	
Coloured Section:		
Stripes	81½%	
Checks	76½%	
Worsted Goods (Cl. 47 of 1924 edition of Uniform List)	77½%	
Fustian and Velvet List 1947	Nett.	
Waste Weaving List	75%	
Bolton Quilt Weaving	72½%	
Uniform Sheeting List	Nett.	
Towel Weaving List	77½%	
Cop Winding List	77½%	
Burnley Beaming List	77½%	

Weavers' Minimum Wages. (running looms)

Ordinary System	151/6	(full complement)
	125/3	(less than full complement)
More than 6 looms	199/11	Basic wage, plus $_5$ of 6 looms price
C.M.C. System	127/4	Basic wage plus 25/7 Flat Rate

Winders'

	per wk.	per hr.
(Manufacturing section) Minimum wage	141/–	42.29d.

Winders' and Reelers'

(Spinning section) Minimum wage	134/10
Average wage not less than (for 90%)	147/2
Day rate not less than	143/6

Beamers'
(Manufacturing section) Minimum wage .. .. .. 151/2 45.34d.

Beamers', Crossballers' (Spinning section)

Average wage 1 machine, not less than	156/-
Average wage 1½ machines, not less than	171/4
Day rate 1 machine, not less than	147/9
Day rate 1½ machines, not less than	164/4

(Agreement of 14th September, 1951, fixes minimum wage for Beamers and Crossballers at 137/5, under conditions therein stated. See Amalgamation Annual Report 1952, p. 14).

Sweepers, Oilers, Labourers, etc.

(Manufacturing section) Minimum weekly wage	218/-
(Spinning section) Weekly minimum wage	218/-

Shift Workers
Where double-day or three shifts are worked all the above rates are subject to 5.6% increase.

ESTIMATED NUMBER OF POWER-LOOMS

(United Kingdom)

Year	*Looms*	
1820	10,000	
1832	75,000	
1844	150,000	
1860	203,000	
1862	240,000	
1882	485,264	(Worrall's Directory)
1890	606,585	" "
1895	627,585	" "
1900	648,820	" "
1905	652,166	" "
1910	741,197	" "
1915	808,145	" "
1920	798,000	(Federation of Master Spinners) *State of Trade Report*, 1928
1925	788,000	
1930	700,000	
1935	530,000	
1940	441,065	(*Skinners' Directory*)
1941	220,000	Licensed to run (F. W. Tattersall)
1945	300,000	(in place) (Cotton Board)
	215,900	(average number running) " "
1948	355,500	(in place) " "
	286,600	(average number running) " "
1949	356,900	(in place) " "
	289,300	(average number running) " "
1950	357,700	(in place) " "
	304,800	(average number running) " "

(NOTE: The Cotton Board figures include all cotton and rayon looms in the country).

AVERAGE NUMBER OF LOOMS RUNNING

	United Kingdom	*Lancashire Area*
1951	311,700	285,300
1952	249,700	228,400
1953	270,600	249,000
1954	280,700	258,100
1955	252,600	231,000
1956	229,400	210,000
1957	222,700	205,400
1958	192,000	177,200
1959	172,100	158,900
1960	149,400	134,400
1961	150,200	134,600
1962	131,000	117,800
1963	119,800	108,900
1964	116,500	105,600
1965	113,700	101,700
1966	107,200	95,600
1967	83,100	75,200

(Source: *Textile Council Statistical Review*)

UNIFORM WEAVING LIST FLUCTUATIONS

	(Pre-legalisation editions)	Grey List	Coloured List	
			Stripes	Checks
		plus	plus	plus
1912—July	(5% adv.)	5%	7½%	2½%
1916—January	(5% adv.)	10%	12½%	7½%
1917—January	(5% adv.)	15%	17½%	12½%
July	(10% adv.)	25%	27½%	22½%
December	(15% adv.)	40%	42½%	37½%
1918—June	(25% adv.)	65%	67½%	62½%
December	(50% adv.)	115%	117½%	112½%
1919—June	(30% adv.)	145%	147½%	142½%
	(Hours reduced from 55½ to 48 per week)			
1920—May	(70% adv.)	215%	217½%	212½%
1921—June	(60% red.)	155%	157½%	152½%
December	(10% red.)	145%	147½%	142½%
1922—April	(40% red.)	105%	107½%	102½%
October	(10% red.)	95%	97½%	92½%
1929—August	(12½% red.)	82½%	85%	80%
1932—September ..	(15½% red.)	67%	69½%	64½%
		Worsted Clause		
1937—April	(10½% adv.)	77½%	81½%	76½%

1935—July: First legalised Uniform List, 15th July, 1935 (red. of 5.72%, Grey basis; revision of clauses; Adv. of 4% in More Looms basis and improvements).

1937—April: Second legalised Uniform List, 12th April, 1937 (adv. of 7.3%, Grey basis and 7.14% Coloured basis). Clause revision and improvements.
Coloured List percentages adv. to 81½% and 76½%. Other Lists increased by 10½% (6.29% on current)

			Total
1939—November	Advance of 5% }		12½%
1940—January	Advance of 7½% }		22½%
April	Advance of 7½%	(Cost of Living advance)	20%
July	Advance of 2½%	,, ,, ,,	22½%
October	Advance of 2½%	,, ,, ,,	25%
1941—January	Advance of 5%	,, ,, ,,	30%
April	Advance of 2½%	,, ,, ,,	32½%
1942—January	Advance of 2½%	,, ,, ,,	35%

1943—January	Advance of 5/-	(Flat Rate advance)	5/-
1944—January	Advance of 4/-	” ” ”	9/-
1945—June	Advance of 7/-	” ” ”	16/-
1946—February	Advance of 10%		45%
1946—December	Reduction in Working Hours from 48 to 45 per week		
	Compensating advance of 6⅔%		54½%
1948—February	Advance of 7/6	(Flat Rate advance)	23/6
1949—March	Advance of 4/6	” ” ”	28/-
1951—January	Advance of 10%	Lists plus	70%
		Flat Rate	30/10
1951—September	Advance of 5%	Lists plus	78½%
		Flat Rate	32/4
1951—Christmas	Special Payment based on 5% of earnings between January and August, 1951.		
1953—August	Advance of 5%	Lists plus	87½%
		Flat Rate	34/-
1954—October	Advance of 6%	Lists plus	98¾%
		Flat Rate	36/-
1956—April	Advance of 5%	Lists plus	108½%
		Flat Rate	37/10
1957—August	Advance of 5%	Lists plus	119%
		Flat Rate	39/8
1960—March	Advance of 7½%	Lists plus	135½%
		Flat Rate	42/8
1961—January	(Hours Reduced from 45 to 42½ single shift, and from 38¾ to 37½ double-day shift). Compensating Advance of 5.88% for single, and 3.33% for double shifts.		
1962—October	Advance of 3%	Lists plus	156¾%
		Flat Rate	43/11
1963—July	Advance 5/9	(Flat Rate)	
		Lists plus	156¾%
		Flat Rate	49/8
1964—July	Advance 4%	Lists plus	167%
		Flat Rate	51/8
1964—July	Advance 0.6%	For Shift Workers	
1965—January	Reduction of hours, 42½ to 42		
	Compensating Rate of 1.2%		
		Lists plus	170.2%
		Flat Rate	51/8
1965—July	Advance 9/-	List plus..	170.2%
		Flat Rate	60/8
1966—January	Reduction of hours, 42 to 41½		
	Compensating Rate 1.2% advance		
1966—January	Advance 1.2%	For Shift Workers	
1966—July	Advance 4%	Lists plus	184½%
		Flat Rate	63/1
1967—July	Reduction of hours, 41½ to 41		
	Compensating Rate 1.2% advance		
1967—July	Advance 1.2%	For Shift Workers	
1968—January	Reduction of hours, 41 to 40		
	Compensating Rate 2.5%		
1968—January	Advance 2.5%	For Shift Workers	
1968—May	Flat Rate Advance 10/-	Flat Rate Now 73/1	

DATES OF ADOPTION OF WEAVING LISTS
and Guaranteed Minimum Wage Agreements.

1843 Ashton, Dukinfield, Stalybridge and Mossley List.
1843 Burnley Weaving List.
1844 Stockport Standard List of Prices.
1834–46 Various Oldham Weaving Lists.

1853	Blackburn Standard Weaving List.
1853	Radcliffe and Pilkington List.
1860	Preston Weaving List.
1861	Chorley Weaving List.
1861	Bolton Quilt Weaving List.
1866	Nelson Plain Cloth Weaving List.
1867	Hyde Weaving List.
1867	Blackburn Standard List Revised.
1887	North and North East Lancashire Fancy List for Grey Goods.
1890	Oldham Velvet List.
1890	Colne Coloured Goods List.
1892	Uniform List of Weaving Prices, 24th June.
1913	Uniform List for Weaving Waste Cloths, 11th March.
1913	Uniform List for Weaving Towels, 16th September.
1916	Uniform List for Weaving Fustians.
1932	More Looms Agreement, 28th December (following "Midland Agreement" of 27th September, 1932).
1934	Legalisation Act. "Cotton Manufacturing Industry (Temporary Provisions) Act, 1934".
1935	First Legalised Uniform List of Weaving Prices.
1937	Amended Legalised Uniform List of Weaving Prices.
1939	Uniform List for Weaving Sheeting Cloths, 2nd November.
1941	First General Minimum Wage Agreement for Weavers, 15th August, which was largely superseded by:—
1942	Essential Work (Cotton Manufacturing Industry) Order, 1942. No. 90, and Joint Agreement under it of 18 November, 1941.
1942	Minimum Wage Agreement of 24th December, for 48/– on Ordinary System, and first Flat Rate payment of 5/–.
1943	Minimum Wage Agreement for Winders (Manufacturing Section), 30th March.
1943	Minimum Wage Agreement for Beamers (Manufacturing Section), 30th March.
1944	Minimum Wage Conciliation Award for Winders, Reelers, etc. (Spinning section). 14th September.

VARIATIONS IN LIST PERCENTAGES— WINDERS, ETC., IN SPINNING MILLS

1940—March	Cost of Living Agrement	
1940—April	,, ,, ,,	13½%
1940—July	,, ,, ,,	4%
1940—October	,, ,, ,,	5%
1941—January	,, ,, ,,	9%
1941—April	,, ,, ,,	4%
1942—January	,, ,, ,,	5%
1943—January	5/– Flat Rate advance	
1944—January	4/– ,, ,, ,, = 9/–	
1944—Sept.	Doughty Award	
1945—June	7/– Flat Rate advance = 16/–	
1945—October	7½% advance (separate)	
1946—Dec.	Reduction in Hours: 48 to 45. 6.66% on current rates	
1948—January	10% advance (separate)	
1949—May	5% ,, ,,	
1951—January	10% ,, ,,	
1951—Sept.	5% ,, ,, plus Xmas bonus	
1953—August	5% ,, ,,	
1954—October	6% ,, ,,	
1956—April	5% ,, ,,	
1957—August	5% ,, ,,	
1960—March	7½% ,, ,,	
1961—January	Reduction in Hours: 45 to 42½. 5.88% on current rates	
1962—October	3% Advance (Industrial Tribunal)	
1963—July	5/9 Flat Rate advance. Flat Rate now 34/9	
1964—July	4% Advance. Flat Rate now 36/2	

1965—January	Hours Reduced: 42½ to 42. 1.2% on current rates
1965—July	9/- Flat Rate advance. Flat Rate now 43/9
1966—January	Hours Reduced: 42 to 41½. 1.2% on current rates
1966—July	4% Advance. Flat Rate now 47/-
1967—July	Hours Reduced: 41½ to 41. 1.2% on current rates
1968—January	Hours Reduced: 41 to 40. 2.5% on current rates
1968—May	10/- Flat Rate advance. Flat Rate now 57/-

ESTIMATES OF AVERAGE WAGES

Year	*Per week*	
1809	12/- to 14/-	(Reelers, Manchester District). (G. H. Wood)
1815	15/-	" " " "
1826	10/- to 12/-	(Factory weavers) (Manchester District). (G. H. Wood)
	9/- to 10/6	(Winders) " " "
	10/- to 12/-	(Warpers) " " "
1834	12/6	(Weavers) " " "
1839	16/- to 17/-	(4-loom weavers) " " "
1845	12/8	(Weavers) " " "
1860	14/6	" " " "
1870	13/10 to 17/-	" " " "
1890	20/-	" " " "
1906	19/3	(All workers). (Government census).
1913	26/3½	(4-loom weavers). (Amalgamated Weavers' census).
1924	36/10	(All workers). (Ministry of Labour census)
1928	37/8	" " " " "
1931	34/6	" " " " "
1935	35/6	" " " " "
1936	31/5	(Weavers). (Amalgamated Weavers' census)
1937	36/6	(Weavers). (Amalgamated Weavers' census)
1940	51/6	(All workers). (Ministry of Labour census)
1942	49/2	(Weavers). (Amalgamated Weavers' estimate)
1944	65/2	(Adult weavers). (Cotton Spinners & Manufacturers' census).
1945	77/11	" " " " " "
1946	84/7	" " " " " "
1947	88/2	" " " " " "
1948	99/2	" " " " " "
1950	103/5	" " 1948 figure plus 4/6 increase
1950	107/5	(Ministry of Labour Inquiry; all sections of workers)
1951	130/6	(Adult weavers. Employers' census, October–November)
1953	137/-	" " " " plus percentage)
1954	145/-	" " " " " percentages)
1956	152/3	" " " " " "
1958	159/10	" " " " " "
1960	171/9	" " " " " "
1963	182/8½	" " " " " " and flat rate).
1965	231/1½	(Ministry of Labour Inquiry. All textile workers)
1965	240/9	" " " (Dec.) " "
1966	278/-	" " " (Oct.) " "
1968	308/-	" " " (June) " "

ESTIMATED NUMBER OF WORKPEOPLE

Year	*Handloom weavers*	*Power-loom weavers*	*All workers in factories*	TOTAL WORKPEOPLE
1788	108,000	—	60,000	168,000
1806	184,000	A few	90,000	274,000
1810	200,000	A few	100,000	300,000
1815	220,000	7,000	114,000	334,000
1820	240,000	10,000	126,000	366,000
1830	225,000	50,000	185,000	425,000
1840	123,000	150,000	262,000	385,000
1845	60,000	150,000	273,000	333,000
1850	43,000	200,000	331,000	374,000

1855	27,000	240,000	371,000	398,000
1860	7,000	—	427,000	437,000
1862	3,000	—	—	—
1870	—	—	—	450,000
1878	—	—	—	483,000
1885	—	—	—	504,000
1890	—	—	—	529,000
1895	—	—	—	539,000
1901	—	—	—	523,000
1904	—	—	—	523,000
1907	—	—	—	572,062
1912	—	—	—	621,516
1924	—	—	—	528,312
1930	—	—	—	379,234
1934	—	—	—	355,093

	Spinning and Doubling	*Weaving*	
1939	193,000	184,000	378,100
1942	108,000	104,000	212,000
1943	103,970	98,000	202,000
1944	97,490	97,600	195,090
1945	95,950	79,090	175,040
1949	137,660	110,740	248,400
1950	147,120	121,740	268,260

(Whole of UnitedKingdom)

	Spinning	*Doubling*	*Weaving*	TOTAL
1951	116,310	29,120	140,320	285,750
1952	92,840	21,250	118,390	232,480
1953	102,860	22,860	124,190	249,910
1954	106,720	23,550	127,060	257,330
1955	97,570	20,810	117,970	236,350
1956	92,590	19,370	108,340	220,300
1957	93,860	18,760	103,510	216,130
1958	84,000	15,590	92,710	192,390
1959	77,320	14,670	84,870	176,860
1960	69,230	14,900	81,260	165,390
1961	61,560	13,340	70,660	145,560
1962	52,310	11,910	66,250	130,470
1963	49,630	11,940	68,340	129,910
1964	47,780	11,640	66,400	125,820
1965	43,770	10,620	64,220	118,610
1966	41,380	10,050	54,360	106,790
1967	34,580	8,600	49,360	92,540

Original Central Committee,
appointed 4th May, 1884, consisted of:

D. Holmes, Burnley
J. Barrows, Padiham
Luke Park, Preston
G. Barker, Blackburn
A. Buckley, Oldham
W. Booth, Ashton.

Original Trustees
appointed 17th May, 1884:

James Craven, Blackburn
Thomas Heys, Haslingden
Andrew Harris, Preston
Joseph Taylor. Burnley
William Hayhurst, Great Harwood
Elisha Reddihough, Church
Eli Pemberton, Ashton-under-Lyne.

ESTABLISHMENT OF DISTRICT ASSOCIATIONS

Owing to fear, records of early years of history of District Associations are very scanty. Clubs and societies existed in most of the districts quoted below before the dates shown, but not in permanent form:

Preston	1842, 1858
Radcliffe	1852
Blackburn	1854
Padiham	1856
Darwen	1857
Great Harwood	1858
Haslingden	1858 (First Amalgamation).
Church	1858
Accrington	1858
Clitheroe	1860
Bolton	1865
Oldham	1867
Ramsbottom	1868
Burnley	1870
Nelson	1870
Rossendale	1873
Ashton	1877
Heywood	1877
Todmorden	1878
Rochdale	1878
Longridge	1878
Colne	1878
Hyde	1880
Whitworth	1882
Bamber Bridge	1884 (Present Amalgamation, 1884).
Bury	1884
Wigan	1890
Skipton	1902
Stockport	1906
Manchester	1908

CONCILIATION COMMITTEE HEARINGS

25th/26th November, 1936.

Claim for Wage Advance of 15%, and Minimum Wage of 7½d. per hour.

Result:

Agreement on second Legalised List, 12th April, 1937; Advance of 7.3% on 4-looms basis, 7.14% on 6-looms basis; Revision of many clauses; Coloured List advanced from 69½% to 81½% (stripes) and from 64½% to 76½% (checks); Other Lists increased by 10½% (6.29% on current wages).

22nd April, 1938.

Claim by Federation of Master Cotton Spinners' Associations, for reduction in Hyde Sheeting List.

Result:

Lengthy negotiations ensued in Joint Prices Committee, resulting in Uniform Sheeting List, incorporated in Sir Charles Doughty's Award of November, 1939.

5th May, 1939.

Claim for Minimum Wage of 8¾d. per hour, or 35s. per week.

Result:

Agreement, for a fall-back wage of 66⅔% of individual weaver's earnings over 4 full weeks; not more than 33s. nor less than 25s. Lengthy negotiations carried on until Agreement of 15th August, 1941.

24th April, 1942.

Claim for advance of 2d. per hour.

Result:

Award, of 5th May, 1942. Operatives' claim "not established either wholly or in part."

18th December, 1942.
Claim for Starting Point Wage of 9d. per hour, plus 50% of List earnings.
Result:
Agreement, of 24th December, 1942, for Flat Rate Payment of 5s. per week (normal complement); Minimum Wage of 48s. (Normal System), 55s. (6-looms system), or 41s. (less than normal system); Wage for Age Scale; Holidays with Pay extended to two weeks.

9th/10th December, 1943.
Claim for 12s. per week advance, 6s. for juveniles.
Result:
Chairman's Recommendation, accepted by both sides. Advance of 4s. in Flat Rate Payment (2s. juveniles), to operate from 10th January, 1944.

29th March, 1944.
Overlookers' application for Standing Wage.
Result:
Chairman's Recommendation, accepted by both sides, "Under the conditions at present prevailing the claim has not been established."

14th September, 1944.
Claim for general agreement with Federation of Master Cotton Spinners' Associations, for 9d. per hour, 58s. 1¼d. per week (Winders); 9½d. per hour 60s. 10d. per week (Beamers & Crossballers), and 10d. per hour, 54s. 5¾d. per week (Beamers etc. on 1½ machines).
Result:
Chairman's Award, of 14th September, 1944, Winders & Reelers' average wage of 51s. 10¼d., after eliminating lowest one-tenth), Minimum wage of 11½d. per hour, (46s. per week).
Varying figures for Beamers & Crossballers, and Wage for Age scale for Learners.

19th/20th April, 1945.
General claim for increase in flat rate payments, to 20s. per week (10s. for juveniles), and pro rata increases to others.
Result:
Chairman's Award, of 9s. increase in flat rate payments, (to 16s. per week) for adults. To operate from 11th June, 1945. Pro rata increases to spinners.

31st October, 1945.
Claim for operation of spinning section increases to our winders etc., in spinning mills.
Result:
Chairman's Award of 31st October, 1945; 10% to male operatives, 7½% to female operatives.

21st December, 1945.
Claim for general advance in manufacturing section, of 7½% in wages.
Result:
Chairman's Award of same date; advance of 10% in piece rates, making 35% into 45% on Lists.

26th September, 1947.
Warehousemen's application for 10% advance.
Result:
Chairman's Award of same date; various increases in base wages, including General Warehousemen (and Loom Sweepers), 47s. base wage, equal to 84s. 2d. per week, (increase of 5s. 3d.).

23rd November, 1948.
Tape Sizers' claim for basic wage of £8 per week, with 10% addition for special work.
Result:
Chairman's Award, fixing county base wage of £7 2s. 6d. Special work to be negotiated locally.

4th March, 1949.
Claim for general advance in manufacturing section of 10s. per week in flat rate payments.
Result:
Chairman's Award of same day. 4s. 6d. per week, making the 23s. 6d. into 28s. per week, to operate from 14th March, 1949 to 31st December, 1949. (Continued afterwards by joint agreement).

17th/18th August, 1950.
Claim for abolition of deductions from weavers' wages for Sweeping, Oiling and Cleaning.
Employers' application for Agreement governing Double Day Shifts on Automatic Looms.
Result:
Chairman's Awards of 22nd August 1950. (Lord Terrington).
Deductions for sweeping, cleaning and oiling abolished.
Previous joint agreement on Double Day shifts was awarded. (Joint discussions followed, on details and date of operation).

9th October, 1956.
Claim for Abrogation of Six-Looms Price.
Result:
Chairman's Award (Lord Terrington) 17th October, 1956.
Abolition of Six-Looms Prices in Uniform List.

25th October, 1962.
Industrial Court.
Claim of Unions for 10% Advance in wages.
Employers offer of 5s. 9d. per week advance.
Court's Award 3% increase in wages.

LIBRARY

THE TEXTILE INSTITUTE
10 BLACKFRIARS ST.
MANCHESTER 3
LIBRARY

THE TEXTILE INSTITUTE
10 BLACKFRIARS ST.
MANCHESTER 3
LIBRARY